INTERNATIONAL THEMES AND ISSUES

VOLUME
4

# BUILDING BETTER BRITAINS?

INTERNATIONAL THEMES AND ISSUES
A joint series of the Canadian Historical Association
and the University of Toronto Press

SERIES EDITOR │ Pierre-Yves Saunier

Canadian
Historical Association

Société historique
du Canada

UNIVERSITY OF TORONTO PRESS

INTERNATIONAL THEMES AND ISSUES
A joint series of the Canadian Historical Association
and the University of Toronto Press

SERIES EDITOR | Pierre-Yves Saunier

# BUILDING BETTER BRITAINS?

*Settler Societies Within the British Empire 1783–1920*

### CECILIA MORGAN

UNIVERSITY OF TORONTO PRESS

Library and Archives Canada Cataloguing in Publication
Morgan, Cecilia, 1958–, author

Building better Britains? : settler societies within the British empire, 1783-1920 / Cecilia Morgan.

(International themes and issues ; volume 4)

Includes bibliographical references and index.
Issued in print and electronic formats.

Co-published by: Canadian Historical Association.

ISBN 978-1-4426-0812-2 (hardcover).–ISBN 978-1-4426-0752-1 (paperback).
–ISBN 978-1-4426-0754-5 (html).–ISBN 978-1-4426-0753-8 (pdf).

1. Great Britain—Colonies—History—18th century. 2. Great Britain—Colonies—History—19th century. 3. Great Britain—Colonies—History—20th century. 4. Imperialism—History. I. Canadian Historical Association, issuing body II. Title. III. Series: International themes and issues (Toronto, Ont.) ; v. 4

DA16.M58 2016 941 C2016-900653-0
C2016-900654-9

We welcome comments and suggestions regarding any aspect of our publications—please feel free to contact us at news@utphighereducation.com or visit our Internet site at www.utppublishing.com.

| North America | UK, Ireland, and continental Europe |
|---|---|
| 5201 Dufferin Street | NBN International |
| North York, Ontario, Canada, M3H 5T8 | Estover Road, Plymouth, PL6 7PY, UK |
| | ORDERS PHONE: 44 (0) 1752 202301 |
| 2250 Military Road | ORDERS FAX: 44 (0) 1752 202333 |
| Tonawanda, New York, USA, 14150 | ORDERS E-MAIL: enquiries@nbninternational.com |

ORDERS PHONE: 1-800-565-9523
ORDERS FAX: 1-800-221-9985
ORDERS E-MAIL: utpbooks@utpress.utoronto.ca

Every effort has been made to contact copyright holders; in the event of an error or omission, please notify the publisher.

The University of Toronto Press acknowledges the financial support for its publishing activities of the Government of Canada through the Canada Book Fund.

Printed in the United States of America.

To Paul Jenkins

# Contents

# Illustrations

*Maps*

# Acknowledgements

Thanking all those who have made this book possible is, I think, the most pleasurable part of getting it into print. First, I am so very grateful to Beverly Lemire and Natalie Fingerhut. In their respective editorial roles—Beverly for the Canadian Historical Association's Short Book Series and Natalie for the University of Toronto Press—Bev and Natalie deserve a very special thanks. Their support, insights, efficiency, and (not least) patience were a constant source of encouragement. Thank you for inviting me to take on this project. Pierre-Yves Saunier, Chair of the Series' Editorial Board, helped see this manuscript through to the end; many thanks for your suggestions, enthusiasm, and sense of humour! I am very grateful to Eileen Eckert for her superb copyediting. Eileen's sharp eye and thoughtful suggestions have made this a much better book.

As well, I owe a special debt to the six anonymous reviewers, who saved me from some embarrassing mistakes and provided a number of suggestions that have improved this book. I appreciate their generosity and the swiftness with which they responded to the draft. A book such as this relies very heavily on a wide body of historiography, so I'd also like to acknowledge the many fine historians whose work I've drawn on in order to create *Building Better Britains?* I hope I have represented their scholarship fairly: I know I learned much from them in researching and writing this book.

Closer to home, Paul Jenkins has lived with this book longer than both of us anticipated. As always, it's for him.

# Maps

**MAP 0.1** Indigenous Communities, New Zealand, c. 1840s

**MAP 0.2** Indigenous Communities, Australia, c. 1780s

Indigenous Australia was distinguished by an extremely wide variety of linguistic groups with ties to traditional territories. It is difficult to represent all of these groups clearly on a small-scale map such as this. Therefore, we have chosen to indicate larger linguistic macro-regions, which contain many individual groups. Readers who wish for more detail should consult the Australian Institute of Aboriginal and Torres Strait Islanders Studies map of Indigenous Australia (http://aiatsis.gov.au/aboriginal-studies-press/products/aiatsis-map-indigenous-australia).

**MAP 0.3** Indigenous Communities, Canada, c. 1820s

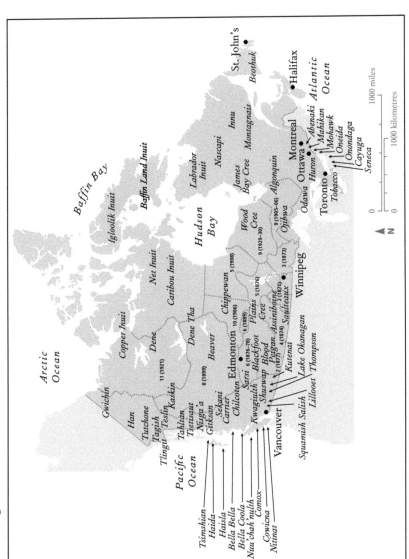

**MAP 0.4** Indigenous Communities, South Africa, c. 1800s

**MAP 0.5** Settler Communities, New Zealand, c. 1860

Bay of
Islands

Waitangi

Auckland

Tasman
Sea

AUCKLAND

NORTH
ISLAND

New Plymouth

Pacific
Ocean

Hawke's
Bay

Cook Strait

WELLINGTON

NELSON

Wellington

SOUTH
ISLAND

Pacific
Ocean

Christchurch

CANTERBURY

OTAGO

0                    150 miles

N

0              150 kilometres

**MAP 0.6** Settler Communities, Australia, c. 1900

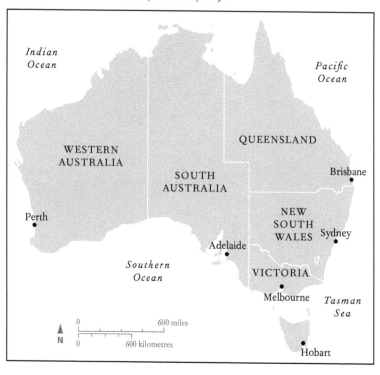

**MAP 0.7** Settler Communities, Canada, c. 1905

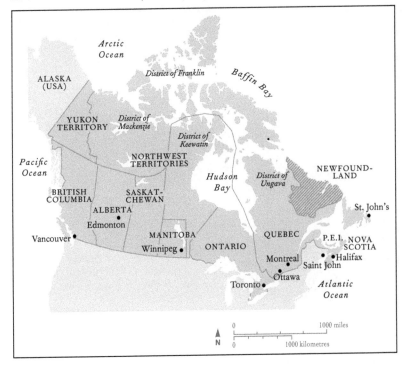

**MAP 0.8** Settler Communities, South Africa, c. 1910

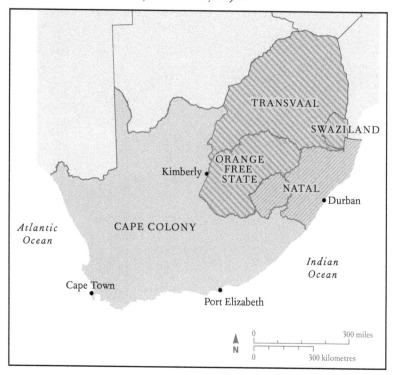

# Introduction
## Better Britains?: Settler Societies Within the British Empire 1783–1920

The spread, persistence, and effects of empires, as well as their lingering presence in today's world, have become a major preoccupation for scholars in the early twenty-first-century academy. Historians, literary specialists, cultural theorists, anthropologists, and geographers (to name practitioners of a few prominent disciplines) have drawn our attention to the ways in which imperial powers reshaped the lives and landscapes of millions of people around the world, both those who became subject to imperial rule and those who were, in various ways, imperial rulers. While the study of imperial expansion and imperial encounters is chronologically wide-ranging and takes in multiple forms of empire, the nineteenth century and, in particular, the expansion of British imperial power around the world during that time have been the focus of a diverse body of scholarship. Although the reasons for scholars' fascination with nineteenth-century British imperial history are multiple and complex, one key factor for the great volume of work in this area can be traced to the rapidity and range of British imperial expansion over this period. Over the course of the nineteenth century, Britain acquired 10 million square miles—a territory that included 400 million people, making it the largest of Europe's imperial powers. It also created a range of colonies and protectorates, ones that encompassed direct governance (the Caribbean, Hong Kong, and, by 1858, India), rule through military occupation (Egypt), and settler colonialism. This book explores the latter subject, examining the spread of settler colonies within the British Empire over the course of the nineteenth century.

Settler colonialism was not a phenomenon limited to the British Empire, of course. Other imperial powers also created colonies in which the formation of new, long-lasting societies for colonists, effected through the dispossession and dispersal of Indigenous peoples, occurred alongside the extraction of resources for the metropole. British settler colonialism, though, was particularly persistent, pervasive, and long-lasting. British settlers also spread outside the boundaries of those colonies that are the subject of this book—Australia, Canada, New Zealand, and South Africa—to places such as Argentina and, of course, the United States, developments that have been explored by historians James Belich and John Weaver. Moreover, settler colonialism was related to the British Empire's global expansion. It took place in a context of other forms of British colonialism and shared a number of features: a range of social, political, cultural, and economic connections to the metropole; a belief in the supremacy of "British" values and institutions; and a willingness to resort to military violence, simultaneously coupled with a staunch faith in the benevolence and humanitarianism of the British Empire. Furthermore, British settler colonies were, like other British colonies, structured by a number of hierarchies. Relationships of race, gender, class, and religion were critical in determining categories of inclusion and exclusion. Who would be considered a "British subject" and in what particular ways would they be seen as such by settlers and various levels of government were processes that were, as in other colonial settings, shaped by relations of power and dominance. These hierarchies might be mutable and were subject to challenges from various groups, both within the colonies themselves and the metropole. Nonetheless, they helped shape these societies and gave them their form and structure.

Yet we can also identity a range of significant differences that, over time, came to distinguish British settler colonialism from the forms of imperial expansion that occurred in other colonies. One of the most critical and important distinctions that shaped settler colonialism was the assumption that the British settlers' presence would be permanent, an expectation that had significant and enduring implications for Indigenous people. Demographics also played an important role in British settler colonies. With the exception of South Africa, white settlers came to outnumber Indigenous people over the course of the nineteenth century. This development had serious political, social, and cultural implications for both colonized and colonizer, a theme that runs through various chapters of this book. While this book explores the ongoing ties between Britain and her settler colonies, it also points to the growth of settler nationalism and demands for a distinct and differentiated status within the Empire, most notably over the question of responsible government.

In addition to differences between settler colonies and colonies whose primary purpose was economic and/or military and diplomatic usefulness to Britain, the societies considered here had their own particular and specific histories. Some had already been affected by European presence and had been marked by warfare between groups of Europeans as well as European-Indigenous conflict. Some negotiated treaties with Indigenous peoples, while others had no formal agreements with the latter. While they all were connected to Britain, their relationships with the metropole were shaped by a range of dynamics, not least metropolitan attitudes concerning these colonies' military, diplomatic, and economic potential and usefulness for imperial goals, attitudes which shifted over time. Moreover, while these colonies were part of a network of "British worlds," those links and connections of people, goods, practices, institutions, and identities that tied them to the metropole (and at times to each other), their histories were affected by other worlds and other sets of networks. Australia and New Zealand, for example, were tied to Pacific routes of trade and migration; by the early twentieth century Australia, in particular, also looked to the United States. Canada had links to Atlantic, Pacific, and Caribbean networks, and it was also connected to the United States. In turn, while South Africa's Cape Colony and Natal were tied to Britain through markets, missionaries, and the military, they also were linked to an Indian Ocean world of migration and labour. Settler societies' constitution over the nineteenth century is best explored, I argue, from multiple perspectives—not least those of settler colonists themselves—so that we can appreciate the dynamic interplay between them and the wider worlds to which they were linked. This dynamism was a significant part of their histories.

*Building Better Britains?* opens in 1783 and spans the nineteenth and early twentieth centuries, ending in the aftermath of World War I. The American Revolution (1776–83) and the Napoleonic Wars (1803–15) were pivotal moments in the founding of these colonies. In a similar vein, the early 1920s saw significant developments in settler nationalism. Such identities had been shaped by both the South African War (1899–1902) and World War I; the commemoration of these events was marked by both an ongoing connection to Britain and a sense of settler societies' individual contributions to these conflicts. As well, the networks and connections between these societies and Britain that developed over the course of the nineteenth century did not end in 1919. Indeed, in the aftermath of World War I emigration from Britain to settler societies continued to occur at relatively high levels. By 1931, though, these colonies had become, for the most part, Dominions. Their twentieth-century histories are sufficiently complex and multilayered to warrant their own treatment.

Chapter 1 explores colonial relationships with Indigenous peoples. A central, defining feature of these colonies was their relationship with their original inhabitants. Indigenous-newcomer contacts involved conflict, negotiation, and—at times—cooperation over land, resources, political governance, intimate relations, and cultural representations. These developments were not one-sided, predictable, or homogeneous. Depending on time and location, they resulted in treaties, formal warfare, informal physical conflict, or some combination of all three. In some contexts, such as Australia or Canada's Pacific coast, treaties were more pronounced by their absence. These relationships were also mediated by factors such as colonists' need for Indigenous peoples' trading networks and knowledge of geography, climate, and topography. Preexisting relationships, whether forged through military alliances and conflicts, trade, or missionary work, also affected nineteenth-century developments. Yet while the Indigenous societies that settlers encountered were marked by their heterogeneity, over the course of the nineteenth century a common theme in settler colonies' history was Indigenous peoples' increased marginalization. They lost more control of land and resources, increasingly inhabited designated areas controlled by colonial officials, saw their physical mobility limited by legislation and practice, and experienced the suppression of their languages and culture. (Simultaneously, Indigenous culture frequently was appropriated by settler civil society as a way of distinguishing its culture from that of the metropole.) Indigenous people reacted to these developments in a number of ways: armed and open resistance, such as the New Zealand Wars (1845–72) or the Cape Colony's 1851 Kat River Uprising; negotiation and cooperation, which might involve intermarriage with settlers, becoming members of missionary societies, or fighting for colonial powers; or engaging in Indigenous revivals of language and culture, thus drawing boundaries (as best they could) between themselves and settlers.

Chapter 2 explores the processes of migration and settlement in these colonies, ones that began in the late eighteenth century and intensified after the end of the Napoleonic Wars. Waves of British, other European, and—in some contexts—African people found their way to the Antipodes, British North America, and the Cape Colony. This migration took a number of forms. It might be forced, as in the case of convict transportation to New

South Wales; it might be the movement of refugees fleeing the aftermath of the American Revolution; or it might be that of men and women who sought better futures as a result of social and economic upheaval in Britain. The chapter also examines the implementation of structures of governance in settler colonies, as they shared British law and legal systems, not to mention colonial governors. The latter, along with members of the judiciary, both travelled from Britain to the colonies and moved between colonial sites. However, while by the end of the nineteenth century settler colonies shared much in their legal structures and methods of policing, these developments also were influenced by local conditions and particular historical contingencies. Questions that surrounded political representation, particularly challenges to the authority of colonial governors and the issue of "responsible government," also became urgent and important to settlers during the nineteenth century. They were shaped by concepts of liberal democracy and the possibility that settler societies might represent new opportunities for white male settlers. By the middle of the century settlers began to form national governments, processes that were primarily conducted through constitutional negotiations between different provincial bodies, whether in 1867 British North America or 1901 Australia. The 1910 Union of South Africa, though, was a different matter. It had been preceded by a war that involved Britain and her supporters in the region, the Boer republics, and other settler Dominions.

Settler economies and the labour they depended on are the subject of Chapter 3. In the late eighteenth and early nineteenth centuries, the imperial state and, to no small extent, the British military were significant actors in shaping settler economies. While the mid-nineteenth century saw the end of mercantilism and the rise of free trade, imperial investments and exchanges within the "British world" were significant, indeed critically important, for the settler societies' economies. By the early twentieth century Australia, British America (Canada), the Cape, and New Zealand were actively engaged in financial networks that intensified their ties to the metropole. Such networks moved credit, technology, and material culture across the British Empire and underpinned the expansion of settler economies. Although the ideal form of settlement for these colonies was that of the small, independent "yeoman" farmer, this model was not achieved in every society or, at least, not in its idealized version. Some contexts, climate, and topography made it far from being feasible. Settler societies' economies were marked not just by agriculture but by pastoralism, whaling, logging, fishing, mining, and, toward the end of the century, industrial production. Accordingly, settler economies relied on and mobilized a wide range of labour: that of the household and family; the unfree labour of slaves or convicts; the coerced and unpaid labour of Indigenous people; South Asian indentured labour; and Chinese contract labour. British migrants also brought with them both the belief that labour had the right to organize collectively and their experiences within the British trade union movement. In settler societies, though, the labour movement was shaped by racial, ethnic, and gendered hierarchies.

Chapter 4 then turns to the domain of "civil society": the family, domesticity, and intimate relations; religion; voluntary associations and institutions; and education. Importing British institutions—whether marriage, churches, or schools—was a concern and, in many ways, a struggle for colonial officials and settlers. For one, they brought with them assumptions about heterosexual marriage and the need for patriarchal households as the "building block" of settler society. Yet in the context of places such as Australia or British America, concerns about marriage were also shaped by the question of interracial sexuality and the presence of other kinds of marriages and intimate relations. As well as trying to regulate marriage, colonial elites also attempted to regulate the behaviour of colonists, Indigenous communities, and racialized people through voluntary institutions; edicts about manners and behaviour; and ordinances that governed disease, drinking, and sexual conduct. Through its dissemination of beliefs, people, and artifacts, the British missionary movement played a role in such practices. It also helped link settler societies to the metropole, to each other, and, in many cases, to other British colonies. Moreover, the drive for spiritual self-improvement also had its secular counterpart, in the spread of both institutions that promoted informal types of learning and those of formal, state-supported and organized education. Settler colonists' arguments for compulsory, state-regulated, and free education were inspired by developments both in Britain and in Europe. They also, however, were shaped by the belief that colonists needed education in order to create "better Britains" made up of "better Britons." Such developments were not seamless or untouched by hierarchies of gender, race, and class, at the level of either primary or university education.

Chapter 5 closes the book with an exploration of identity and culture in settler societies. Settler colonists thought of themselves as "British," albeit in multilayered ways and in ways that were informed by conceptions of settler nationalism. Settler constructions of identity took a number of forms: they were expressed in attitudes toward the Crown, forms of cultural representation, the press, and concepts of both the future and the past. From the mid-nineteenth century on, settler societies also began to display themselves in industrial and imperial exhibitions. Such displays highlighted themes of agricultural development, the richness of colonial resources, the progress of manufacturing, and the advance of settler "civilization" (in some cases, through the exhibition of "civilized" Indigenous people). Finally, settler societies' participation in war, particularly in South Africa and World War I, also led to the creation of narratives, monuments, prose and poetry, and other forms of representation that valourized the Dominions' participation in such conflicts. These cultural genres suggested that such experiences were not only important testimonies to imperial devotion and loyalty but also part of the process of nation-building. As with many other aspects of settler societies' construction, the creation of such identities was not a neutral process, devoid of relationships of power. For one, it was profoundly gendered. Although white, middle-class women often were keen participants, they were limited to certain images and narratives, usually cast as "mothers of the nation" or represented as allegorical or mythical figures. While at times working-class men and women supported imperial and nationalistic ventures, they often had little or no control over dominant narratives of empire and nation. Racial minorities and Indigenous people were by no means silent in asserting their own identities and distinct cultures and histories. Nevertheless, in general their experiences were overlooked and subsumed, particularly as settler nations became increasingly structured by more restrictive and racially exclusionary policies and practices.

*Building Better Britains?* explores the shared histories of these societies, while simultaneously being sensitive to the nuances that at times differentiated them from each other. Often seen within national frameworks, the histories of these settler colonies provide us with another means of conceptualizing the multiple ways in which the British Empire reshaped the nineteenth-century world. As we will see in Chapter 1, such reshaping had profound effects on the worlds and societies of Indigenous people.

# 1

# Colonial Frontiers and Contact Zones: Indigenous Peoples and Settler Encounters

*It appears to me to be the finest country I have yet as seen.... The habitations of the Indians are pretty close on each side of the river as far as I could see, with a very few white people interspersed among them, married to squaws and others of half blood, their offspring. The church in the village is elegant, the school house commodious, both built by the British government, who annually order a great many presents to be distributed among the natives; ammunition and warlike stores of all the necessary kinds; saddles, bridles, kettles, cloth, blankets, tomahawks, with tobacco pipes in the end of them; other things, and trinkets innumerable, provisions and stores; so that they may live, and really be, as the saying goes, as happy as the day is long.*
—Patrick Campbell, *Travels*, 1793[1]

*Forasmuch as we the poor oppressed Hottentot race are objects of the present war which is going on here, who have now been for a considerable time oppressed by the unrighteous English settlers, who have so continually petitioned the Government, by memorials, for consent and execution of irregular and oppressive laws, such as vagrant laws, which tend to oppression and complete ruin of the coloured and poor of this land, a land which we, as natives, may justly claim as our mother land, it is my aim and object, by this opportunity, esteeming it my duty ... to give information that this war which is going on here, is declared against us Hottentots because we defend ourselves against above-mentioned laws, or will not let them pass. Thus it is my earnest wish and request to you (since the poor and ruined of our race here have employed me to represent to you*

1

*this their deplorable condition) to hear your determination regarding this matter
as a nation, and who ought to bear and feel with one another in hardship; and
what your plans and intentions are, as the principal portion of our nation have
earnestly requested me to entreat from you to favour them as soon as possible
with an answer or decision.*

*Beloved, rise manfully and unanimously as a nation and children of one
house to engage yourselves in this important work, a work which concerns your
mother country, for not a single person of colour, wherever he may be, will
escape this law. Trust, therefore, in the Lord (whose character is known to be
unfriendly to injustice), and undertake your work, and he will give us
prosperity—a work for your mother-land and freedom, for it is now the time,
yea, the appointed time, and no other.*

—Willem Uithaalder, 1851[2]

English traveller Patrick Campbell's account of his visit to the late
eighteenth-century Haudenosaunee community of the Six Nations on the
Grand River, a territory located in what is now southern Ontario, depicted
a society marked by hospitality, politeness, and—not least—degrees of cultural mingling and adaptation. The latter was practised not just by Indigenous
people but also by those Europeans who had chosen to live among them. In
contrast, Willem Uithaalder, leader of the Khoekhoe people who in 1851
took up arms against the British at the Cape Colony's Kat River, saw his
and his people's situation in a very different light. Uithaalder's letter was a
plea to Griqua leader Adam Kok to join forces with the Khoekhoe to combat
the rule of settlers. While Campbell's travelogue suggests how Indigenous
communities might affirm their identities and presence in the face of settler
colonialism, Uithaalder's letter testifies to some of the important changes
that Indigenous societies faced during the nineteenth century as settlers
became a more numerous—and permanent—force in their territories.

As a number of historians have pointed out, one of the more distinctive
features of settler colonies was the relationship between Indigenous peoples,
settlers, and land. Unlike other colonies in the British Empire in which the
extraction of resources—sugar, cotton, minerals—or diplomatic and military considerations were the main reasons for Britain's presence, in places
such as New Zealand or British America settler society was forged through
the creation of new "homes" for British migrants and the accompanying
dispersal and dispossession of Indigenous peoples. While these processes
at times involved the acquisition of Indigenous labour, most notably in the
Cape Colony and in some Australian colonies, nevertheless the ideal that

motivated the formation of "better Britains"—the creation of an agricultural society settled by independent farmers—meant that Indigenous peoples' experiences need to be considered in light of such processes.

However, Indigenous peoples in the Australian colonies, British America, the Cape, and New Zealand were by no means homogeneous groups. Their societies encompassed a range of social, economic, political, and cultural structures and ideologies, not to mention a wide range of languages. As well, the timing of their encounters with settlers played a role in nineteenth-century developments. Whether they had longer histories as military and trading allies or whether their meetings with Europeans were abrupt confrontations mattered for Indigenous societies, at least so far as short-term developments were concerned. Moreover, these encounters were also influenced by Europeans' own histories and the concepts they brought with them to the shores of New South Wales or the interior of British America. It also made a difference, at least initially, who those Europeans were: traders, military leaders, land speculators, and humanitarians came with a range of motivations, beliefs, and practices.

Yet despite these differences, Indigenous people were confronted with similar problems over the course of the nineteenth century, ones that revolved around questions of land and governance and that frequently involved military and settler violence. Indigenous peoples' histories in nineteenth-century British settler societies were marked by attempted dispossessions of their land, culture, language, and autonomy and, overall, their containment by the steady expansion of settler communities. Nevertheless, Indigenous peoples were far from passive in the face of such depredations. The nineteenth century was also marked by their resistance, negotiation, and at times cooperation with colonial and imperial powers, means by which they attempted to cope and contend with changes Europeans brought to their doors. Furthermore, as later chapters will explore, even though the nineteenth century was one of increased settler power, it also was marked by Indigenous political and social activism.

### Indigenous-European Encounters, 1650s–1790s

In the late eighteenth and early nineteenth centuries, British and other European settlers encountered a vast range of Indigenous societies. Historians and anthropologists who have studied Indigenous communities and their relationships to different settler societies and nation-states— Australia, Canada, New Zealand, and South Africa—have provided us with a wealth of national, regional, and local studies. Such scholarship makes it clear that Indigenous societies are quite heterogeneous and complex in their histories; their social, political, and cultural structures and beliefs; and, in particular, their relationships to land and place. These societies might be hierarchical, ranked by status and birth, and practise slaveholding of those captured in warfare. Alternatively, they could be more egalitarian in their structure, with descent reckoned matrilineally or through paternal lines; residence could be determined by matrilocal or patrilocal principles. Extended families or clans often played an important role in a range of areas, such as the choice of marriage partner, use of hunting and fishing territories, political decision making, religious ceremonies, and healing practices, thereby structuring virtually all aspects of the community's life. While gender relations shaped Indigenous societies, as they did European ones, the form they took might vary considerably. In some communities serial monogamy was the norm, which often resulted in women having considerable autonomy in their choice of husband; they also could leave a marriage should they choose to do so. Other societies, though, were polygamous, while in some societies wives' freedom to leave unsuitable marriages might be limited and women's adultery could incur severe penalties. Furthermore, Indigenous communities supported themselves through a broad range of activities, ones that included hunting and gathering, pastoral farming, agriculture, and fishing. Some communities also possessed multiple languages, cultural beliefs, and practices.

However, we can identify some common themes that shaped Indigenous societies' histories over the course of the nineteenth century. One question leading to the identification of such themes was that of previous encounters with Europeans. Had they already come into contact with members of the military, imperial authorities, explorers, traders, and missionaries? And if so, what were the circumstances of those meetings? By the 1790s, for example, a number of Indigenous communities on the northeastern seaboard of North America had approximately two centuries of relationships with European powers, both as military allies—and enemies—and as liaisons in the fur trade. They also had witnessed the effect of Christianity, both Protestant and Catholic, on their societies, a religious encounter that had mixed results for their own spiritual beliefs and practices. Moreover, the American Revolution (1776–83) had catastrophic results for the Haudenosaunee (Iroquois) people. No matter which side they picked, Loyalist or Patriot, members of the Iroquoian Confederacy were faced with upheaval and dislocation. They either became refugees, forced to relocate to

Quebec, or had to contend with the loss of their traditional lands as the new United States government sought to expand into the continent's interior. Others, though, such as northern Pacific societies or the Cree and Ojibwa living in the northwestern interior of the continent, did not experience such catastrophic disruptions until later in the nineteenth century. They too, though, had contact with Europeans (and, for coastal peoples, Kanaka and other members of Pacific Indigenous communities) through fur and other forms of trade.

Indigenous people living in southern Africa had equally lengthy and complicated histories of contact with Europeans. They also experienced their own histories of change and conflict before the expansion of British settlement at the Cape Colony occurred in the late eighteenth century. In 1652 the Khoisan, nomadic pastoralists, encountered the Dutch East India Company (VOC) when it established a small settlement, including a fort, at Table Bay in the Cape peninsula's extreme southwest; it was intended to serve as a station for ships en route to the Dutch East Indies. Over the next century and a half, settlement spread into the northern and eastern regions of the Cape, not at the instigation of the VOC but because Dutch settlers wished to obtain more land for themselves and their cattle. Once the Khoisan people realized the intruders did not intend to leave, they retaliated by attacking their farms; however, their lack of firearms and insufficient fighters led to their defeats in 1659 and in the 1670s. The Khoisan situation then became even more dire, as a major smallpox epidemic eroded their numbers. By the late eighteenth century, the Khoi had lost the vast majority of their society's communal structures and their own language was increasingly replaced by Afrikaans, the Dutch dialect spoken by the settlers. They also found themselves working for the Dutch as farm servants, serving as colonial soldiers in so-called Hottentot (the Dutch word for the Khoisan) regiments, scraping a living on the margins of Cape Town, or relocating to mission stations. Between 1652 and 1807 the Dutch changed the Cape's demographics as they transported slaves from the Dutch East Indies, islands in the Indian Ocean, and Africa's east coast to work in Cape Town and the colony's surrounding farms. A new society thus was formed at the Western Cape, one composed of Khoisan, slaves, ex-slaves, and the mixed-race children of Dutch farmers and Indigenous women.

As the population of the southern Tswana people grew substantially in central and eastern South Africa, they expanded their trade with Muslim and Portuguese merchants, since their territory along the eastern coast lay at the convergence of a number of Indian Ocean trade routes. While trade might lead to conflict, since communities disputed who would control the routes and the ways in which goods were dispersed, it also helped contribute to a "rough and ready" equality, as different groups needed to negotiate their relationships in order to obtain goods. Yet not all Southern African communities were able to maintain the kind of equilibrium that trading relationships might bring. In the continent's southern interior, the expansion of Dutch settlement resulted in both the Khoisan and the San (Bushman) people being pushed further into the middle and lower ranges of the Orange River. There they found themselves in competition for resources with groups already resident in the area. As well, Dutch farmers raided Indigenous communities for livestock and female and child slaves, the latter taken to work as domestics and shepherds. Over this period, then, pastoral and hunter-gatherer communities in the interior began to break up. Their replacements were more fluid and, historians argue, unstable, as they were forced to support themselves with a range of hunting, gathering, herding, trading, and raiding.

In the southern Pacific, Indigenous meetings with Europeans became more frequent over the course of the eighteenth century. Although not without tensions that erupted into violence, this process took a different trajectory than in the case of southern Africa and British America. Exploration and trade, not settlement, brought Europeans to Indigenous peoples' attention in the eighteenth century. Such processes might include Captain James Cook's three voyages between 1768 and 1779; the whaling and sealing enterprises in which Indigenous sailors from both New Zealand and Australia participated; and Britain's increasing commercial expansion in the area, one that became particularly significant in the context of Atlantic upheaval in the 1770s and 1780s. The first European landing was that of Abel Tasman, whose 1642 stop on New Zealand's South Island was notable for its brevity and bloodiness. Cook's voyages, dedicated to scientific exploration and discovery, drew both Europeans and Indigenous peoples more firmly into each other's orbit. Moreover, Indigenous people did not meet only Europeans. British trade routes stretched from Australasia to China and India, linking the Pacific and Indian Oceans. Those who worked on sealing vessels, for example, might meet lascar crews from India, hear new languages, and encounter new kinds of food and drink, such as rum from Bengal or tea from China.

Such patterns of fluidity, along with a different balance of power than in other colonial settings, continued into the early nineteenth century. From about 1810 small numbers of settlers started arriving in New Zealand;

however, before the arrival of British authority in the mid-1830s the narrative of Māori-European encounters in New Zealand was one of the latter's dependence on the former. This dependence might take the form of needing Indigenous help in supplying ships and Indigenous labour to crew them—though without, it seems, the kind of forced labour that occurred at the Cape—or, in the case of settlers, Indigenous knowledge of topography, climate, vegetation, and wildlife. In such exchanges Māori people frequently held the upper hand and often quickly took advantage of the economic opportunities that work on whaling vessels, for example, afforded them. As well, marriages between British, European, and non-European crew members and Māori women resulted in a culture distinguished by its polyglot, multi-ethnic, often cosmopolitan flavour, one that could not be easily pigeonholed in the binary categories of whites and Indigenous peoples.

By the 1790s, then, Indigenous people in settler societies created by the spread of the British Empire had developed varying degrees of contact and familiarity with Europeans. The nature and extent of these meetings was shaped by a number of variables and contingencies. These encompassed geographic location, the motivations that underlaid Europeans' presence, and the state of Indigenous communities' demographics, economies, and political structures, not to mention the presence—or absence—of conflict with other Indigenous peoples. All of these factors would play important roles as Indigenous societies contended with increasingly larger numbers of British migrants. For the most part, the latter arrived with the intention of not just trading or exploring: they wished to found new homes on Indigenous territories.

### Indigenous and European Perceptions of "the Other"

When Indigenous people looked at these newcomers and the material culture they brought with them—food, plants, animals, clothing, tools, and other artifacts—what did they see? A definitive answer to that question remains elusive, either because some communities have left no record of their thoughts or because settlers did not care too much about their effect on others. Yet it is possible to glimpse a range of perceptions and reactions to the presence of a large number of outsiders. For one, Indigenous communities created their own oral histories, ones that were passed down from generation to generation and helped educate Indigenous youth about these encounters. From the mid-nineteenth century on, anthropologists and, later, historians gathered these histories; such narratives have alerted us to a wide range of Indigenous reactions to the strangers on their lands. Furthermore, Indigenous historians such as the Anishinabe writers Kahkewaquonaby/ Peter Jones and Kahgegagahbowh/George Copway from the British American colony of Upper Canada (Ontario) published histories of their peoples. These narratives appeared in the mid-nineteenth century; they were not limited to Anishinabe encounters with Europeans, but they provided valuable information about such meetings. As well, in some cases, a few of the new arrivals were indeed struck by Indigenous peoples' responses to them. In other accounts, we can glean such reactions by reading between the lines of settlers' thoughts and deeds to catch Indigenous peoples' curiosity, fascination, exasperation, and at times outright anger at the behaviour of these strangers.

In the Australian colonies of New South Wales, Victoria, and South Australia, Indigenous people displayed a range of attitudes toward Europeans. In some cases, they were simply quite curious, both about the people themselves and about the material culture they brought with them. Explorer G.A. Robinson wrote of being watched by young Aboriginal women during his first trip to western Van Diemen's Land (Tasmania). Others noted that Aboriginal people would scour newcomers' camps for goods that Europeans had abandoned, putting them to use for their own needs. One site in Gippsland, southeast of the city of Melbourne, produced clothing, sewing materials, blankets, tools, a thermometer tube, muskets, a sealskin hat, a Bible, and British newspapers. Iron and glass were particularly prized by Aboriginal people, as the former was durable, could be worked more easily than stone, and kept sharp, while glass was better suited to use in stone-working techniques than iron. Travellers' journals also suggest that Aboriginal people could extend assistance and friendship toward them, providing them with information about waterholes, springs, and shortcuts through unfamiliar terrain.

Yet good-natured inquisitiveness did not characterize all of these encounters. Unlike Indigenous people in British America, for example, or at the Cape, Australian Aborigines had not become accustomed to the large domesticated animals brought by settlers. Europeans' livestock strayed into their camping and hunting sites, scaring away game and fouling waterholes that had both physical and spiritual meanings for Aboriginal communities. Cattle, in particular, were at the very least disconcerting, if not terrifying, with their large horns, loud bellows, and at times hostile behaviour. People in South Australia told missionary George Taplin of their fear of wandering bullocks, calling them *windwiyere*, or beings with spears on their heads. Furthermore, Aboriginal people also were puzzled by the very nature of whites. While community protocols might prevent Aboriginal people from inquiring too closely about Europeans' differences, at times their curiosity might win out, especially when it came to determining the gender of these strange beings. They also could not decide if they were ghosts, as the colour white was linked to death. Possessing kin systems in which all were related, it was unthinkable to Aboriginals that these people might be true strangers or that they could come from another land beyond the sea other than the realm to which humans travelled after their deaths. However, if the latter was the case, Aboriginal communities could not fathom why the settlers did not recognize them as their relatives and friends; some then decided that the trauma of death and an unexpected resurrection had damaged settlers' memories and intelligence. They therefore treated them in a sympathetic and good-natured way, seeing them as simple-minded relatives whose slow acquisition of Aboriginal languages might be explained as the gradual relearning of lost skills. However, such a perspective started to change as Aboriginal communities gradually saw settlers as truly strangers, not reborn community members. Others maintained their belief that the settlers were indeed a type of spirit but instead—and with good reason—thought of them as evil ones, even devils. In Australia, the dissemination of such beliefs and of European goods was facilitated both by traditional trade routes, which crossed the continent and might move goods hundreds of miles from their point of origin, and by tribal messengers, who covered long distances quite quickly in order to pass information between clans.

If Indigenous peoples' reactions might cover a spectrum that ranged from open-mindedness, curiosity, and hospitality to suspicion, distaste, and fear, how did settlers view them? Such a phenomenon is difficult to quantify, not least because only a minority of these large waves of immigrants left impressions of their new homes. In many cases, though, it seems that settlers often were not that interested in those whose traditional lands they now lived upon. Arrivals from England, for example, who came to Upper Canada between 1815 and 1840 had little, if anything, to say about Indigenous people, even though those who took up uncleared land in the colony might well live next door to Indigenous communities. However, some of the colony's prominent literary figures, such as Susanna Moodie and her sister Catherine Parr Traill, noted the presence of Indigenous people, particularly women, around them. They could be quite fascinated by their lives and work. (The fact that Moodie had been involved in humanitarian work in

England, transcribing the memoirs of the former slave Mary Prince, might have made her more sensitive to their presence.) Those who served in military campaigns in which Indigenous people were allies recorded a range of impressions. Major John Richardson, for example, who fought alongside a range of Great Lakes peoples in the War of 1812 admired many Indigenous warriors for their tenacity, intelligence, and physical bravery. He was also repulsed by some of their practices and thought that at least one nation, the Chippewa, were cowardly and spiteful.

Travellers' accounts, such as that written by Patrick Campbell, also had much to say about Indigenous people. By the late eighteenth century, travel writing was a genre that had its own long-standing history of observing and commenting on these communities. In the early nineteenth century, though, such accounts were also written to provide information about colonial conditions for those considering emigration from Britain, so their descriptions often downplayed tensions between Indigenous and non-Indigenous people. Despite this tendency, at times these writers approached Indigenous communities with more curiosity and, in some cases, empathy—witness, for example, Campbell's appreciation of the hybridity of Joseph Brant's Mohawk Village—than did settlers. The latter tended to see Indigenous people as a nuisance, obstacles who stood in the way of Europeans' claims to land and control of resources. Moreover, unlike other Europeans, Campbell expressed considerable admiration for Mohawk women, as he saw them as physically striking and commanding in their appearance.

Explorers might also realize how dependent they were on Indigenous communities. In 1833, the 17-year-old Edward John Eyre, the third son of a Yorkshire clergyman, arrived in New South Wales. While in the colony, Eyre's travels took him to a number of areas unfamiliar to Europeans, as he journeyed as far west as the Swan River settlement, 200 kilometres west of Adelaide in South Australia. Although Eyre would be known for his harsh conduct as the Governor of Jamaica and his brutal suppression of the 1865 Morant Bay Uprising, as a young man he was more open-minded about the communities he saw on his travels. In his account of his expedition between Adelaide and King George's Sound, published in 1845 in London, Eyre noted Indigenous peoples' willingness to help his party. As well, while he saw them as "others," he also noted the features that Aboriginal people and Europeans held in common. Moreover, Eyre insisted that any Aboriginal brutality settlers experienced had to be seen as the consequence of imperial expansion: for the most part, Aboriginal people did not resort to violence unless they were provoked. Eyre's travelogue demonstrates a desire to learn from Indigenous people and, too, an understanding of the effect that settler colonialism was having on them. Yet in other contexts Indigenous people were seen as being close to subhuman. The treatment of the Khoi woman Sarah Baartman, for example, who in the early nineteenth century travelled to Britain and France and who appeared for audiences as a kind of racial spectacle, shows how European curiosity could become racial voyeurism. As we will see, missionaries, humanitarian organizations, and government officials had their own perspectives on Indigenous societies.

## Indigenous Communities and Early Nineteenth-Century Colonial States

Over the course of the nineteenth century, Indigenous communities generally felt the impact of the colonial state most keenly, as colonial governments increasingly played a central role in reshaping their relationship to traditional territories and homelands. The imperial government played a critically important part in this process; the Colonial Office, established in 1801, was charged with running the daily affairs of the Empire. The Secretary of State for the Colonies became a senior cabinet minister and was assisted by a junior minister or parliamentary undersecretary. During the 1830s these individuals were crucial in shaping colonial policy in settler colonies.

Other factors, though, were significant, such as existing patterns of relationships between Indigenous people and British imperial power and the reasons for British expansion into particular areas. In the context of the late eighteenth century, global warfare often played a particularly important role. At South Africa's Cape Colony, for example, which Britain had seized from the Dutch in 1795 as part of its military strategy in the French Revolutionary Wars (1792–1802), the imperial power's military concerns came to the fore. Britain set up military and naval bases and also deployed troops to support settlers on the colony's frontiers, displacing Indigenous farmers who were resisting white attempts to push them from their lands. The question of which imperial power would rule the Cape was not determined until 1806, as the colony was returned to the Dutch in 1803 and then recaptured when the Napoleonic Wars (1803–15) resumed. Nevertheless, during the wars British troops were crucial in displacing Xhosa people along the colony's eastern river. While the end of the Napoleonic Wars resulted in the confirmation of British rule, it was not until 1820 that British immigrants began to arrive in large numbers; 5,000 of the arrivals settled in the eastern part of the Cape. Unlike British America or the Australian colonies, in the first half of the nineteenth century British immigration to South Africa was relatively small in scale. Dutch settlers outnumbered the British at the Cape itself, while African communities along the colony's frontier waged war on settler incursions.

Transatlantic warfare also brought British settlers, in the form of parties of convicts and their overseers, to New South Wales, as Britain's loss of her American colonies brought an end to the transportation of British prisoners to North America. The 1788 arrival of the First Fleet in New South Wales brought 1,000 men and women, a group that by 1815 was still only 15,000. Yet settlement spread into the colony's interior, reaching up its rivers and across the Bass Strait into Van Diemen's Land. The initial meeting at Sydney Harbour was quite friendly, as Aboriginal people helped the British come ashore. Lieutenant William Bradley's sketch of one such encounter, at Broken Bay, demonstrates the tone of these meetings. It, and subsequent landings in New South Wales, was marked by dancing, singing, and playful roughhousing, as well as British combing of Aboriginal peoples' hair (see Figure 1.1). Later British incursions onto Aboriginal land, though, made without consultation or offers of compensation, resulted in ongoing conflict.

FIGURE 1.1 "View in Broken Bay New South Wales March 1788," by Lieutenant William Bradley. Bradley's note for his sketch states, "These people mixed with ours and all hands danced together."

Source: Mitchell Library, State Library of New South Wales.

Aboriginal peoples' resistance was met with even greater amounts of settler violence in which Aboriginal warriors' skill with spears was outmatched by the blunt force of the settlers' rifles. European diseases also proved devastating to communities that had not been exposed to them. These patterns would be replicated in the 1820s—and beyond—as pastoralist entrepreneurs, or squatters, moved with their convict workers and herds of sheep and cattle into the plains beyond the Blue Mountains, an area beyond the boundaries of official settlement. Furthermore, the colonial government's use of the Native Police, first formed in 1837 in Port Phillip, added to the violence, as the force became known for its brutality toward fellow-Aboriginals.

In neither colony, then, was there much incentive or, it seems, desire to negotiate with Indigenous communities, possibly because they had no history of military alliance with Britain and were not seen in the early nineteenth century as strategically useful to the imperial power. Such was not the case in British America. As previously noted, a longer history of British contact, rivalry with other European powers (most notably France) that necessitated alliances with northeastern Indigenous communities, and relationships with Indigenous people in the fur trade had set a pattern of diplomatic negotiations that culminated in a number of treaties. For one, the Royal Proclamation of 1763 established limits on settler expansion into the Ohio Valley. This document arose from the Crown's desire to set out the foundations for peaceful coexistence between Indigenous people and settlers; it involved the former in its design and ratification. The Royal Proclamation declared that all lands that had not been ceded to or bought by the British would be considered reserved for Indigenous people, no lands were to be taken without Indigenous consent, and their territorial integrity and decision-making powers over their lands would be respected and protected. The Proclamation also stated that colonial governments, private individuals, and British subjects could not survey, grant, or settle on unceded lands. Only Crown officials could purchase land from Indigenous people at public meetings and assemblies. The Proclamation, however, also included provisions to extinguish Indigenous peoples' title to their lands. Ratified at a 1764 assembly in Niagara by both the British and multiple Indigenous nations, the Proclamation provided the basis for relationships between the British Crown and Canada's First Nations and the procedure for the treaties that would follow it.

Not all British American colonies, though, were settled by treaty. The Maritime colonies did not recognize the Proclamation. In Nova Scotia, for example, the only Indigenous rights that were acknowledged were those of hunting and fishing (albeit only at "the sovereign's pleasure"), and the Mi'kmaq people had to petition the colonial government for reserves. Newfoundland saw the extinction of the Beothuk people, and in Quebec the influx of Loyalist settlers in 1783 led to the Proclamation also being disregarded. In Upper Canada (present-day Ontario), though, treaties were made with the Anishinabe people. However, these treaties did not always meet the Proclamation's stipulation that they must be negotiated with large councils and their content was not always explained properly to Indigenous people; moreover, the colonial government's oral promises would not be honoured. The northern half of the colony (by then the province) also would be the subject of treaties in the mid-nineteenth century, although in those cases—the Robinson Treaty, for example—it was more business and industry's access to mineral resources, less so settler access to farmland, that was at stake. After Confederation in 1867, the Dominion government, keen to "open up" western Canada for agricultural settlement, struck seven treaties with Indigenous nations in the 1870s and four more in northern Canada (the last being negotiated in 1921). It also acquired the Hudson's Bay Company's lands in 1870. This latter acquisition took place without any consultation of the Indigenous and Métis people who lived in those territories, and it sparked considerable resentment on the part of the Métis, a resentment that flared into open rebellion in 1869–70.

In the case of New Zealand, British settlement occurred slowly and sporadically. Some escaped convicts, as well as others who were seeking adventure in the south Pacific, made their way across the Tasman Sea to New Zealand, yet Māori demographic, military, and social strengths left Europeans at a distinct disadvantage. Unlike the more scattered and isolated nature of Australian Aboriginal communities, the organized nature of Māori clans, their occupation of the island's best lands, and the fact that their trade with ships' crews had outfitted a number of them with guns left them able to attack Europeans and drive them away. Although missionaries established stations in New Zealand, starting with the London-based Church Missionary Society in 1809, until the late 1820s they operated under terms set by the Māori, few of whom converted. Missionaries made their greatest inroads into areas such as trade and agriculture, in teaching literacy, and as peacemakers who helped a number of Māori end tribal warfare. British colonial control, however, came from Sydney. Not surprisingly, given the distance involved and the small scale of the Sydney settlement, it was sporadic and exercised only in response to Māori complaints. In 1813 the Governor of New South Wales, Lachlan Macquarie, issued an order that extended British protection over Māori and stipulated that ships that put in at New Zealand must post a bond for their crews' good behaviour. In response to missionary complaints about mariners, escaped convicts, and traders' violence and disorderly behaviour, in 1817 the Secretary of State for the Colonies allowed courts to try cases of murder and manslaughter committed by British subjects outside British territory. Six years later this decision was followed by the authorization of New South Wales courts to try offences that had taken place in New Zealand.

Growing concerns at the Colonial Office about violence and possible threats to British dominance led to the 1832 appointment of James Busby as British Resident at the Bay of Islands. Busby was charged with preventing European violence toward Māori, protecting settlers and traders, taking escaped convicts into custody, and fostering good will toward Britain among Māori leaders. While Busby had little in the way of armed force to back his authority, he was able to provide London with a growing amount of news about the situation in New Zealand, dispatches that told the Colonial Office of the possibility of intertribal conflicts that threatened the security of British trade. Yet along with the more alarming descriptions of tension and conflict were those that painted a picture of a temperate climate, fertile and available land, and possible mineral riches. In 1835 Busby also helped 35 northern chiefs to sign a declaration that committed them to resisting invasion by other nations. Such positive news about New Zealand attracted the attention of colonization promoter Edward Gibbon Wakefield. In 1837, supported by a group of financiers, politicians, and businessmen, Wakefield founded the New Zealand Association (later known as the New Zealand Company). At this point the Colonial Office, pressed by various actors with differing concerns—promoting settlement, protecting Māori interests, establishing peace and order—could no longer argue for minimal British involvement. In response, it appointed as Consul-Designate William Hobson, a British naval commander who would become the colony's first governor in 1841. Instructed to establish British sovereignty over part or all of New Zealand, Hobson's role was to prevent further conflict between Māori and settlers, a role that culminated in the signing of the Treaty of Waitangi in 1840. Seen as the pivotal document for founding New Zealand as a bicultural society, the Treaty was signed by more than 500 high-ranking Māori men and women. It drew on British constitutional and legal history to set out three critical areas that would govern future relationships between Māori and *Pakeha* (non-Māori New Zealanders). Chiefs would recognize

British sovereignty, and Māori would be guaranteed possession of their lands, forests, and treasures (the Māori text) or fisheries (the English version). As well, Māori land sales would be offered exclusively to English buyers, and Māori would receive the rights and privileges of British subjects.

The Treaty was the subject of great debate within Māori communities. Those opposed to it warned it would lead to a loss of land and political and economic autonomy, while three important chiefs, Hone Heke, Patuone, and Tāmati Wāka Nene, argued that increased contact with Europeans would lead to some degree of compromise. They also believed the Treaty would protect Māori and give them more control in their dealings with Europeans. Their support turned to disillusionment and anger in the years just after the Treaty's signing, though. It became clear that the Colonial Office had not fully understood the promises it had made to the Māori or could not enforce the Treaty's provisions in the face of settlers' desire for land. In 1842 and 1843 Māori reacted to these problems with attacks on surveyors and military challenges to British authority. While Hobson and his successor, Governor Robert Fitzroy, attempted to calm matters through conciliation and the return of land bought before the Treaty, by 1845 the Colonial Office recalled Fitzroy and sent George Grey. Backed by imperial troops, Grey arrived with a policy of assimilating Māori into European economic, domestic, and legal structures and practices. Although Grey recognized Māori claims to tribal land, he also resumed land purchases and established a number of Māori reserves; like those in other settler colonies, these were generally insufficient for Indigenous needs. In 1846 Grey stated that acknowledging Māori ownership of uncultivated land was essentially pointless, a sentiment with which many settlers in the British Empire would have concurred. Māori, though, believed that uncultivated or not, their lands should not be alienated from them. Using a range of tactics and strategies, they would continue to oppose British land sales.

## Indigenous People and the Abolition of Slavery in the British Empire

By the 1830s and 1840s, Indigenous people in settler societies were undergoing similar experiences of conflict, dispossession, and attempts to assimilate them into European manners and habits (although the latter did not mean encouraging them to enter the colonial middle class). It is important not to overstate or exaggerate similarities, as each colony differed in the degree and timing of these processes. Indigenous people in British America's settler colonies, for example, were not seen as a valuable source of labour, free or unfree. In New Zealand settlers and colonial government arrived later than in, for example, British America or the Cape Colony. Treaties were signed in both New Zealand and British America, agreements that continue to resonate, particularly with Indigenous communities. Settler aggression and expansionism in both New Zealand and the Cape was met by organized military resistance; conversely, Indigenous peoples in both the Cape and New South Wales experienced often horrific levels of settler violence and cruelty.

Yet other shared patterns emerged, such as the fact that by the late nineteenth century Indigenous people were often outnumbered by settlers. Certainly demographic ratios and changes in them varied across these societies. Indigenous people in Upper Canada, for example, became a minority in that colony because of the sheer number of British immigrants who arrived after 1815. In contrast, at the signing of the Treaty of Waitangi there were 70,000–90,000 Māori in New Zealand and fewer than 2,000 Europeans. By 1858, though, declining fertility and rising mortality rates among the Māori left them with a population of around 56,000, while Europeans numbered 59,000, a ratio that became more uneven by 1896, with 42,000 Māori and 701,000 Europeans. In British Columbia, Indigenous people remained numerically dominant into the late nineteenth century, not least because the province's settler population did not reach the numbers hoped for by British officials and colonial promoters. In the Cape Colony, Indigenous Africans and mixed-race (coloured) people consistently outnumbered whites, a demographic reality realized only too well by a number of British and Afrikaans political leaders. Yet despite these important distinctions, Indigenous people in settler colonies shared the loss of their ancestral lands and sustained attacks on their historic ways of life, ones that occurred on a number of fronts.

The Cape Colony stood out in at least one respect: its relationship to slavery and its abolition in the British Empire. Although slavery existed in New France and elite Loyalists brought slaves with them to British America, it was phased out in Upper Canada by its first Lieutenant-Governor, John Graves Simcoe. In 1793 Simcoe championed legislation that in many ways foreshadowed slavery's 1833 abolition in the British Empire. At the Cape, though, slavery was more widely practised. Khoi and San people were either chattel slaves, who could be bought and sold, or treated as serfs who, although not legally slaves, experienced conditions that differed little from those endured by the former. There were fewer slaves at the Cape than in other parts of the Empire—40,000 as compared to 167,000 in Jamaica—and many were from the Indonesian archipelago and South Asia. Nevertheless, slavery in the Cape differed from the situation in other settler colonies, where obtaining Indigenous peoples' labour usually came second to seizing their lands. However, its abolition foreshadowed future developments in the treatment of Indigenous people, most notably in its combination of liberal ideologies that were coupled with paternalism.

Legislation passed in the 1820s helped ameliorate conditions for the Khoi and San people, and slavery was phased out between 1834 and 1838. Yet, as in Jamaica, the apprenticeship system that replaced slavery was aimed not at outright freedom for slaves but, rather, at imposing new forms of control on workers and reinforcing their dependency on employers for their survival. Apprentices could still be bought and sold, albeit not at public auctions; however, unlike the past, their duties were clearly spelled out, as were infractions and punishments (flogging for men, the stocks for women). In turn, employers saw their right to punish apprentices taken away by the colonial state and instead placed in the hands of magistrates. Although employers often resented these measures, they also used them to their advantage, as they charged apprentices with violation of their contracts and pressed for punishments that differed little from those they had inflicted as slave-owners. They also withdrew support for elderly and infirm apprentices and refused to extend it to slave women's children unless they were formally indentured to them. Apprentices also attempted to use the new system to their advantage. At times they refused to leave employers even when the latter wished for their departure, stole portable goods that they could sell in urban markets, or, in some cases, took employers before magistrates to demand redress for the former's violation of contracts. Nevertheless, the passage of the Masters and Servants Act in 1841 set in place restrictions on black workers' mobility, ones that were harsher than similar legislation in the Caribbean and that were not abolished in South Africa until 1974.

## Missionaries, Humanitarians, and the Report of the Select Committee on Aborigines

While settler and state intervention in Indigenous peoples' societies was aimed at securing their lands—and in some cases, most notably at the Cape, their labour—the story of missionary and humanitarian relationships with them is a complex one. Of course, by the late eighteenth century missionary work with Indigenous communities was by no means a new or novel phenomenon. Roman Catholic missions, most notably those of the Jesuit and Ursuline orders, had been part of seventeenth-century New France's colonial landscape (arguably, though, their greatest success in that period was with the colony's French population, less so than with its Indigenous residents). In eighteenth-century New England colonies, Protestant missions to Algonquian and Iroquoian people had led to their conversion. However, the global expansion of missionary work in the early nineteenth century, sparked by the surge of Britain's late eighteenth-century evangelical movement and coupled with the upheavals Indigenous peoples endured in this period, led to a growing prominence of missionaries within Indigenous society. Historians have cautioned that we must not confuse the increased missionary presence with a simple or straightforward acceptance of Christianity and a corresponding rejection of Indigenous spiritual beliefs and practices. The late eighteenth century also saw a number of Indigenous revivalist movements, such as the Haudenosaunee Code of Handsome Lake or that of the Shawnee spiritual leader, the Prophet. These movements explicitly rejected Christianity and those secular features of settler society—such as alcohol—that Indigenous leaders believed harmed their people. Moreover, Indigenous people might combine their own cultures' spiritual beliefs and practices with Christianity, resulting in syncretic religions that offered alternatives to the stark choices often presented by the missionaries.

Nevertheless, over the course of the nineteenth century missionaries made inroads into Indigenous communities, both at a quantitative and qualitative level, in unprecedented ways. For one, the early modern association between Christianity and European identity began to break down. Although this link was not as clear in British America, given its longer history of Christian proselytization among Indigenous people, Christianity in places such as the Cape was the province of Dutch settlers (and in other nearby areas, Portuguese slave traders and settlers). The 1799 arrival at the Cape of the London Missionary Society (LMS), an interdenominational organization founded in 1795, marked the beginning of Christian mission activity among Indigenous African communities. By the 1830s the Khoekhoe people, the recipients of much LMS attention, had developed their own robust and autonomous form of Christianity, one that did not rely on missionaries for its sustenance. In British America, one of the "hotbeds" of missionary activity was in the Great Lakes area. Haudenosaunee people who took up land along the banks of the Grand River had already been exposed to Christianity, particularly Anglicanism. As well, the early nineteenth century was marked by the arrival of American-based Episcopal Methodist preachers among neighbouring communities of Anishinabe people, particularly the Mississauga of the Credit River. The 1820s were marked by a wave of conversions and the creation of Christian villages. These were sparked by the dislocation and upheavals suffered by the Mississauga, who experienced settler encroachments on their lands and fisheries, disease, and problems with alcohol. Although in the following decade the Americans were replaced by British-based Wesleyan Methodists, a strong link was created between Indigenous communities and Christianity in the colony. Furthermore, not all missionaries were American or British. The Mississauga community had its own Methodist missionaries and produced prominent and well-known religious—and, in the case of Kahkewaquonaby, political—leaders, such as Kahkewaquonaby, Shahwundais/John Sunday, and Kagegagahbowh. As Figure 1.2 suggests, the missionary movement promoted such success stories as proof of its effectiveness.

Missionaries have been charged with reshaping Indigenous communities in ways that damaged their economies and political autonomy, altered domestic and sexual relations in ways that were harmful to Indigenous women, and undermined Indigenous languages and, in particular, spiritual practices. While there is certainly a degree of truth in such a characterization, historians have pointed out that such a narrative is too simplistic. Not all changes to Indigenous peoples' situations can be attributed to the presence of missionaries: settlers, traders, and colonial governments could be equally, if not more, detrimental to Indigenous communities' independence and survival. Moreover, at times missionaries lent their support and moral authority to Indigenous communities' struggles over land rights when colonial governments were determined to move them from their territories. Such was the case in Upper Canada in the mid-1830s. The Methodist church backed the Mississauga peoples' fight against colonial governor Francis Bond Head's attempt to move them from good farmland in the colony's southern region to a more isolated—and less agriculturally viable—location.

As well, missionaries were prominent, and in some contexts the sole, voices—other than those of Indigenous people themselves—raised in protest against settler violence. After the abolition of the British slave trade in 1807 and then slavery itself in 1833, British evangelicals turned their attention to the situation of Indigenous people in Britain's colonies. The Anti-Slavery Society, founded in 1823, began to lobby Westminster for an inquiry. Led by Thomas Fowell Buxton, who had been a significant force in abolition, in 1835 this group of humanitarians convinced Parliament to set up a Select Committee on the topic. Buxton and his fellow-evangelicals

**FIGURE 1.2** Shahwundais/John Sunday

Source: *Wesleyan-Methodist Magazine* (March 1839), London, England.
Image courtesy of Victoria University Library, University of Toronto.

(often dubbed the "Exeter Hall" set, a reference to one of their meeting places in London) were fortunate in their timing. The Colonial Office was led by prominent evangelicals or those sympathetic to humanitarianism, such as Colonial Secretary Lord Glenelg (Charles Grant), Parliamentary Secretary Sir George Grey, and Permanent Undersecretary James Stephen, who was extremely influential in shaping colonial policy. The Select Committee's hearings produced a vast amount of information about the abuse Indigenous people suffered in settler colonies. Missionaries, military officials, and colonial administrators testified to the decline of Khoisan people's status at the Cape, violence between colonists and Xhosa people in the Eastern Cape, the near-genocide of Aboriginal people in Van Diemen's Land, and (although to a lesser extent) the problems of Indigenous people in North America and New Zealand. The Committee summed up Indigenous peoples' condition in the following manner:

It is not too much to say, that the intercourse of Europeans in general, without any exception in favour of the subjects of Great Britain, has been, unless when attended by missionary exertions, a source of many calamities to uncivilized nations. Too often their territory has been usurped; their property seized; their numbers diminished; their character debased; the spread of civilization impeded. European vices and diseases have been introduced amongst them, and they have been familiarized with the use of our most potent instruments for the subtle or violent destruction of human life, viz. brandy and gunpowder.[3]

In the Committee's eyes, the British Empire would be judged most unfavourably by a divine power if matters did not change.

Can we suppose otherwise than that it is our office to carry civilization and humanity, peace and government, and, above all, the knowledge of the true God, to the uttermost ends of the earth? He who has made Great Britain what she is, will inquire at our hands how we have employed the influence He has lent us in our dealings with the untutored and defenceless savage, whether it has been engaged in seizing their land, warring upon their people, and transplanting unknown disease, and deeper degradation, through the remote regions of the earth, or whether we have, as far as we have been able, informed their ignorance, and invited and afforded them the opportunity of becoming partakers of that civilization, that innocent commerce, that knowledge and faith with which it has pleased a gracious Providence to bless our own country.[4]

With such considerations in mind, the Committee recommended a greater missionary presence in the colonies. Not only should they preach the gospel, they should educate Indigenous people in the ways of European society, persuading them to wear European clothing, live in European housing, and adopt the capitalist work ethic. By forswearing communal property and nomadic ways of living, and taking up the more "advanced" norms of individual property ownership, Indigenous people would vastly improve their situation. The Committee eagerly offered examples where, it was felt, these developments had occurred, most notably the Kat River settlement in the Cape. At the Kat River, Khoisan people (living on land taken from the Xhosa) had been growing crops, paying taxes, and attending the local church, school, and temperance society. Similar events had occurred among Upper Canada's Mississauga people. Missionaries based in the colony had noted that the Mississauga had also reshaped gender relations in their society, so that men's and women's roles as husbands and wives, fathers and mothers, more closely resembled those in European society. Furthermore, their Mohawk neighbours had gone from being a drunken and violent people to ones noted for their sobriety, honesty, and industry. As well as the missionaries' "civilizing mission," as it would be called, the Committee also called for better protection of Indigenous people from settler violence. It recommended that the office of Protector be set up, a position that was subsequently established in New Zealand, the Cape, and Port Phillip (the precursor of the Australian colony of Victoria).

Clearly the Committee believed that Indigenous people were human beings with the right to be treated with compassion and humanity: they could not be slaughtered like wild animals or merely pushed aside. So far as the evangelicals were concerned, the British government had a moral obligation to ensure that Indigenous people were kept safe from the worst excesses of colonial expansion. However, it was assimilation to European ways, not the return of Indigenous land or the promotion of racial equality, that seemed to the Committee to be the most reasonable solution. Indigenous people were seen as children, incapable of making rational choices without European guidance and education. While such a stance may seem to a twenty-first-century audience to be a straightforward instance of racism, it is important to realize that it also came from a particular notion of history, that of the Scottish Enlightenment's stadial theory of civilization. This concept of social organization ranked societies according to their economic base and the historical stage at which they had arrived. At the bottom lay nomadic hunter-gatherers and at the top mercantile capitalists, with nomadic pastoralists and subsistence agriculturalists in between. In order to reach the top level, societies had to progress through each stage, thus experiencing a greater division of labour and a more complex form of social organization, culminating in the most advanced form, that of European capitalism. Indigenous societies were seen by the Committee—and many others—as having reached subsistence agriculture at best; Australian Aborigines were perceived as resting at the bottom of the scale. Only after these societies had reached the highest scale could their residents be granted the advantages of full citizenship. Racism also played a significant role in discussions of Indigenous peoples' enfranchisement and settler societies' treatment of Indigenous agriculture. Over the course of the nineteenth century notions of racial hierarchies shaped Europeans' assessments of Indigenous peoples' potential and abilities.

## War and Violence: New Zealand, the Cape, and Australia

The Select Committee's *Report* was a turning point in Indigenous peoples' relationship with the Colonial Office and settler societies, not least because it was presented at the height of evangelical influence in the Colonial Office. One important consequence of the *Report* was the formation of the Aborigines' Protection Society. Founded in 1837, the Society lobbied for Indigenous peoples' rights and welfare in both British settler and other colonies in South America, the Pacific, and Africa until 1909. However, evangelical sway over colonial affairs would begin to diminish in the 1840s and into mid-century. In the aftermath of the *Report*'s publication, increased waves of British settlers arrived first in British America and then in the Australian colonies, New Zealand, and the Cape, a movement that brought about even greater pressures on Indigenous lands, resources, and rights. As well, the granting of responsible government to settler legislatures, which began in the 1840s in British America and then spread to other colonies throughout the nineteenth century, had mixed results for Indigenous communities. While the achievement of "adult" status within the Empire was often heralded as a significant step for these colonies, as it meant controlling their internal affairs, responsible government had other consequences for Indigenous people. As we shall see in Chapter 2, although voting rights in the majority of the colonies were ostensibly colour-blind, the way in which they were implemented tended to exacerbate and sharpen racial inequality.

The violence that so concerned humanitarians did not vanish with the publication of the *Report*. In a number of colonies more British settlers arrived; correspondingly, racial divisions became even more clear-cut and began to serve increasingly as markers of boundaries between different groups. To be sure, in a number of colonies conflict could also encompass armed resistance on Indigenous peoples' part. At the Cape, the outbreak of the eighth English Frontier War in 1850—one of a series of wars between settlers and the Xhosa that began in 1779 and did not end until 1879—resulted in the breakup of the Kat River settlement, the very site praised by the Select Committee for its confirmation to assimilation and the civilizing mission. Members of the settlement refused to fight alongside the British; in 1851, a significant minority of its Khoisan members banded together with the Xhosa to oppose the settlers. In retaliation, the British government disbanded the settlement, confiscating its members' land and selling it to white settlers. Matters were somewhat different, if no less tense, in the eastern colony of Natal. The powerful Zulu nation, formed in the 1820s and 1830s under the leadership of Shaka and, following him, his half-brother Dingane, had been defeated by Afrikaners (Dutch settlers) who had founded the republic of Natalia. British authorities, concerned that the republic's presence would mean more armed conflict with nearby

Africans and the enslavement of defeated tribes, annexed Natalia through military force in 1842 and renamed it Natal. Fearing the loss of their language, culture, political autonomy, and, in particular, their slaves, Natalia's settlers decided to depart in 1843 for the interior, where they established the Orange Free State and the Transvaal republics. From 1849 to 1852 the British brought approximately 5,000 British and Irish settlers to Natal. Further immigration took place in the 1860s, when Indian migrants arrived as indentured labourers for the area's sugar plantations. Natal, then, was marked not by the Cape's more mixed population of Africans, coloured or mixed-race people, British, and Afrikaners, but, rather, by a much sharper and clear-cut division between non-Europeans and Europeans. Until the British army's defeat of the Zulus in 1879 and the shattering of the latter's kingdom, white settlers were constantly concerned about the military and political threat of an African majority.

In New Zealand, Māori resistance to the growth of the settler population took the form of the Māori King Movement and armed resistance, the New Zealand Wars of 1845–72 (formerly referred to by historians as the Māori Wars). The King Movement, a federation of Māori tribes on the North Island, was forged out of a context of growing European settlement and land losses; those Māori involved in it hoped chiefly to regain *mana*, or control over lands and people, and to form a block that would prevent further land sales. While the governor and his ministers, who believed that sovereignty over New Zealand now rested with the British, were gravely concerned about this challenge to their authority, they were confronted with an even more immediate one in Taranaki in the southern part of the North Island. A confrontation over land sales at Taranaki resulted in the declaration of martial law in 1860 and the area's occupation by British troops. Although the confrontation ended in an informal truce, the situation worsened. Reappointed as governor, in 1863 George Grey attempted to curb the growing strength of the King Movement by trying to persuade moderate groups to abandon the king, P tatau Te Wherowhero. He set out to improve roads in Waikato, the Movement's stronghold, and demanded that Māori in the area swear a loyalty oath to the Crown and surrender their arms. Grey then moved imperial troops into the king's territory and began a series of battles with the Māori that lasted into 1864. Grey encountered opposition from the Colonial Office over the use of imperial troops, since Britain had begun to withdraw its armies around the Empire. Nevertheless, he was able to secure a limited victory over the King Movement. Britain withdrew all but one regiment between 1865 and 1866 but the fighting continued, shifting on the east and west coasts of the North Island to smaller and much more dispersed, highly effective guerrilla strategies by the Māori, attacking colonial militias.

By 1869, though, the prominent Māori leader Titokowaru had lost his peoples' support, while Te Kooti, another Māori military and religious leader, avoided capture by the British by moving into the King Country, which was closed to Europeans. The British authorities and settlers believed they had won the New Zealand Wars and had asserted their sovereignty over New Zealand, justifying their subsequent land-grab of 3.25 million acres on the North Island as the confiscation of rebel property (around half was later returned or paid for). The Māori, though, saw this confiscation as a major grievance. As well, Māori resistance continued in the form of spiritual movements or the formation of separate villages. The latter were destroyed by the government in the early 1880s, concerned that they had become the locus for another resistance movement. Some also decided to become involved in settler politics and took up Māori parliamentary seats established in 1867 to give Māori a sense that they had a voice in New Zealand politics. Despite their military defeat, Māori did not abandon their hopes of a separate Māori polity. They kept discussions of this body alive, leading to the founding of the Māori Parliament in 1892, which met for 11 years.

In the new Australian colonies of Queensland and West Australia, Indigenous people had similar experiences to those in New South Wales, Victoria, Tasmania, and South Australia. Settlers squatted and seized control of land and resources, wreaking violence on Indigenous communities. While early nineteenth-century settlers' perspectives on Indigenous people were far from egalitarian, from the 1860s on their notions of Aboriginal people were influenced by ideas about their racial inferiority. These concepts were shaped by evolutionary theory and a notion of Australian Aborigines as the most "primitive" of human beings. Such an ideology would lead to the collection of skulls, especially those of Tasmanians, and the exhumation and, in some cases, museum display of Aboriginal bodies (despite the government's intervention with legislation aimed at regulating—albeit not banning—the use of human remains). It would also result in the growing popularity, first seen in British America, of the "doomed race" theory, one that argued Indigenous culture was too fragile to withstand the advance of European civilization. Significantly, this theory was used to justify assimilationist policies in settler colonies around the Empire.

From the 1860s to the 1880s settler governments in Northern Queensland, Central Australia, the Northern Territory, and the Kimberley region asserted control over, mapped, and opened up for pastoral settlement Indigenous lands without any negotiations. These regions were quite different from the more temperate southern part of the continent or even southern Queensland, whose tropical climate made it suitable for plantation agriculture. Dry and harder to reach, the northern and western portions of Australia attracted a smaller and much-dispersed European population. However, fewer settlers also meant less oversight of their behaviour; new technology also meant rapid-fire, more accurate, and multi-shot guns; and the spread of responsible government meant settler legislatures, not the British Crown, were in charge, motivated by a desire to clear Aboriginal people quickly from their lands. The situation in Northern Queensland was that of an armed camp, fortified with Native Police sent from New South Wales (a force that would be disbanded in 1896 for its brutality). Aboriginal people mounted a strong defence of their country, as they resisted by killing settlers and their cattle and stealing horses and supplies. Settlers' vigilante raids in Western Australia and the Northern Territory ended in multiple Aboriginal deaths. Aboriginal resistance was ultimately met by the state with arrests, convictions, and imprisonment. When they were released, Aboriginal people found their connection to their land, or "country," had been severed by the government. On Australia's northern coasts, where pearl diving predominated and cheap convict labour was not available, it was Aboriginal people's labour, not their land, that employers desired. Between 1866 and the 1880s, Aboriginal divers were brought in to work in the pearl diving industry, often as forced labour. Aboriginal people thus found opportunities for work and, in many cases, intermarriage with Asian workers; however, those who ran the pearl-diving industry replaced them as divers in the 1880s, hiring Asian workers instead.

### Paternalism and Protection: The Mid-Nineteenth Century to the Early Twentieth Century

Wars and violence, though, were not the only significant forces that reshaped or affected Indigenous communities throughout the nineteenth century. Humanitarians' and missionaries' concerns about violence and a desire to assimilate Aboriginal people resulted in the creation of protectorates by the British Parliament in a number of colonies and communities such as the Kat River settlement. In 1839 George Augustus Robinson became the Chief Protector of Aborigines in Port Phillip, with four assistants who were assigned to specific regions within the colony. The journal of William Thomas, sent to the Melbourne and Westernport regions, suggests that the Kulin people of the area saw this new office as being far from benign. They realized that the Protector and his office lacked the power and authority to prevent settler raids on their communities. As well, while the Kulin intervened to protect Thomas when they felt he was threatened by other, more hostile groups, they believed that his primary goal was to remove them from their homes and threaten their culture and ways of life.

Although Thomas was unable to either protect or directly assimilate his supposed charges, from 1859 on members of the Kulin started to farm in the Melbourne area, clearing land, putting up fences and buildings, and planting wheat and vegetables. Their efforts, though, were seen as threatening to local settlers and resulted in them moving to another location further away. The creation by the Victoria government of the Board for the Protection of Aborigines, aimed at creating reserves to be run by local managers and appointing local guardians to oversee Aboriginal peoples' affairs, led to the formation of six reserves in the colony. These included Corranderk, which was on a traditional camping site at Badger Creek (northeast of Melbourne). In 1863 a number of Kulin, including Simon Wonga, a leader of the 1859 group, had occupied the area and petitioned for land to establish another farm. They received 930 hectares, which was increased to 1,960 hectares three years later, and were joined by the Bangerang people from the Murray River area. By 1874 Corranderk consisted of 32 cottages, outbuildings, 450 head of stock, and 65 hectares of crops; by the 1880s the community boasted 1,215 hectares of crops and won prizes for its hops at the Melbourne International Exhibition. Observers noted that its residents' homes were furnished with rugs, sofas, rocking chairs, clocks, pictures, and wallpapers; their gardens featured flowers and fruit trees, ringed with picket fences. As well, Aboriginal women had adopted European clothing and hair styles. Yet these shifts in material culture did not mean wholesale assimilation or acceptance of European ways. People maintained ties of kinship and observed their obligations to their kin networks, practised customary funeral rituals, hunted and collected bush food, and remained deeply attached to land and country. Their ability to create a syncretic form of Christianity can be attributed both to Aboriginal resistance and creativity and to their trust in the resident missionary, C. John Green, who worked alongside—not over—Corranderk's residents.

In the 1870s and 1880s Indigenous people either moved to or set up communities that were inspired by Corranderk. Some, such as the government reserve Cummeragunja, were thriving by the early 1900s, as their prosperity and stability provided a safe and secure place, particularly for children. Yet such communities also encountered a range of problems: lack of government support that would allow them to acquire more land, discrimination from nearby settlers, insufficient capital to expand industry and skilled trades, and, in some cases, reserve managers who were too controlling. Aboriginal people reacted to the latter problem with petitions, letters to local newspapers and interviews, strikes, contact with sympathetic whites, and two 70-kilometre walks to Melbourne to meet government ministers. Their protests were not met with a sympathetic response. Victoria's Royal Commission of 1877, followed by a parliamentary inquiry of 1881, led to the state's passage in 1886 of the Victoria Aborigines Act and the expulsion of mixed-raced people from the ages of 8 to 34 from the reserves, a practice New South Wales adopted in 1909. Those who were expelled in the 1890s faced a major economic depression, discrimination, and racially motivated hostility, conditions that made supporting large families on seasonal and poorly paid rural labour almost impossible. The extreme poverty faced by these families forced the Victoria government to change its policy in 1910 and allow people to return to the reserves. However, the Board for the Protection of Aborigines decided to sell significant portions of reserve lands and close all but two reserves, a decision that resulted in Aboriginal people losing an important source of protection.

Matters became even worse in 1915. New South Wales passed legislation that would allow its Board for the Protection of Aborigines, founded in 1883, to remove mixed-race children from their families and place them in foster care and then in apprenticeships or domestic service; Aboriginal girls, in particular, provided a cheap source of labour for white Australian homes. Board members were not required to obtain parental consent, nor did they have to prove neglect or abuse. Until 1940, between 5,000 and 6,000 children were removed from their homes merely because of their racial heritage. While child removal would become the focus of considerable political activism in the twentieth century, in this period Aboriginal people coped with such onslaughts by retreating into private life, focusing on kinship obligations, holding mourning rituals, and continuing to hone and, where possible, hand down skills in hunting and living on the land.

Missionaries, sometimes supported by settler governments, called for similar combinations of protection and paternalism in the Northern Territory, Western Australia, and Queensland. Western Australia's Protector, Reverend John Gribble, denounced settler brutality toward Aborigines, including forced labour, placing workers in neck chains, and rape, while in the Northern Territory J.L. Parsons called for the establishment of reserves to protect Aboriginal people. In Queensland, the 1887 Aborigines Protection and Restriction of the Sale of Opium Act was aimed at ending the starvation and exploitation of Aborigines. Simultaneously, though, the Act saw them as a dying race and as children whose lives needed to be controlled. For the next three generations, Aboriginal people in Queensland could be forcibly moved to reserves and made to stay on them. They also were not allowed to vote, drink, or have sexual relations with Europeans and Asians and were forbidden to work for Chinese employers. They could only enter into an interracial marriage with the approval of a Christian minister. Moreover, Aboriginal people did not work under freely negotiated contracts; instead, their labour was compulsory. The Queensland act was the model for similar legislation in Western Australia (1905), South Australia (1911), and the Northern Territory (1911). Areas with fewer government officials and smaller police forces were not able to enforce these acts as thoroughly as settler governments wished. Nevertheless, by the early twentieth century the majority of Australian Indigenous people saw their lives defined by these special acts, their civil rights denied by the racism that structured the legislation.

As we have seen in the treatment of emancipated slaves, the Cape Colony was no stranger to similar mixtures of paternalism and protection. Moreover, like settlers in Australia's colonies, settlers in southern Africa were often quite hostile to missionaries' calls for better treatment of Africans. Yet demographic differences in Indigenous populations, coupled with a greater threat of Indigenous armed resistance, might result in colonial authorities having to modify their policies. In Natal, for example, the colonial government set up African Locations in the 1840s; in these areas chiefs took over local affairs and land tenure was held communally. Different denominations received Mission Reserves; South African High Commissioner George Grey (former Governor in South Australia and then New Zealand) devised a plan for African education, with grants given directly to the missions. Settlers, their numbers growing and—most importantly—their representation on the colony's Legislative Council increasing, called for the government to shrink the number of Locations, raise taxes on Africans, push more of them into low-paid labour, and abolish "savage" customs such as Indigenous spiritual practices and polygamy. However, the first Secretary of State for Native Affairs, Theophilus Shepstone (1853–75), faced with supervising a black population of 100,000 with a tiny staff and well aware that the settler population was less than one-tenth the

size of the African, opposed settler demands. Shepstone believed that alienating land, increasing taxes, and attempting to abolish traditional customs
would result in armed rebellion. Gradually the settler population realized
the benefits of Shepstone's program, since if Africans were confined to
Locations the authorities were able to maintain order and provide a regulated
supply of labour to white mines and farms. Moreover, maintaining a rule
of law on the Locations that, in the settlers' eyes, was despotic allowed the
latter to continue to treat Africans in a dictatorial and undemocratic manner.
Settlers attempted to justify their behaviour with the argument that Africans
were accustomed to such treatment from their own chiefs.

Yet although white supremacy had been secured by 1893, by which time
Natal had achieved responsible government and introduced a racially based
franchise, the presence of more than a dozen missionary societies meant
that late nineteenth-century Natal experienced one of the highest rates of
evangelization in the British imperial world. Since the societies could not
hope to make large-scale conversions with a limited number of white missionaries, they followed patterns set out earlier in the nineteenth century
in other colonies, such as British North America, and ordained Indigenous
evangelists who then took charge of Indigenous congregations. Along with
their independent counterparts in the Transvaal and the Cape Colony,
Indigenous missionaries raised alarms for both white missionaries and the
government. The former saw them as threats to their religious authority,
while the latter perceived them as a challenge to white supremacy. Despite
these fears, the narrative of Indigenous control over Christianity is not
entirely one of successful challenges to white paternalism. The government's measures included taking over administration of Native reserves,
refusing to fund education for anything but basic reading, arithmetic, and
manual training, restricting black ministers' right to perform marriages,
curbing their preaching in African Locations, and preventing others from
entering Natal or expelling those believed to be preaching without official
denominational approval. The Mission Reserves also became sites of struggles between the government and the missionaries in matters such as the use
of educational funds and taxation; the white farm lobby succeeded in having
Reserve rents raised to the same level as those paid by the farmers' African
tenants. Tensions erupted between the white and black missionaries and
between black missionaries and their congregations. Black missionaries felt
that their white colleagues had betrayed them, while black congregations
accused their ministers of not doing enough to protect them. However,
Indigenous missionaries also set in motion currents that white churches had

not intended: when the African National Congress was founded in 1912, many of its leaders came from Natal's Christian communities.

Indigenous peoples' experiences with both humanitarians and settler governments in British America and the Dominion of Canada were similar in many ways to those of their counterparts in other parts of the Empire: they were not, however, identical. As we have seen, missionaries had a much longer history of contact with Indigenous North Americans. Missionaries were not always welcomed by others who dealt with Indigenous people. Fur traders, for example, resented them for interfering with Indigenous peoples' mobility and cultural practices, which were integral to the trade's survival. Yet as colonial legislatures and, then, the national government sought to create spaces for European settlers, they also created ones for Indigenous peoples that were marked by restricted mobility and increased state and missionary surveillance. With Canadian Confederation in 1867, the federal or Dominion government took responsibility for Indigenous people. Unlike the situation in Australia's colonies, its Indian Department, not provincially run boards, oversaw their lives. Such supervision was set out in the (frequently amended) Indian Act of 1876 and covered education, health and welfare, treaty payments, treaty rights (access to resources such as hunting and fishing), reserve agriculture, and interracial marriage. Although these matters were governed by legislation, the latter was interpreted and mediated by Indian agents, located on or near reserves. While the agents' relationship with Indigenous peoples was shaped by paternalistic ideologies—ones that could range from benevolent to dictatorial—in some circumstances Indigenous people were able to exercise degrees of control. In the 1840s, for example, the Six Nations reserve at the Grand River in southern Ontario hired their first supervisor, David Thorburn. Thorburn's geographical distance from the reserve (he lived 60 miles away), combined with the Confederacy's determination to run its own affairs, resulted in a more egalitarian relationship. However, his successor, Jasper Gilkison, who lived in nearby Brantford, was more interested in directing and controlling reserve affairs. Although some of Gilkison's ideas were seen as helpful (improving roads and providing better health care), a number of the Confederacy chiefs found his style far more abrasive.

Others, though, saw their lives become more restricted, hedged by both agents and missionaries. For Indigenous people in the western provinces, one of the more frustrating aspects of agents' application of the Indian Act was their attitude toward agriculture. The Dominion government envisioned that ultimately these communities, ones that had supported themselves through hunting, trapping, and gathering, should become self-sufficient through farming. It also adhered to the stadial theory of evolution, which meant that Indigenous communities were denied the seeds and equipment that would allow them to achieve self-sufficiency quickly. Instead, believing that these supposedly "nomadic" people needed to work through economic stages gradually and in a supervised, regulated manner, government officials provided them with implements and seeds that would keep them dependent until they were perceived to warrant better equipment. This attitude persisted despite Indigenous communities' agricultural success. Just as Indigenous farmers at Corranderk proved more than able to produce prize-winning hops, western Canadian Indigenous farmers competed alongside white settlers in local agricultural fairs, often winning prizes for their produce. Settlers' fear of such competition, though, led to government restrictions on the kinds of markets for Indigenous farmers' produce and the subsequent strengthening of settlers' and the government's belief that Indigenous people were not "naturally" suited for agriculture. All of this occurred despite Indigenous peoples' demands that the government follow through on its treaty promises to provide them with proper support for agriculture and ranching, support they believed was crucial to their communities' economic security and stability.

It was in the area of education, though, that the Dominion government was most intrusive. Prior to Confederation, missionaries had worked to provide day schooling in communities organized around missions or on Indigenous reserves, at times doing so at the behest of local chiefs. Although a few attempts were made to educate Indigenous children in boarding schools, these generally proved ineffective and were rejected by Indigenous communities. Starting with mid-nineteenth-century treaty negotiations, Indigenous leaders, mindful of the need for their people to be equipped for a changing society, stipulated that in exchange for land the government would be obliged to provide formal education for Indigenous children. Working with missionaries from both Catholic and Protestant churches, the Dominion government established a network of residential schools, primarily in the western provinces and in British Columbia. These institutions were ostensibly aimed at supplying Indigenous children and youth with European-style education, which could be provided more efficiently in a boarding school. However, underfunded by the government and run by often poorly trained members of religious organizations, both lay and ordained, these schools did not live up to Indigenous communities' hopes for their children's future.

The list of ways in which the schools and those who ran them failed Indigenous children is a lengthy one. For one, children were taken, either forcibly or by other means of coercion (such as threats to cut off food rations), from their parents, extended families, and communities, their contact with them often limited to a few weeks or, at best, months in the summer. The gender-segregation practised in the schools separated brothers and sisters. Children also had their own clothes taken from them in exchange for European-style uniforms, while boys' hair, an important symbol of masculinity in many Indigenous communities, was cut. In many schools missionary staff (who, with some exceptions, did not speak, read, or write Indigenous languages) forbade the use of children's mother tongues; children who broke this rule might suffer severe and brutal corporal punishment. Physical conditions were frequently harsh, with inadequate food, heat, and medical care: the numbers of children who died in residential schools from diseases exacerbated by malnutrition is only now coming to light. The schools' staff saw their ultimate goal as the assimilation of Indigenous children; while some attempted to do so with kindness, others believed that harsh treatment was the most effective method. As in other institutional settings, the control that school staff had over vulnerable children also provided scope for a range of physical and sexual abuse, crimes that had far-reaching consequences for the victims and their communities. While not all children experienced severe beatings or sexual violence and some remembered individual teachers, nuns, and priests as kind and caring, the schools' greatest failures were their separation of children from their cultures and their inability to provide Indigenous children with an adequate education. The training they provided was rudimentary, not least because children were used as cheap labour to help run the institutions: boys did agricultural work while girls provided domestic services.

As in other Indigenous communities that experienced the force of settler state policies, Indigenous people in Canada were not passive in the reaction to the schools. Parents attempted to keep their children out of the schools through a number of strategies: hiding them in the bush when missionaries and police came for them in late summer, for example, or marrying daughters at a young age. Although children's agency can be more difficult to discern for this period, school archives contain complaints from staff about them running away, being insubordinate, and refusing to "learn" European ways. Oral histories from the twentieth century also contain accounts from former students about strategies they used to circumvent school rules:

passing notes to siblings, for example, in the hat of an unsuspecting visiting priest. However, despite parents' and children's resistance, it is clear that residential schools disrupted and damaged Indigenous communities' cultures and social relations, not least those between parents and children. Their impact is still felt in Canada to this day.

## Conclusion

The histories of Indigenous people in settler colonies for this period can be characterized as ones of struggle, war, and changes over which they often had little or no control. Historians have pointed to the loss of land and resources, in particular, and to the various forms of settler and state violence as central features shared by Indigenous people, whether from southern Africa, Australia, New Zealand, or British America. Such were the experiences of Willem Uithaalder, faced with ever-growing restrictions on his peoples' lives by white settlers at the mid-nineteenth-century Kat River: for Uithaalder, armed resistance seemed the only option. Yet, as Patrick Campbell's description of the Grand River community suggests, oppression and violence were not the entire or only story. Campbell's account, along with other, similar narratives, points to Indigenous peoples' negotiations and at times resistance to settler encroachments, ones that demonstrate creativity and resourcefulness that persisted well into the twentieth and twenty-first centuries. Chapter 2 explores the demographic, legal, and political changes brought about by the arrival of European newcomers.

## Notes

1 Patrick Campbell, *Travels in the Interior Inhabited Parts of North America in the Years 1791 and 1792* (Edinburgh: 1793), 209–11.

2 Robert Ross, "The Possession and Dispossession of the Kat River Settlement," in *Indigenous Communities and Settler Colonialism: Land Holding, Loss and Survival in an Interconnected World*, eds. Zoë Laidlaw and Alan Lester (Basingstoke, UK: Palgrave MacMillan, 2015), 97.

3 British Parliamentary Papers, *Report from the Select Committee on Aborigines (British Settlements); with the Minutes of Evidence, Appendix and Index* (London: 1837), 5.

4 Ibid., 76.

# 2 | "Peopling," Settling, and Governing

*To a parent country, colonization is, in a philosophical view, highly interest-*
*ing; and, commercially considered, productive of important benefit: not only*
*relieving it from a redundancy of population, but securing to it for many*
*years to come the advantage of an exclusive trade with the new settlements.*
*That our language, customs, and manners, should be transplanted into*
*distant portions of the globe, and the pure worship and undefiled region of*
*Christianity be disseminated where the horrors and atrocities of paganism*
*have prevailed, are subject-matter of pride and gratification.... At first, a*
*hard task awaits the colonist: he must hew down immense forests; he must*
*dig up the roots of these trees; construct habitation; break the yet untilled*
*soil, and, above all, must drive before him the native possessors of the*
*district, who, however, yearly decrease in numbers and strength. The alien,*
*having overcome first difficulties, enjoys a career of rapid prosperity.*
                                   —Thomas Dyke, *Advice to Emigrants*, 1832[1]

*Dear Sisters,*
    *When we came out here there was houses provided for us to go in to which we*
*were to remain in till we had built our house. As for provisions we could get any-*
*thing almost the same as in England but most things at that time much dearer.*
*You wished to know in your letter if we were near a church and school and I*
*am happy to inform you that we have been living near to both and Sarah and*
*Anthony have gone to school ever since we came out, and sometime John. There*
*is a Sunday school in Wellington and different places of worship the same as in*

*England.... Of course being separated so far from all thats near and dear to me causes me at times to be turning my mind to the objects I have left behind but so as we can get an honest living and do our duty I don't think that it matters so much considering the short time we have to sojourn here, whether in England or New Zealand.... I think it is a very healthful climate. We have very beautiful weather at this season of the year. We have not so much thunder and lightning as in England but we have Earthquakes at times.... We have no frost or snow, the trees and bushes are always evergreen.*

—Susannah Wall to Hannah Wall, 1842[2]

Thomas Dyke's "philosophical view" of emigration, its benefits to Britain, and the inevitable transformation of faraway lands into prosperous British settlements was one shared by many of his contemporaries. Along with many of his fellow emigration promoters, Dyke saw innumerable opportunities for his countrymen ("the colonist" in such writing was almost always male), should they be willing to work hard and contend with both natural and human obstacles. Although he acknowledged that these "distant portions of the globe" were already inhabited, Dyke did not perceive their dispossession as anything other than natural and desirable. Overall, Dyke's "impartial guide" to emigration is notable for its dispassionate tone toward emigration and settlement. In contrast, Susannah Wall's letter to her sister differs from Dyke's perspective on emigration in a number of ways. Hers is not the "top-down" view of emigration promoters but, rather, provides us with the details—of schools, churches, climate, and topography—from one who has engaged in the daily work of creating a new society. Moreover, Wall's rather wistful reference to the "objects I have left behind" reminds us of the emotional and affective dimensions of emigration, as does her reassurance of her sisters that they need not worry about their sibling's new home. Between them, Dyke and Wall remind us that nineteenth-century colonization was a process with many dimensions.

From the late eighteenth century on, waves of European and African people found their way to the Antipodes, British North America, and the Cape Colony. In some cases this migration either was forced, as in the case of convict transportation to New South Wales, or was the movement of refugees fleeing the aftermath of the American Revolution (1776–83). Some arrived as a result of economic upheaval in Britain, often in familial networks of migration, while others travelled to New South Wales or Upper Canada when military postings in India, Europe, or the Caribbean ended. Assisted migration, either through the settlement schemes of Edward Wakefield or the work of other promoters of migration to settler colonies, brought those who might lack the resources to migrate independently: this was particularly the case for groups of single women sought as either domestic servants or future wives (or both) in colonies where men outnumbered European women. These patterns of migration were not always unilinear, as some found life in colonial settings difficult and returned to Britain.

How to govern these new colonies and order relationships among the new arrivals, existing European communities, and Indigenous populations was a question that preoccupied imperial and colonial governments. A common, shared experience of these colonies was that of British law and legal systems: discourses of "British justice" were brought to settler societies, along with the structures and processes of the British legal system. As well, colonial governors and, in a number of cases, members of the judiciary travelled from Britain to the colonies and then moved between colonial sites. However, implementing British law was not a straightforward process. While by the end of the nineteenth century settler colonies may have shared much in their legal structures and methods of policing, these developments also were influenced by local conditions and particular historical contingencies. Furthermore, challenges to the authority of appointed governors or lieutenant-governors and their executive councils, the establishment of elected bodies, and the issue of "responsible government" were central to colonial politics for much of the nineteenth century. The mid-nineteenth century saw the confederation of four British American colonies into the new Dominion of Canada, a development followed by Australia in 1901 and South Africa in 1910. South Africa's union, though, came only after a number of wars, one that involved British and Dutch settlers, Indigenous people, Britain, and members of other settler societies.

### Assisted Migration to Settler Colonies

Migration from the British Isles was not a new phenomenon. The seventeenth century had seen the movement of men, women, and children from England; in the eighteenth century, the majority came from Scotland and Ireland, and many ended their voyages on Irish and American plantations. For some, this was an unwelcome form of exile; others, though, saw it as an opportunity to improve their lives and seize new opportunities. The aftermath of the Napoleonic Wars (1803–15), which brought social dislocation to a number of regions in the British Isles coupled with an increased desire for imperial expansion, brought about an even greater wave of migration.

Furthermore, Britain was also experiencing an unprecedented increase in population growth, one markedly higher than any other European country (as historians point out, an increase in population is an extremely influential force in large-scale migrations). Emigration was thus perceived not as the hallmark of those who lacked any other options—indentured servants, for example, or, worse, convict transportation. Instead, it represented opportunity, a chance for Britons to improve their lives and, for some, to create "better Britons" in "better Britains." Between 1815 and the 1850s, the number of those leaving Britain for North America and Australasia totalled around 5 million. Although the vast majority chose to emigrate to the United States, nevertheless, as Table 2.1 shows, British America saw a constant stream of migrants. By 1867 around 60 per cent of Canadians were of British origin.

The ways in which these men, women, and children reached their new homes varied. After 1815, imperial authorities and colonial elites argued over the kinds of strategies the British Parliament might use to assist emigration and promote colonial settlement. In 1819, the government organized a small-scale scheme to send British settlers to South Africa; it sent 4,000 emigrants, a small proportion of the 80,000 who applied to migrate to the Cape. In 1823 and 1825, groups of Irish Catholic farmers were offered such assistance to emigrate to Upper Canada, where they created the Robinson settlements near Peterborough, northeast of Toronto. Two years later the Select Committee on Emigration recommended that Parliament should adopt a national plan for emigration for the benefit of both Britain and her colonies. The hopes of its chief proponent, Wilmot Horton, would be disappointed, though, as Parliament decided to leave emigration to private bodies and individual Britons' discretion. Instead, Parliament regulated trade with America with the Passenger Act of 1817, legislation designed to encourage emigrants to go to British colonies and not the United States. It was not the first such piece of legislation (nor would it be the last): the first Passenger Vessels Act of 1803 had attempted to improve conditions for passengers by setting standards for hygiene, food, and comfort. In the 1820s the cost of travel decreased and a greater number of emigrants landed at Quebec City and Saint John. After considerable controversy in 1827, when the suspension of the Passenger Act and the corresponding lack of government oversight meant that emigrants suffered shipwrecks and starvation onboard ships, a new Act was passed in 1828. This legislation spelled out requirements for accommodation and provisions onboard ships carrying emigrants. Unfortunately for passengers, these requirements were not consistently enforced, and in some cases ships' captains ignored them completely.

**TABLE 2.1** Outward Movement from Britain, 1815–1925, to British America, Australasia, and South Africa

| Year | British America | Australasia | South Africa |
|------|-----------------|-------------|--------------|
| 1815 | 680 | ———— | ———— |
| 1820 | 17,921 | ———— | 1,063 |
| 1825 | 8,741 | 485 | 114 |
| 1830 | 30,574 | 1,242 | 204 |
| 1835 | 15,575 | 1,860 | 325 |
| 1840 | 32,293 | 15,312 | 266 |
| 1845 | 31,803 | 830 | 496 |
| 1850 | 32,961 | 16,037 | 4,624 |
| 1855 | 16,110 | 47,284 | 487 |
| 1860 | 2,765 | 21,434 | 2,516 |
| 1865 | 14,424 | 36,683 | 1,037 |
| 1870 | 27,168 | 16,526 | 1,005 |
| 1875 | 12,306 | 34,750 | 5,628 |
| 1880 | 20,902 | 24,184 | 9,059 |
| 1885 | 19,838 | 39,395 | 3,268 |
| 1890 | 22,520 | 21,179 | 10,321 |
| 1895 | 16,622 | 10,567 | 20,234 |
| 1900 | 18,443 | 14,922 | 20,815 |
| 1905 | 82,437 | 15,139 | 26,307 |
| 1910 | 160,205 | 45,000 | 27,297 |
| 1915 | 16,772 | 12,379 | 5,700 |
| 1920 | 118,837 | 43,827 | 15,157 |
| 1925 | 40,523 | 48,102 | 7,174 |

Source: Modified from N.H. Carrier and J.R. Jeffrey, *External Migration: A Study of the Available Statistics, 1815–1950* (London: Her Majesty's Stationery Office, 1953), 94–96, 99–100.

Although the national government did not, then, become involved in helping emigrants, other arms of the British state and private individuals stepped in. Parishes in southern England, faced with unemployed labourers left destitute by changes in agriculture, sought to find ways to keep poor rates down (rates were charged to local residents to provide minimal support for those unable to support themselves): assisting individuals or families to leave for British America seemed to landowners a logical choice. Voluntary organizations aimed at helping groups such as artisans and urban labourers leave Britain for British America also were active in the 1830s and 1840s. While only about 10 per cent of those who arrived at Quebec City or Saint John between 1815 and the 1860s did so under the aegis of such organizations, such efforts demonstrate the range of approaches to emigration. Moreover, in Upper Canada, where the majority of settlers welcomed fellow-arrivals from Britain, many communities organized committees or some form of group to assist them. Initially these were supported in an ad hoc manner with private benefactors' donations, but by the 1820s these individuals professed themselves to be overwhelmed by the scale of emigrants' needs. At that point the provincial legislature, with some help from London, began to make such assistance available in more formal ways. By the 1830s a network of societies and government agents was organized, most notably in Toronto, to ensure that emigrants could move onto the land, find work, and be reunited with their family and friends. While the help provided by the immigration agents was rudimentary, nevertheless it signalled an important shift in the development of state institutions in the colony.

Furthermore, the concept and practice of assisted emigration did not end in the mid-nineteenth century. Although British workhouse authorities initially were opposed to the emigration of workhouse inmates, by 1848 their policy shifted to allow orphans, aged 14 to 18, to emigrate to New South Wales and South Australia. (Workhouses were institutions set up under Britain's New Poor Law of 1834 for those unable to work, whether because of age, illness, or other disabilities.) The Colonial Land and Emigration Commissioners set certain conditions for this group, which they hoped would number 10,000 from British workhouses and 4,000 from Ireland. They needed to be industrious, of good character, and healthy (which included having been vaccinated against smallpox), to possess basic literacy and numeracy, and to understand the principles of Christianity. The Commissioners also preferred female orphans over their male counterparts. Although the scheme was less successful in Britain, it proved popular in Ireland, where between 1848 and 1852 more than 8,000 female workhouse emigrants left, many of them for Quebec. In the early 1870s, amidst concerns that British emigration to New Zealand had slowed down (the result of economic recession, unemployment, weak social infrastructure, and reports of conflict with the Māori), the colonial government hired a recruiting agent, Caroline Howard, to bring three ships of migrants to the colony. A number of colonial officials objected to the arrival of more Catholic migrants to the colony. However, both the minister for immigration and the first bishop of Dunedin, each of whom had ties to Ireland, overruled such objections. Out of the 466 passengers who arrived in Otago in April 1874, 263 were Irish; 37 of this group were women recruited by Howard, many from Cork's workhouse. Young, single, and lacking in work experience or employable skills, these women's presence in the colony set off a storm of complaints that New Zealand had allowed in prostitutes, thieves, and vagrants (unfortunately, once in Otago the young women often found themselves in front of the magistrates on such charges). While small in number, the "Asiatics," as the young Irish women were known (as the ship they arrived on was the *Asia*), demonstrated the ways in which gender, class, and ethnic tensions shaped concepts of who was the "ideal" emigrant.

Child emigrants, a group that received even more press coverage than workhouse residents, made up almost 100,000 arrivals in Canada between 1870 and 1930. Brought over by philanthropic individuals and organizations such as Dr. Barnardo, parish guardians, or institutions, these boys and girls were intended to receive new opportunities in the Dominion. Some were orphans and some had run into trouble with the law in Britain, while yet others had been abused and/or abandoned by their parents. These new opportunities, though, usually consisted of agricultural work for boys and domestic labour for girls (not unlike the situation of Indigenous children in residential schools and training programs). Canada, the evangelical promoters of child emigration argued, would provide the healthier environment needed to save these children from the moral and physical deprivation of urban slums. Furthermore, the country would in turn benefit from the cheap farm and domestic labour provided by these children. At the turn of the twentieth century, proponents of British child emigration were increasingly influenced by the eugenics movement and its quest for racial purity, one that influenced early twentieth-century imperialism. From the perspective of eugenicists, Canada's environmental benefits, less so its moral ones, would further the work of empire-building.

Canadian commentators, though, were not as confident about such benefits. They cited a range of objections such as the children's supposed "immoral" backgrounds and the threat of "contagion" that they represented to Canadian society, the need for Canada to improve its own child welfare provisions, and the heartlessness of "child savers" taking young children away from their families and communities. Furthermore, like their British counterparts, Canadian officials were influenced by the language of eugenics. In their case, though, they used eugenics to oppose Britain ridding itself of children who might carry venereal disease or had inherited susceptibilities to crime and degenerate behaviour. Promoters of children's emigration, such as Britain's Maria Rye who brought 75 young girls to the Niagara area in 1869 to work on farms, were also attacked for undermining Canadian workers' wages with cheap labour and seeking to turn a profit from their enterprises. Rye was specifically accused of abandoning the children to unscrupulous and abusive employers. Prior to becoming involved in child migration, Rye had co-founded the Female Middle-Class Emigration Society, which brought parties of girls and women to Australia, New Zealand, and Canada.

One of the most active organizations of the early twentieth century in resettling British families and youth across the Dominions was the Salvation Army. Between 1903 and 1936 the organization, whose work in Britain focused on assisting impoverished urban dwellers, sponsored 250,000 British emigrants to Canada, Australia, New Zealand, and South Africa. By 1914 Canada had received 150,000, since from 1903 the Canadian government paid a bonus for every adult and child recruited by the Army. As well, it helped the Army with advertising; in Manitoba and Saskatchewan, provincial governments provided annual grants for the Army's emigration services. Yet just as the other "child-saving" organizations were not always viewed favourably by settler governments, the Army's work was also met with degrees of opposition. The Australian government felt that the Army was "dumping" destitute urban Britons on its shores at a time when its economy needed skilled workers and experienced farmers. It responded by writing provisions into 1901 immigration legislation that guarded against such developments; later the government stipulated that immigrants—with the exception of youth and domestic workers—needed to arrive with some form of capital. Canada followed suit: its 1906 Immigration Act allowed for the deportation of anyone who, two years after their arrival in the Dominion, had become a charge on public funds. Two years later 70 per cent of deported immigrants were recent arrivals from Britain.

Australian officials continued to be dissatisfied with Britain's handling of emigration societies. In 1910 the agents-general for Victoria and New South Wales refused to attend the Royal Colonial Institute's conference on emigration, which was intended to establish permanent standing committees that represented the societies. Both provinces believed their own officers were qualified, objected to Britain's involvement in the matter, and were concerned that providing more leeway for philanthropic agencies to work in the area would lead to the entry of cheap labour that would undermine Australian workers (other colonies, including New Zealand, cooperated with the scheme). Although juvenile immigrants continued to enter Australia before and after World War I, doing so with the help of both voluntary societies and various levels of governments, their arrival was hotly contested by the Dominion's Labor Party (a stance also taken by organized labour in Canada). Their wages and working conditions, opponents argued, amounted to not much more than slave labour: the argument that these were not the "better Britons" that the Dominions needed continued to resonate for many. It was not until the 1920s, with concerns over increased European migration to Australia and the provisions of the Empire Settlement Act, that the philanthropic organizations' work was seen by the Australian government in a more favourable light. The Act spelled out financial cooperation between Britain and the Dominion governments and approved private organizations' involvement, with the Salvation Army foremost. Between 1922 and 1927, 14,000–20,000 children between the ages of 12 and 18, sponsored by groups such as the Army, the Child Emigration Society, the Young Men's Christian Association, and Big Brothers, arrived in Australia under the Act's terms. The impact of the global depression of the 1930s and Dominion governments' restrictions on immigration curtailed such movement. Moreover, as we shall see, by the late nineteenth century restricting immigration between Dominions and other colonies also became an important means of establishing racial boundaries.

## Unwilling Migrants: Loyalists and Convicts

Other arrivals to British America and the Australian colonies did not choose their new homes freely, coming as either refugees or as transported prisoners. The aftermath of the American Revolution saw the departure of 60,000 Loyalists from the new republic between 1781 and 1784. While their exodus spread across the Atlantic to England, down the eastern seaboard to Florida, south to the Caribbean, and across the globe to Sierra Leone and India, as far as settler colonies were concerned the Loyalists made their strongest impact in British America. More than 30,000 refugees arrived in Nova Scotia (which at that time encompassed present-day New Brunswick, created in 1784), while between 6,000 and 8,000 located in Quebec. Their presence would result in the colony's division into Upper and Lower Canada.

Although the late nineteenth century would see the creation of a "Loyalist myth," one that emphasized uniform devotion to the Crown and the imperial tie, those who settled in British America were a heterogeneous

**FIGURE 2.1** "Dancing between Decks." This sketch depicts emigrants en route from Liverpool to North America.

DANCING BETWEEN DECKS.

Source: *London Illustrated News*, 6 July 1850. Mary Evans Picture Library, Picture Number 10239552.

group. A few were members of a colonial elite who had left behind considerable amounts of property and attempted to recreate their former positions in their new communities. However, the vast majority were farmers, tradespeople, and labourers, men and women who spoke a range of languages, came from different ethnic communities, and worshipped in a variety of churches. They also were racially diverse, as the Loyalist influx included the Six Nations and African slaves who had been promised freedom and land by Britain, promises that tended to be broken more often than kept. While some Loyalists felt a keen sense of duty to the Crown and to Britain, theirs were not necessarily knee-jerk or reactionary conservative sentiments: a number had been distressed by British corruption and continued to express such feelings once they settled in their new homes. In British America they were not a quiescent or passive group. In both Nova Scotia and Upper Canada, "ordinary" Loyalists spoke out against elite pretensions and privilege, demonstrating their desire for more egalitarian societies than those envisioned by either Loyalist leaders or colonial officials. Moreover, many black Loyalists in Nova Scotia demonstrated their unhappiness with receiving either inferior land or no land, and with the persistence of slavery in the colony, by moving en masse to Sierra Leone in 1792. Overall, then, supporting the British Crown did not mean acquiescing in the colonial government's desire for a hierarchical society. Indeed, not long after their arrival in British America a number of disillusioned, bitter, and homesick Loyalists made their way back across the border.

However, for transported convicts, returning "home" was, if not impossible, a far more difficult prospect to entertain. Britain's loss of her American colonies and subsequent overcrowded prisons forced imperial authorities to search for new destinations. At first the solution appeared to be found in the Gold Coast slave forts located in western Africa. Over the objections of their owners, the Company of Merchants Trading to Africa, who feared both damage to their establishments' security and that the presence of convicts would undermine African respect for Europeans, the government used convicts in the regiments that supported the forts. The experiment was not successful, though, and the convicts were transferred to the Company's employ as indentured servants. While other destinations, such as Honduras Bay and southwestern Africa, were considered, they also failed.

In 1787 New South Wales became the government's choice for transportation: the First Fleet docked at Botany Bay in January 1788. Starting in 1791, convicts were also transported from Ireland, a practice that ended in 1853. Transportation from England came to a close in 1868, when the last group of convicts arrived in Western Australia. Approximately 163,000 convicts were sent to the Australian colonies. Most convict settlements were located in New South Wales, while 67,888 men and 12,116 women went to Van Diemen's Land (Tasmania) between 1803 and 1852. Colonial authorities attempted to set up a small convict settlement at Port Phillip in 1803 but abandoned it the following year, while Norfolk Island served as a penal colony from 1788 to 1794 and from 1824 to 1847. For those who arrived on the First Fleet, conditions were harsh; they endured crop failures, livestock deaths, and the delayed arrival of the Second Fleet, with its extra provisions. However, by late 1792 matters had improved. The population had grown to 2,500 colonists, crop production had increased substantially, and the number of livestock being raised had expanded.

### Unassisted Emigrants

Stories of convicts, "home children," and Loyalist refugees have provided considerable drama and colour to the story of the British Empire's spread and reconfiguration in the late eighteenth and nineteenth centuries. A far more common experience, though, was that of the unassisted emigrant who, as Figure 2.1 suggests, departed Britain as part of a family group or as a single man or woman, seeking work and, possibly, reunification with family and friends from home. They left for a number of reasons. In some cases, emigrants were persuaded by the many printed guides that promised them rosy futures in lands whose names were fast becoming recognizable to residents of Essex, Tipperary, Inverness, and Swansea (that such depictions might be far off the mark would become evident once the guides' readers landed in Upper Canada or Victoria). Emigration promoters hosted local meetings, for example, in which they told glowing stories of the "better Britain" that awaited those in attendance. Travellers' accounts and settlers' narratives also provided prospective emigrants with descriptions of topography, climate, relationships with Indigenous people, and, where applicable, the state of roads, churches, and schools. While the majority of emigrants' guides were written by men, Upper Canadian settlers Susanna Moodie and her sister Catherine Parr Traill published accounts of "life in the bush" that described the kinds of possibilities—and, in Moodie's case, obstacles—that prospective "gentlewomen" settlers might encounter.

However, letters from those who had gone before may have provided the most significant and, in many cases, accurate portraits of the lives British emigrants could expect to create. Of course, such letters were affected by their authors' own situation. Their feelings about their new home might be shaped by whether their departure had been eagerly anticipated and their new lives approached with optimism and hope, or if they had felt pressured to leave and had done so with regrets and sadness. As well, those who had found work, a home, and community support relatively easily might be far more encouraging about the prospects of emigration than those who had struggled just to survive. Regardless of their personal feelings about their new situation, immigrants' letters home were frequently far more useful than the published guides for those considering departing Britain. Letters from family and friends provided more practical advice about the material goods that would be needed on the voyage and in the colony.

It is easier to understand why children, workhouse inmates, and convicts left their home country: for them, emigration was not a matter of individual choice. In contrast, assisted emigrants might decide to move to other villages, towns, or regions in Britain, rather than risking their fortunes on an uncertain future overseas. Determining why unassisted emigrants chose to leave Britain is even more complex. Changes in the economy and the effects of war, industrialization, and transformations in agriculture have to be considered carefully, as they affected different regions, communities, and classes in diverse ways at different times. People's choices to emigrate also were shaped by their individual circumstances and changes in their family's situation, such as death, illness, and marriage. A family member's decision to leave might prompt relatives left behind to do the same. For example, in the late 1830s Duncan McTavish, born in Rupert's Land and sent by his Scottish father to Inverness as a child, decided to follow his brother Donald to Australia upon hearing that Donald was doing well in New South Wales. Duncan was able to travel there with a close (and well-connected) older family friend. He did not end up in New South Wales, though, but in Port Phillip (Melbourne), where he found work in the colony's jail. While the trajectory of their voyages around the British Empire followed a less-common path, members of the McTavish family were not alone in connecting Britain with British America. A number of Scottish families from the Highlands departed for British America, building on earlier ties and networks developed in the fur trade and in the transatlantic trade in fish and timber.

An even larger number of emigrants from Ireland found their way to British America. They were not the first to make the voyage across the Atlantic: over the course of the eighteenth century the Irish had already established significant communities in the American colonies. The majority of the Irish who arrived in British America between 1815 and 1845 were Protestant farmers, artisans, and labourers, whose move to the colonies was not a "push" but, rather, was shaped by the opportunities to obtain land and join family and friends. They were followed by young, predominantly single Irish Catholic labourers and artisans who arrived in British America with the intention of eventually making their way to the United States; about two-thirds of this group stayed. Although the migration of Irish people fleeing famine from 1846 to 1851 is well-established in popular memory as the central, defining feature of Irish immigration, it was not a typical experience for the vast majority of those who arrived in British America. It was, however, alarming to colonists and a wrenching experience for the immigrants because of their destitute state. While more than 100,000 arrived in 1847, approximately 60 per cent of the Famine migrants made their way to the United States; those who stayed found their way to Irish communities in Quebec City, Montreal, and Toronto. Irish emigration to settler colonies did not end in the 1840s: during the 1860s a number of literate and skilled Irish arrived in New Zealand via Australia. Unlike the young Irish women who in 1874 came to New Zealand from their country's workhouses, they tended to be literate, have some degree of access to capital, and possessed the skills to establish themselves in colonial society.

Another identifiable and much-desired, if smaller, group of emigrants were half-pay officers and "gentlemen" emigrants, such as John Dunbar Moodie and Thomas Traill. Such men's influence, colonial authorities felt, was needed in setting the correct social, political, and cultural tone in settler colonies. (Moodie, who emigrated to Upper Canada, had previously spent time at the Cape as part of a group of Scottish settlers led by his elder brother Benjamin Moodie.) While fewer of these men emigrated than those from artisanal, labouring, or agricultural backgrounds, those who did often wielded considerable influence in colonial societies such as Upper Canada or Vancouver Island.

### Acquiring Land

Who would have access to land was a central concern in the creation of settler societies, a question that new immigrants had to face whether they arrived in New South Wales, the Cape, or Upper Canada. As Chapter 1 has shown, this process was not straightforward. In some colonies it involved negotiations and the creation of treaties between Indigenous people and imperial authorities. Even in colonies where no treaties were signed and no formal recognition of Indigenous peoples' inhabitation of territory took place, as in the Australian colonies where the doctrine of *terra nullius* (empty, unoccupied land) predominated, colonial governments and settlers were faced with various degrees of Indigenous resistance to their appropriation of traditional territories. Colonial officials and settlers perceived their acquisition of Indigenous land as part of the natural order of things, a process that was predictable, expected, and would contribute to the colonies' (inevitable) development. In their eyes, settlers would "improve" lands seen as wasted by their Indigenous inhabitants. However, as Chapter 1 has discussed, Indigenous people had other ideas: colonial settlement could be messy, complicated, and at times quite violent.

In a number of colonies, colonial governments used land grants as a means of rewarding and encouraging certain types of settlers. By 1792 in New South Wales, for example, officers of the garrison were permitted to receive land grants. In British America, Loyalist refugees received land grants in compensation for their suffering and losses during the Revolution and, too, for proving their continued allegiance to the

Crown. In New Brunswick, Governor Thomas Carleton, who arrived in the colony in 1783, issued grants only to those who were prepared to swear an oath of loyalty, as a way of preventing "'any Persons disaffected to us and our Government from becoming settlers.'"[3] In Upper Canada, members of the provincial regiments who had fought on the New York frontier and then fled to Quebec and Niagara received land, first allotted by regiment; approximately 6,000–8,000 refugees were assisted. Yet colonial governors' notions of the order and stability that land grants to the "right" sort of colonists would bring about were at times challenged by other Loyalist refugees. In New Brunswick, "ordinary" Loyalists expressed their anger at a petition of 55 elite New Yorkers who requested grants of 5,000 acres. If granted, such grants would force the rest of the Loyalist community "'to content themselves with barren or remote Lands Or submit to be Tenants to those, most of whom they consider as their superiors in nothing but deeper art and keener Policy.'"[4]

As well as colonial governments, consortia of politicians, financiers, and businessmen saw opportunities to increase settlement through large-scale purchases of land. In British America, the colonial government's concern that too many British emigrants were choosing the United States, where the cost and labour of establishing farms were lower and less onerous, created opportunities for private land companies. Although the government saw middle-class settlers as the most desirable—including in that definition well-established farmers and master craftsmen, as well as capitalists—it also realized that hard-working labourers, smaller-scale farmers, and artisans were capable of achieving "manly independence" on the colony's frontier. With such goals in mind, the Canada Company was founded in 1826 to purchase Crown land and offer cheap lots to recent immigrants. Its example was followed in the 1830s by the British American Company of Lower Canada and the New Brunswick and Nova Scotia Land Company. The Canada Company was the most effective of these organizations; it also offered services such as forwarding mail and sending funds back to Britain for prospective emigrants.

Perhaps the most striking and influential promoter of these schemes was Edward Gibbon Wakefield, an energetic and well-connected advocate of emigration and settlement through "systematic colonization." Although not the first to call for such a strategy, Wakefield has garnered much attention from historians, possibly because his advocacy coincided with large surges of emigration. Wakefield became interested in emigration while serving a three-year prison sentence for the abduction of Ellen Turner, a well-off silk merchant's daughter (Wakefield, who wished to stand for Parliament but lacked the funds, hoped to marry her and gain access to her family's money). During his incarceration Wakefield read widely about Britain's colonies and became interested in developing more effective strategies for settlement; he was particularly influenced by Scottish reformer Robert Gourlay's critique of British policy in Upper Canada. Wakefield's promotion of New Zealand as an ideal location for this practice came to fruition in 1836 with the creation of the New Zealand Association (later New Zealand Company). The organization's aggressive promotion of buying land cheaply from the Māori and sending out settlers alarmed missionaries and humanitarians, who were concerned that rapid and unregulated contact between Māori and Europeans would lead to the former's destruction. The Crown's subsequent intervention—the appointment of William Hobson as Consul and a decision that land purchases would need a Crown title to be valid—resulted in the Company quickly sending out a survey party to purchase land, followed by a shipload of settlers. In the aftermath of the Treaty of Waitangi, though, many of the land purchases—including those of the Company—were returned.

The Company continued to be active, however, in recruiting emigrants with cheap passages, land at low prices, and promises that employment would be abundant and wages high. Wakefield's conception of a "better Britain" involved recruiting a solid middle-class base of settlers, such as gentry families and members of the professional classes (doctors, lawyers, and clergymen), which would not include members of the working class or the aristocracy. New Zealand became known, in the words of one of its governors, as a "'gentleman's colony,'"[5] even though such a perspective conveniently omitted the colony's rural and working-class settlers. Moreover, while European men outnumbered women in New Zealand until the 1920s, the colony also was seen as being an eminently suitable place for white women, one in which their domestic and moral capacities would be celebrated. In Wakefield's eyes, "'a colony that is not attractive to women, is an unattractive colony.'"[6] The Company targeted prospective female emigrants in its advertising; women were offered free passages and positions in domestic service when they arrived. Yet despite the rhetoric of New Zealand as a haven for middle-class domesticity, from the 1850s to the 1870s labour migration schemes run by both local and central governments put the colony's economic needs first. They sought to attract single women workers who were needed in pastoral, gold-mining, and then industrial settlements as domestic servants.

From these women's perspectives, emigration to New Zealand might hold out the promise of a brighter, better future. Such was the case for 17-year-old Lizzie Daniels, an orphan from a London suburb who had been left without any family and without experience in the paid labour force, who left England for Canterbury in 1867. Other young women, charged with caring for aging parents, faced a difficult, often wrenching decision, one that pitted their familial responsibilities against their hopes to improve their lives. Still others seized the opportunity to leave an unhappy marriage or abusive relationship. Ann Dunn, for example, a Sussex laundress, sailed for the other side of the world to escape her violent partner. Once in New Zealand, opportunities for work in domestic service were plentiful and, given the shortage of female servants, domestic work was well-paid in general (although women were still paid less than male workers). Gaps in mid-nineteenth-century marriage records make it difficult to determine precisely the percentage of women who fulfilled Wakefield's dream of settler domesticity; however, approximately half of the women who arrived in Canterbury province in the 1860s and 1870s married, many of them to men they met at their workplaces.

In addition to land grants and land companies, individual settlers and missionaries also purchased land. In New Zealand, Church Missionary Society chaplain Samuel Marsden bought land in 1815 from the Māori *rangatira* (chieftain) Te Uri-o-Kanae, as he wished to establish a legal claim to lands on which the Church had already begun to build. He also hoped to expand his mission and put it on a more permanent footing. Marsden thus initiated a pattern of land purchases in New Zealand that would be followed by other settlers and missionaries even before Edward Wakefield's company began its work. Moreover, speculation in land also occurred, particularly during periods of rapid growth in settler economies, fuelled by a sense of unlimited possibilities and inexhaustible resources. Of course, land speculation on colonial frontiers was not a new phenomenon. A considerable body of scholarship, not to mention contemporaries' complaints and concerns, documents its widespread existence in eighteenth-century American colonies and its persistence in the new republic, as it spread into the continent's interior and to the western territories. Speculation in British settler colonies, then, occurred alongside more widespread, global investments in land. In a number of colonies speculators bought up both rural and urban land, a process that increased its value; they also invested in mines, business, and other resources. In Upper Canada's southwestern Enniskillen Township, for example, an oil boom during the 1860s attracted speculators, whose buying and selling of land resulted in great—although quite temporary—fluctuations in its value.

While speculation helped contribute to "boom and bust" economies, it also affected Indigenous communities in a variety of ways. Land speculators at Upper Canada's Grand River in the late eighteenth century, for example, bought plots of land from Indigenous residents, some of whom did not have the legal or community authority to sell. Such practices, combined with settlers squatting on Indigenous land, undermined Indigenous peoples' control over the (often quite scanty) land base left them by the advent of settler colonization. Indigenous communities resisted settlers' encroachments with both symbolic or actual violence. For example, in the mid-nineteenth century Plains people on the Canadian prairies sometimes defecated on top of the survey stakes; in 1843 Māori burnt surveyors' huts near Nelson; and in 1840 Aboriginal people in New South Wales's Port Phillip District killed two members of a surveying party. Settlers' acquisition of Indigenous land did not always proceed as smoothly as imperial governments might have wished.

Emigration promoters and colonial governments valued male emigrants who symbolized the independent yeoman ideal and, therefore, wished to acquire farmland to achieve such a goal. However, not all emigrants either lived up to this archetype or even wanted to do so. Irish immigrants in Upper Canada, for example, were more concerned with ensuring that their cultural values and ideals accompanied them across the Atlantic and that they would be able to pass them on to their descendants. Community land-holding, not that of individuals, was in some cases more important. Furthermore, men might refuse to conform to the ideal of the yeoman farmer. For example, the single men who flocked to mid-century gold rushes in Victoria and British Columbia worried colonial authorities precisely because they rejected a "settled," domestic life of a frontier farm or of a solid, middle-class urban career. Instead, they preferred the homosocial, working-class environment and the "get rich quick" mentality that the gold fields encouraged. The archetype of the yeoman also did not address women's perspectives on land. To be sure, women's presence was either implicit or explicit in discussions of family farms, and widowed or single women might own land in their own right. Nevertheless, British common-law assumption of coverture—that a married woman was covered by her husband and had no separate, legal being under the law—meant that married women could not receive land grants or purchase land on their own behalf. Other government programs discriminated on the basis of sex. Unlike their counterparts in the United

States, white women on the Canadian prairies were deemed ineligible for homesteads (a form of land grant).

## Establishing English Legal Culture

Private property needed a legal and judicial system to oversee its convey-ance and settle the (almost inevitable) disputes that accompanied such transactions. As historians have pointed out, turning land into the kind of commodity desired by imperial authorities—and many settlers—required the introduction of English law in British settler colonies; furthermore, successive groups of settlers called upon colonial authorities to implement "British justice." (It was the English common law, not Scots law, that was put into place in settler colonies.)

However, the new English common law was not the first or sole form of legal system. For one, Indigenous people had their own legal codes and practices. In the North American northwest fur trade, marriage *à la façon du pays* (according to the custom of the country) was recognized as legitimate. In parts of the Eastern Cape, payments of bride wealth by the groom's family to that of the bride persisted, despite European attempts to abolish them. As well, in New France and at the Cape, English officials were faced with the laws and practices of other European countries. In British America, the Quebec Act of 1774 recognized French civil law, which was a source of considerable concern to Anglo-American merchants in the colony and, later, Loyalist refugees. The new government, though, introduced other forms of English legal culture, such as English public and criminal law, a judiciary modelled after England's, and trial by jury. Matters were equally complex at the Cape. While the British introduced English common law, Dutch-Roman civil law also persisted, a legacy of the colony's original Dutch settlers. After 1843 this legal system also spread into the interior, being brought by the Dutch settlers who set up the Orange Free State and Transvaal republics after the British annexed Natal. Moreover, in some cases British imperial authorities had already established other forms of judicial structures. Newfoundland, for example, had a lengthy history of rule by seasonal fishery admirals and the Royal Navy, traditions that did not die out in that colony even with the appointment of a governor and justices of the peace in 1729. In "fur trade country" the Hudson's Bay Company's legal structure dominated; its rules and practices were administered under the rubric of master-and-servant law, buttressed by the constant threat of corporal punishment.

Yet over the course of the nineteenth century, English common law came to dominate in the vast majority of settler colonies. British American colonies were the first to set up superior courts based on Westminster's courts of common law, starting in Nova Scotia in 1754 and then in Quebec in 1764. From the 1770s to the 1790s they were followed by the other Atlantic colonies, with Upper Canada establishing its court in 1794 (Vancouver Island and British Columbia's courts were set up in 1858). Despite an overall pattern of following England, though, colonial legal regimes differed from English practices in a number of important ways. For one, settler colonies' attitude to law as it pertained to land became increasingly liberal; individual rights and the mobility of capital, rather than community needs, occupied a more central place than in England.

The case of British America, in which the question of liberalism and its influence on the legal system has been closely studied, demonstrates that liberalization took place in a number of ways. In Upper Canada and the Maritimes, land became subject to seizure; primogeniture (the right of the eldest son to inherit an estate) was abolished in the Maritimes and, later, in Upper Canada; and the formation of land registries meant that the status of land titles became the subject of public knowledge. Yet, as historians have noted, even with such changes the particular context of agricultural society also came into play. Farm families' need for security, stability of credit, and the smooth transfer of land through the generations helped modify liberal ideology. For one, dower for widows, which consisted of a one-third share of the husband's property, was kept in both Ontario and the Maritimes until the late twentieth century (it was, however, abolished in the Canadian prairie provinces). Without rights to dower, widows would have been left to rely on the state, the church, or the goodwill of their children: dower thus provided them with a type of social safety net. Until the early twentieth century Ontario courts upheld conditions on wills that prevented heirs from selling land or mortgaging it in ways that might endanger the entire family's security. Many of the province's judges had come from agricultural backgrounds themselves and believed in the sanctity of the family farm being handed down between the generations. Finally, Ontario debtors who were about to lose their property were given a degree of assurance that it would go to the highest bidder at public auction: a mortgagee could sue if a sale did not cover the mortgage debt, interest, and costs (in Nova Scotia a mortgagee could also buy back property at a public sale).

Other aspects of colonial law differed from that of England. The British American colonies looked not to English but, rather, American and other colonial laws that governed water, timber, and mineral exploitation and the development of rail networks. Moreover, while the administration of criminal law in the settler colonies resembled that of England, threats to the state were dealt with in a more repressive and often brutal manner by colonial regimes. As well, British American colonial societies generally preferred not to adopt the English practice of splitting legal duties between barristers and solicitors. They also developed different models of legal education, ones that ranged from apprenticeship to formal legal training at a university-affiliated law school. British America, then, demonstrates the ways in which settler colonies both resembled and deviated from the metropolitan models its settlers inherited.

## Colonial Politics and Responsible Government

For colonial legislation to be implemented it had to be drafted and passed in colonial legislatures. From the mid-eighteenth century, with the foundation of Nova Scotia's assembly in 1758, until the middle of the nineteenth century, settler colonies were governed by a combination of a governor or, in the case of British American colonies, a lieutenant-governor, executive and, in some cases, legislative councils, and colonial assembly. As representatives of the Crown, sent out to colonies with instructions concerning the management of colonial affairs, governors were invested by the imperial government with considerable powers over colonial politics. They appointed members of the council and local magistrates and could send legislation passed by assemblies to England for the imperial authorities' approval. Colonial governors, then, could be very close to their prime ministers. Circulating around the British Empire, moving between both settler colonies and other British colonies, these governors at times also became entangled in partisan colonial politics. In the case of British America in the 1820s and 1830s, lieutenant-governors were perceived by reform politicians as siding with colonial elites. In the Canadas, matters became so fraught that in 1837 armed rebellion erupted. The rebellion was suppressed by both colonies' colonial governments, and captured rebels were either executed or transported to Van Diemen's Land. Those who managed to escape took refuge south of the border, while a number returned to the Canadas in the following decade.

Alarmed by the rebellion—which occurred at the same time that humanitarians in England were receiving reports from settler colonies of the violent treatment of Indigenous people—the imperial government sent John George Lambton, the Earl of Durham, to investigate and suggest solutions to the colonies' political tumult. Durham's report of 1839 made a number of recommendations, most of which were designed to promote the assimilation of Quebec's French-speaking population, which Durham believed was uneducated and backward. Calling for the union of the two colonies and the formation of municipal institutions in Lower Canada—first to ensure English dominance, second to educate Lower Canadians in British forms of government—Durham also recommended the introduction of responsible government, in which governors and executive members would need to be supported by the majority of the legislative assembly's members. The imperial government, Durham believed, should focus primarily on matters such as trade and defence and leave internal colonial matters to settler governments. While his call for responsible government was not immediately heeded, nevertheless his report helped to promote and legitimize changing currents in settler societies regarding their governance throughout the British Empire. In 1847 Britain instructed Nova Scotia's lieutenant-governor to choose advisers from the majority party in the assembly; after an election in 1848 in which reformers triumphed, the colony saw the first "responsible" colonial administration in the Empire. Between 1848 and 1855, the Canadas and the Atlantic colonies followed Nova Scotia's example. In turn, it was picked up in New South Wales, Tasmania, Victoria, South Australia, and New Zealand between 1855 and 1857. Responsible government came later to South Africa, being instituted in 1872 at the Cape and in 1892 in Natal.

Nineteenth-century reformers often heralded the advent of responsible government as an important stage in the colonies' inevitable transformation into self-governing Dominions, a claim that early twentieth-century historians who championed settler nationalisms were often eager to repeat. With responsible government representative governments became more democratic, at least for certain groups of men, as authority shifted from imperial authorities and colonial elites to a broader swathe of settler society. Settlers made up an increasingly larger share of the population and benefited from the expansions of the franchise; responsible government also helped promote the development of political parties.

However, for Indigenous people representative and responsible government did not necessarily bring progressive, positive changes. For one, shifting direct control to settler colonial governments often had disastrous results for Indigenous communities. Such governments acceded to settler communities' demands for increased access to Indigenous land and resources, ones that, moreover, directly benefited members of legislative assemblies and councils. As Chapter 1 has discussed, humanitarian influence within the Colonial Office had been also shaped by a paternalistic attitude toward Indigenous people. Humanitarians wished to mitigate the worst effects of settler violence but did not acknowledge Indigenous peoples' own agency and activism. Even as humanitarian influence waned, the concept of Indigenous people as wards of the state not only persisted but, as we have seen, spread across settler societies throughout the nineteenth century. Such an ideology was reflected in debates over enfranchisement. As increasingly larger numbers of white men were included within settler societies' franchises, Indigenous people (specifically men) found themselves faced with choices in which they were forced to renounce their communities—and governments' obligations toward them—if they wished to vote. In Canada, acts passed in 1850 provided a distinct legal status for "Indian people" as wards of the state. This legislation paved the way for the 1857 Gradual Civilization Act, which stated that those still "uncivilized" could enjoy the special status provided for them in treaties. However, those who wished to qualify for Canadian citizenship needed to demonstrate an acceptable level of "civilization," a process which included renouncing communal payments, holding land as individuals, and separating from their home communities: this legislation provided the basis for the Dominion Government's 1876 Indian Act. Such stark choices did not appeal to even those Indigenous men who had accepted various aspects of European society's mores. For example, despite their eligibility both Mississauga chief Kahkewaquonaby/ Peter Jones and his son, Peter Edmund Jones, a medical doctor, refused to become enfranchised. Such a decision would have cut them off from their communities.

Matters were little better in the Australian colonies. The Aborigines' Protection Society lobbied the Secretary of State for the Colonies in 1850, asking that Aboriginal rights be entrenched in the New South Wales constitution in order to avoid the mistakes made in British America. However, the Colonial Office responded by stating that Aboriginal people were British subjects and therefore already qualified for the franchise. The Society's response—that conditions in the Australian colonies prevented them from exercising it— was ignored, with the result that the Australian constitutions omitted references to human rights and contained no special provisions for Aboriginal people's political rights, despite their rapid and ongoing loss of land.

However, in New Zealand demographics played a role in modifying— although not radically altering—Māori relationships to emerging forms of settler governance. The 1852 New Zealand Constitution Act made provisions for governors to set up Native Districts governed by Māori law if colonial officials did not deem it to be "repugnant" to the laws of humanity. However, because of the property requirements attached to the colony's franchise, most Māori were disenfranchised. Settlers in the legislature argued for the abolition of the position of Native Secretary and moved that funds earmarked for native affairs should only go toward mission boarding schools that would teach Māori English. Nevertheless, throughout the 1850s Māori still made up 56 per cent of the population, unlike the situation in Australia or Upper Canada where Indigenous people were outnumbered by Europeans. For example, in the North Island province of Hawke's Bay, a site depicted in Figure 2.2, there were 3,600 Māori to 2,600 European settlers. Furthermore, English law did not reach areas with dense Māori populations, as communities in Native Districts founded committees that dealt with moral, practical, and criminal matters. By the 1860s, in the aftermath of the New Zealand Wars (1845–72) and Māori King Movement of that decade, settler governments could no longer avoid Māori representation. The 1867 Māori Representation Bill created three large Māori electorates

FIGURE 2.2 "Meeting of Settlers and Māori, New Zealand, 1863." The meeting was held at the Māori village of Pah Wahkairo, Hawke's Bay.

Source: M. Jackson engraving, based on photographs by Charles H. Robson, *The Illustrated London News*, 31 October 1863. Mary Evans Picture Library, Picture Number 10237944.

in the North Island and one in the South Island, enfranchising Māori men over 21 (those who lived in white areas and met the Constitution's property laws were also enfranchised). Although at times hailed as indicative of Māoris' special status and compared favourably to the disenfranchisement of Indigenous people elsewhere, Māori themselves were either unaware of their new seats, indifferent to settler government, or angry at the small number of seats and wished to see every tribal group represented. Upon their arrival in Parliament, the new Māori members created a stir by speaking in Māori. As well, settler legislators were surprised to discover that because the overall number of representatives was small and political factions could be unstable, the Māori could vote as a bloc, influencing bills and, possibly, toppling the government.

In South Africa, Indigenous peoples' relationship to the franchise was shaped by the length of white settlement, the position of non-white populations, and colonial economies. The arrival of representative government in the Cape Colony in 1853 and Natal in 1856 sparked discussions of Indigenous peoples' status as citizens. In the Boer republics of the Transvaal and Orange Free State, though, franchise regulations explicitly excluded non-whites. In comparison with the situation in British America, the Cape franchise was fairly open: it included any adult man who, for at least a year, had occupied property worth £25 per year or whose annual income was at least £50 per year. The colony's large mixed-race or coloured population—the descendants of white settlers, European traders, Africans, and Asians who became a significant and distinct population at the Cape— saw their political position shift with the new franchise. A number of coloured men who lived in urban centres and who had become integrated into the colony's European-dominated economy qualified. It was not until 1887 that the Cape Parliament started to place obstacles that blocked Africans from registering to vote; five years later it raised franchise qualifications in order to limit or exclude African voters in the Eastern Cape.

Natal, however, was a different story. As Chapter 1 points out, a large Indigenous population in Natal and a steadily growing South Asian community outnumbered Europeans, a demographic very different from that at the more racially heterogeneous Cape. White settlers' anxieties, stemming from both their position as a racial minority and the fear of Zulu attack, underpinned decisions about the franchise. The colony's Royal Charter set out a male franchise based on property qualifications—the threshold being either ownership of fixed property worth £50 or payment of £10 per year in rent—and not colour. However, the racial segregation that developed under Theophilus Shepstone's land system, in which many Africans lived on reserves governed by Native Law, was exploited by settlers. Only men subject to English colonial law were able to vote. Similar to the situation in Canada, any African who wished to do so was obliged to apply for an exemption from Native Law on the basis of his having reached a state of civilization; in the process, he was forced to publicly disown his culture and traditional laws. Perhaps not surprisingly (again, like the Canadian situation), those who wished to become enfranchised were the *kholwa* or Christian converts, residents of mission stations. Yet despite their adaptation of European values and practices and the fact that they were able to either rent or purchase property, very few were able to attain political rights. At the advent of responsible government in 1893, only a very small minority of Africans in Natal were able to vote. The 1903–05 Inter-Colonial Commission found that only three could do so, a number that by 1907 had risen to only six out of an electorate of 24,000 men.

Indigenous men in all of the settler colonies thus saw their political rights either contract or at best expand very slightly; Indigenous women suffered even greater diminishment of political status and responsibility over the course of the nineteenth century. Prior to European contact, Indigenous women's political roles and capacities varied a great deal. In northeastern America, Haudenosaunee women, for example, had traditionally enjoyed a range of political, diplomatic, and military decision-making powers in their role as clan matrons. In Natal women such as MaNthatisi, from the Batlokwa clan (part of the Sotho-Tswana people), had exercised chiefly authority and were respected by their communities. In other societies, though, women did not participate directly in clan or tribal governance. Indigenous women's political status was often linked to the ways in which their communities defined membership and descent. In Haudenosaunee society, for example, descent and residence was matrilineal and matrilocal, factors that anthropologists argue helped contribute to women's roles in decision making. Furthermore, in societies where adoption was normal and frequent, an Indigenous woman in a relationship with a man outside of her community, whether Indigenous or not, did not necessarily lose her social and political standing within it. However, in legislation such as Canada's 1876 Indian Act, Indigenous women's relationship to their communities was redefined along lines of marriage and race. Women who married non-Indigenous men lost their "Indian" status, while the opposite situation applied to non-Indigenous women married to Indigenous men. The flexibility demonstrated by a number of Indigenous societies around questions of membership and affiliation was overlaid and, in some cases, replaced by colonial governments' determination to regulate and limit membership in their communities.

In some settler societies, Indigenous women's relationship to suffrage changed as a consequence of European women gaining the vote. In New Zealand, women's enfranchisement included Māori women. They joined Māori men in the four Māori electoral districts, but could only attend and speak in Parliament, not vote. In Australia, where educated, middle-class women had created a grassroots woman's suffrage movement through the Women's Christian Temperance Union (WCTU), the implications of women voting were hotly debated. White Australian women argued that manhood suffrage made white women's exclusion not just unfair but unconscionable, given such women's contributions to settler society and the need to maintain white dominance. Such arguments held considerable sway in South Australia, where in 1894 women were both enfranchised and permitted to run for office. These provisions included Aboriginal women, although their inclusion received little attention. Western Australia followed suit five years later. As politicians began to discuss Australian federation in the 1890s, women's enfranchisement in some states but not others became a matter of contention: the federal parliament decided fairly quickly that the solution was to enfranchise all women.

The difference between white women's and Aboriginal people's enfranchisement at a national level was stark, though. The 1902 bill that proposed a universal franchise met little opposition so far as women voting was concerned. However, the prospect of enfranchising all Aboriginal people was unthinkable to representatives from Queensland and Western Australia. In 1905 Queensland rescinded the small number of provisions that allowed Aboriginal people to vote at the state level; two years later Western Australia declared that both Aboriginal men and women, even if they held property, were ineligible to vote. Politicians in both states argued that their small number of white settlers would be overrun by larger Aboriginal populations. Using blatantly racist language that relied on images of Aboriginals as savages who could not be trusted to conduct themselves responsibly, they raised the spectre of ignorant voters being manipulated by unscrupulous political parties (usually those of the speakers' opponents). Although those Aboriginal people who were already entitled to vote at the state level—in Victoria, New South Wales, South Australia, and Tasmania—could vote for the new Commonwealth, only those enfranchised in 1902 were permitted to do so. Thus, over time the number of eligible Aboriginal voters—literally—died out.

The scenario in Canada differed. Between 1809 and 1840, a small number of propertied women voted in elections in Lower Canada and Nova Scotia; by Confederation, though, women were explicitly excluded from the franchise. Women's suffrage was debated in the Canadian Parliament with the introduction of Prime Minister John A. Macdonald's 1885 Franchise Bill. Meant to enfranchise single women and widows who held property, the bill generated considerable controversy over Macdonald's inclusion of Indigenous people, regardless of their eligibility under the Gradual Civilization Act. However, Macdonald quickly dropped women's inclusion after MPs from Quebec objected. After fractious debate over Indigenous people's "fitness" for citizenship, the bill that passed included only a minority of Indigenous men from the Dominion's eastern provinces. The spectre of Indigenous women voting while white women were excluded resulted in a very gender-specific, as well as racially limited, franchise.

As in Australia and New Zealand, woman's suffrage activists, along with social reform groups such as the WCTU, lobbied for the vote primarily on the grounds of white, middle-class women's moral capacities and their contributions to nation building. Unlike other settler societies, though, Canadian women who were British subjects were enfranchised in different stages: those with family members serving overseas received the Dominion vote in 1917, with the rest enfranchised in 1918. Between 1916 (starting in Manitoba) and 1940 (Quebec), they also received the provincial vote. Yet, along with Indigenous men, Indigenous women would not be enfranchised until 1960—Macdonald's franchise had been repealed in 1898 by a Liberal government. Insofar as provincial elections were concerned, Indigenous people were either directly prevented from voting, excluded if they lived on a reserve, or needed to meet property qualifications reintroduced after the repeal of Macdonald's Franchise Act.

In South Africa, white women would not be enfranchised until 1930. While the WCTU, the Women's Enfranchisement League (founded in Durban in 1902), and prominent writer and activist Olive Schreiner called for the vote, their demands were overshadowed by white men's need to sustain minority rule by containing the size of the electorate. Yet citizenship and political rights were not dependent on solely gender or Indigenous status: settler governments and their supporters also decided that maintaining white dominance was also dependent on the exclusion of Asians and South Asians. In many ways Natal provided others with an example of how to control, limit, and if possible directly prohibit South Asians from attaining full political rights. Although Natal's franchise was, in theory, not racially based, nevertheless in 1894 the government crafted a version of its Native Law in order to bar South Asians from voting. It declared that those of the "Asiatic race" who were not used to exercising their rights under a parliamentary system could not vote. Despite active opposition from the colony's South Asian community and the objections of Colonial Secretary Joseph Chamberlain, who feared that it would create problems for British rule in India, once the bill reached London in 1896 it was approved, albeit in a modified form. As a compromise, the bill substituted "Native" for "Asiatic" while maintaining provisions excluding those "Natives" (and their male descendants) from countries lacking elected institutions based on the parliamentary franchise, unless they received a gubernatorial exemption from the Act. Equally importantly, the following year Natal passed an Immigration Restriction Act that required a language test for all new arrivals in the colony. Those who could not write in a European language of the attending immigration officer's choice were refused admission. Natal's legislation was picked up by Australia, which in 1902 passed its own Immigration Restriction Act that required a dictation test in a European language. It was followed by deportation legislation targeting South Sea Islanders whose work had provided the foundation for Queensland's sugar industry. Racially based immigration would have a long history in Australia and formed the basis of the "White Australia" policy, the last trace of which would not be abolished until 1973.

Australia was not the only settler society that, in the words of historians, helped to construct the "global colour line" through selective immigration policies and franchise legislation that excluded certain groups. In the late 1890s and early 1900s Canada's Liberal government actively promoted the immigration of central and eastern Europeans in order to "settle" and farm its western prairies. Yet not all immigrants were welcomed by Canada. In 1875, anti-Asian racism in British Columbia led to a panoply of legislation aimed at preventing Chinese Canadians from participating in settler society. They were not allowed to acquire Crown lands, could not work underground in mines or on public works projects, were banned from entering provincial homes for the elderly and infirm, and were prevented from voting at the provincial level. Upon completion of the Canadian Pacific Railway in 1885, a project on which many Chinese Canadians had worked and died, the Dominion government imposed a head tax on any new Chinese immigrants; between 1885 and 1924, 86,000 Chinese immigrants paid $23 million to enter Canada. That amount might well have been higher had it not been for the 1923 Chinese Immigration Act, which banned further Chinese immigration and required every resident Chinese Canadian to register with the government; this legislation would not be repealed until after World War II. Japanese Canadians fared little better. Starting in 1907 and continuing into the 1920s, the government put in place a number of discriminatory immigration policies and, until 1947, refused Japanese Canadians the vote. Xenophobic fears of "dangerous foreigners" in World War I led to police surveillance, internment, and, in some cases, deportation of those suspected of radical political beliefs.

## Creating Settler Nations

Discussions of enfranchisement and immigration did not, of course, take place in a vacuum, as they were tied to changes in the colonies' status. Responsible government may have "set the stage" for the creation of Dominions, yet the process was not inevitable or assured. Discussions of a union of the British American colonies began in the 1780s with the arrival of the Loyalists, and the Canadas were united in 1841; during the 1850s colonial political leaders began to explore a transcontinental union. Those negotiating the union's terms accepted "Confederation" as a way of blending the Liberals' preference for an American-style federation and provincial autonomy with the Conservatives' desire for a more centralized, British form of union (which would subordinate French Canadians). In the case of British North America, the Confederation celebrated on 1 July 1867 included only four provinces: Ontario, Quebec, Nova Scotia, and New Brunswick. Between 1870, with the creation of the province of Manitoba, and 1905, when the provinces of Saskatchewan and Alberta were formed out of the North-West Territories, two other provinces joined Confederation (Newfoundland would not enter until 1949). Historians have offered various explanations for Confederation occurring at that moment, not least the crisis of the American Civil War and the subsequent Fenian raids into New Brunswick and Ontario. The raids were conducted from the United States by Irish-American Civil War veterans protesting against Britain's policies in Ireland. British Columbia, for its part, joined Canada in 1871 with the promise of a transcontinental railroad and the new Dominion's assumption of responsibility for its debt. Yet it is difficult to identify a singular or clear-cut motivation that united British North American politicians, for there was just as much opposition to it as there was support for it.

Australia's 1901 Federation resembled Canada's union in some ways, insofar as the role of external threats was concerned. French and German imperial expansion in the Pacific during the early 1880s, as well as the need to deal with intercolonial trade, prompted Australian governments to open discussions of federation. The initial conference devoted to it, held in 1883 in Sydney, led only to a Federal Council that did not include South Australia or New South Wales. By the end of the decade, however, the nationalist vision of Henry Parkes, New South Wales's premier, helped precipitate the 1891 Convention. The meeting produced an initial draft of an Australian Constitution, but it was not approved by New South Wales's assembly. The impetus for federation was revived by Federation Leagues formed in 1893 and continued throughout the decade. Unlike the situation in Canada, where Confederation was not put to a vote, referenda were held on the Constitution in the various provinces between 1898 and 1900 and the Commonwealth of Australia was proclaimed on 1 January 1901. Like Canada, however, Australia's Federation was crafted primarily by an elite of urban, male politicians, drawn primarily from the professional classes. While nationalist sentiment was present, it was overshadowed by loyalty to both Britain and individual states. As well, provincial economies remained more closely linked to Britain's economy, not to each other. Moreover, while New Zealand participated in initial discussions of federation with Australia, after 1891 it did not attend other meetings, believing that it would become a junior and subordinate partner in such a union. Preferring to pursue a status independent of Australia, New Zealand became a Dominion on 26 September 1907.

Although the events and processes that surrounded settler colonies' shifts to Dominion status—the exclusion of Indigenous people, women, and racial minorities from political membership, and the violence that underpinned settler expansion into Australia's Northern Territory, for example—were charged with relationships of power and dominance, the constitutional crafting of colonial unions was a relatively peaceful affair. In the case of South African union, however, such was decidedly not the case. To be sure, the South African War (1899–1902) was not inevitable: in 1897 Britain did not desire to annex the Transvaal by military force. While British Prime Minister Joseph Chamberlain wished to unite South Africa under white minority rule and British dominance, he and the cabinet hoped for a peaceful solution to the tensions between Britain and Boer political leader Paul Kruger's Transvaal Republic. Although Britain's access to gold mines in the Transvaal has been cited as a motivation for the war, it is far more likely that the imperial government wished to establish its power and influence over the Transvaal as a way of ensuring South African unification. While Britain anticipated a short, decisive war with deployment of only 75,000 troops and a few hundred casualties, the conflict lasted two years and eight months, cost £230 million, and killed 22,000 British soldiers, 34,000 Boer civilians and combatants, and around 14,000 Africans. British soldiers died of typhus and in guerrilla raids by Boer fighters, while Boer civilians—many of them women and children—died of epidemics in the concentration camps set up by the British. The latter also burned around 30,000 Boer farms and livestock in a "scorched-earth policy" meant to sap their opponents' will. By 1902, with weekly costs for the war at £1.5 million and British public support for the war waning as news of its army's tactics reached home, the British government was willing to negotiate a peaceful settlement.

The cost and devastation of the South African war was not its only notable feature. It brought together volunteers from Australia, Canada, and New Zealand and, as Chapter 5 will discuss, helped strengthen imperial identities in those Dominions. Moreover, although non-white troops were barred from serving in the British forces, at least 100,000 Africans were drawn into the conflict, working as scouts, labourers, messengers, spies, transport drivers, and patrols. The war also provided work and higher wages and prices for agricultural goods and livestock. Furthermore, in a number of areas the British armed Africans in order to keep Boer commandoes (militia members) out of their areas; some were able to take over Boer land and cattle. African support for the British stemmed from the hope that a British victory would mean the extension of the franchise, along with other civil rights, as existed in the Cape Colony.

However, not all Africans benefited from the war. Those who lived in areas burned by the British lost their farms and were placed in concentration and labour camps (separate from Boers), where many died from disease. Furthermore, black Africans' hopes for a better future were dashed during the peace negotiations, as the Boers would not countenance African enfranchisement. Although the South African Native Congress expressed its concerns to Joseph Chamberlain about black political rights, in 1906 Britain's Liberal government reinstalled self-government, based on an adult white male franchise, to the Orange Free State and the Transvaal. Offering the examples of Canadian Confederation and Australian Federation, the imperial government worked with settler politicians to press for the unity of South Africa's self-governing colonies. Promoted by politicians in the Transvaal and the Cape, and prompted by fear of the Zulu population's Bambatha Rebellion of 1906, the colonies of the Transvaal, Cape, Natal, and Orange Free State formed the Union of South Africa in 1910.

The Union's creation was accompanied by discussions of "racial reconciliation": not that of black and white, but of Boer and British. Indigenous political rights remained a divisive issue, as Natal had excluded non-Europeans, and the Transvaal and the Orange Free State refused to entertain the concept of black enfranchisement. It was only politicians from the Cape, with its history of 56 years of a non-discriminatory, qualified franchise, who wished to see it continue: they did so from a practical basis. According to John Merriman, the dominant Cape politician behind the push for union, the black population was numerically superior, becoming educated and better off; moreover, they were workers, a group Merriman believed would be influential in the twentieth century. While Merriman disliked Indigenous people and wished there were no blacks in South Africa, nevertheless he thought it was incumbent on whites to do their duty toward them while simultaneously maintaining white superiority. The resulting compromise permitted each province to maintain its colonial franchise laws, resulting in coloured and African men in the Cape retaining their ability to vote. However, the government also restricted membership in the Union parliament to white men. South Africa's franchise would remain shaped by fears of its Indigenous and mixed-race populations for the next 80 years.

## Conclusion

The quotes that opened this chapter point to a number of the historical developments that marked the peopling, settling, and governing of these societies. Susannah Wall's hopes and dreams of creating a new home in New Zealand were ones shared by countless other emigrants, their experiences shaped by encounters with the strange and unfamiliar as they struggled to recreate aspects of "home" and to maintain their links with family and friends left behind. For his part, Thomas Dyke saw colonization as a means of transplanting British mores, values, and practices around the world, a process that he believed would inevitably mean the displacement of Indigenous peoples. However, Dyke thought their dispossession would be worth it, not least because of the benefits to Britain that, in his opinion, would result in the elimination of the metropole's surplus population and the "advantages of trade." Chapter 3 turns to the subject of colonial economies, forged both in local contexts and through imperial and transnational networks.

## Notes

1 Thomas Dyke, *Advice to Emigrants: or, An Impartial Guide to the Canadas, New Brunswick, Nova Scotia, the United States, New South Wales, Van Diemen's Land, the Swan River, and the Cape of Good Hope, Pointing Out the Advantages and Disadvantages of the Several Locations: With the Latest Government Instructions* (London: W. Simpkin and R. Marshall, 1832), 2–4.

2 Susannah Wall to Hannah Wall, from Wellington, New Zealand, 18 Dec. 1842, in *"My Hand Will Write What My Heart Dictates": The Unsettled Lives of Women in Nineteenth-Century New Zealand as Revealed to Sisters, Family and Friends,* eds. Frances Porter and Charlotte Macdonald with Tui Macdonald (Auckland: Auckland University Press and Bridget Williams Books, 1996), 79.

3 Maya Jasanoff, *Liberty's Exiles: American Loyalists in the Revolutionary World* (New York: Alfred A. Knopf, 2011), 182.

4 Ibid., 183.

5 Raewyn Dalziel, "Southern Islands: New Zealand and Polynesia," in *The Oxford History of the British Empire*, Vol. 3, *The Nineteenth Century*, eds. Andrew Porter and Wm. Roger Louis (Oxford: Oxford University Press, 1999), 582.

6 Ibid.

# 3 Settler Economies: Local Contexts and Imperial Networks

*I have been greatly bothered with my servants lately my old one left and I got a young girl but she did not answer then I got another and last night she asked me to let her go to a small party I told her not to stay out late and sat up till half past 12 but she did not come. I then went to bed but I could not sleep thinking she would want to be let in every minute but she did not arrive until 8 in the morning after I had got the breakfast half dressed for I dare not take time to dress for the boys had to be in town by nine, I have given her a piece of my mind I can tell you when she did come. For some time I was without any [servants] so you can fancy how tired I am.*
—Caroline Boultbee, 7 December 1875[1]

*Freedom of Contract ... what a nice, high-sounding title.... Freedom for a man to do as he likes! Freedom for the employer to pay what he likes, and you work as many hours as he likes! Freedom for the worker, who is homeless, houseless, and breadless, and a family crying for food, to accept whatever pittance is given to him! Freedom for twenty men to look for the one job and the lowest to get it! Freedom for the worker who dares to get married, and has a family, to send his wife out washing, and his little ones selling papers to help to augment the pittance the head of the household receives.*
—Samuel Lister, 1891[2]

While emigration promoters might write enthusiastically of the economic opportunities that awaited new arrivals in settler colonies, not all agreed.

Colonists such as Loyalist descendant Caroline Boultbee, living in southern Ontario, or New Zealand's Samuel Lister, a Scottish immigrant, skilled worker, and editor, publisher, and printer of the weekly *Otago Workman*, had less rosy perspectives on such matters. Like many white middle-class women in settler societies over the course of the nineteenth century, Boultbee found the hiring and keeping of female servants a trial, one attributed by her contemporaries to a greater range of opportunities for single women and the loosening of notions of deference that governed domestic service in Britain. Writing during the throes of New Zealand's Long Depression of the 1890s, it is unlikely that Lister had much sympathy for Boultbee's complaints. From his perspective, the situation for married, working-class men in the colony was far from the utopia promised by colonial promoters. Instead of being able to exercise their prerogatives as breadwinners, artisans such as Lister were being forced into poverty and dependency, the antithesis of the "better Britain" they had hoped to create.

Despite their different class positions and their different concepts of the meanings of "freedom" for workers, in all likelihood Boultbee and Lister shared a belief in one key concept: the permanence of the capitalist economic structures and institutions in which they lived. British settler colonies were marked by the expectation that such structures would guide their societies into the future and would underpin their future development and prosperity. Unlike colonies where the extraction of resources—sugar, minerals, cotton—or the defence of strategic military interests were the rationale for Europeans' presence, settlers generally thought they were building the foundation for societies that would outlast their creators. While the dispossession and containment of Indigenous people, the peopling of the land with Europeans, and the creation of political and legal institutions were critically important components of that process, so too was the fashioning of settler economies. Permanence might be more honoured as an ideal than in reality, as settler colonies were far from being immune to cycles of "boom and bust." Settlers might find that, after all, their better future could be found back in Britain, the United States, or Argentina. Nevertheless, the creation of economic structures and institutions was intricately bound up with the creation of a "better Britain" in the Antipodes, British America, or South Africa.

Focusing on settler economies also helps us understand another important question, that of the similarities between these colonies and the various ways in which local conditions and historical contingencies led them to differ from each other. The different timing of economic development, variations in topography and climate, and the degree to which Indigenous people were drawn into waged and/or coerced labour: such factors helped differentiate settler economies from each other. Furthermore, proximity to other economies, such as British America's to the United States, Australia's to Pacific trading networks, or Natal's links to the Indian Ocean, also created a range of opportunities and challenges. While it is important not to homogenize these societies' economies, nevertheless their overall patterns bore a number of striking resemblances. For one, they were tied to the metropole not just through imperial policies but also through those commercial networks that grew over the course of the nineteenth century and into the early twentieth. As well, settler societies within the British Empire shared common cultural assumptions about the economy, its meaning and significance, and, in particular, the belief that private property and capitalism were the best economic and political foundations for settler society. The use of certain practices, such as political patronage or imperial preference, that might appear to contradict such tenets of economic faith should not detract from the latter's power in shaping settler economies.

## Trade, Markets, and the Growth of Financial Structures

As we have seen in previous chapters, the ideals that settlers and imperial governments brought to the British Empire's expansion were important, no less (or perhaps particularly) so when they came into conflict with colonial material realities. Early nineteenth-century emigrants' guides held out the promise of the fertile land and plentiful resources that would transform frontier bushland into neat, tidy, and prosperous farms. Promoters of assisted colonization, such as Edward Gibbon Wakefield, were equally enthusiastic about the prospects of agricultural settlement. Later in the nineteenth century, representations of abundant apple orchards and rippling wheat fields became a staple for the Canadian Pacific Railroad's emigration promoters, whose lectures to voluntary societies and a range of institutions around Britain were accompanied by stereopticon slides. As colonial societies became self-governing Dominions, agricultural motifs became a frequently used symbol of nationhood, appearing in commemorative ceremonies, flags, crests, poetry, prose, paintings, and sculpture. By the late nineteenth century a number of political parties in settler societies identified themselves, at times quite explicitly, with the "farmer's interest" and rural society's concerns. They did so often at the very moment when provincial demographics and economic trends were beginning to tilt toward urban centres and industrialization.

The ideology of rural settler society was also grounded in the image of the independent yeoman farmer, a figure heralded for his essential contribution to community and nation-building. Yet over the course of the period covered here, agricultural policies and practices in settler colonies were also linked to imperial policies, imperial trade, and, in particular, imperial warfare. After the conquest of New France in 1759, for example, colonial business in British America became linked to Britain, and trade in Quebec was dominated by those with ties to British merchants or the army. In New Brunswick, Napoleon's blockade of trade with Britain, and the latter's loss of Baltic timber for ship-building, led to preferential tariffs in 1809, ones that helped expand the colony's already-present timber trade and shipbuilding (although, as economic historians have noted, imperial policy was not the only reason for their expansion). Upper Canada's agricultural sector was itself the product of imperial conflicts; its export trade, in both wheat and wood products, was subsequently tied to British markets. At the Cape, provisioning the military was an ongoing theme throughout the nineteenth century, not least because of the series of wars in the region. For farmers at the Cape during the 1840s, for example, the British army created a welcome market for their goods. They also believed the army should be used to gain more land from African farmers, whose practices British farmers saw as unproductive and wasteful. Merchants in Cape Town also benefited from the army's presence, as they were able to supply and provision it. In this instance, ties to Britain and the imperial state helped forge networks of supply and demand; they also helped shape a lobby of wool farmers in the region that would exercise considerable influence in colonial politics.

Not all colonies' trade was with the metropole, though: Newfoundland was an exception to the larger pattern. Although settlement had been actively discouraged by the imperial authorities and the West-Country English merchants who controlled trade, from the mid- to late eighteenth century settlement began to occur, mostly in an informal and protracted fashion. By 1810, Newfoundland's population was more than 20,000; its imports, controlled primarily by merchants in St. John's, came from other parts of the Empire. While Newfoundland sent fish to the British West Indies, 80 per cent of its catch went to Portugal, Spain, and Italy; the fishery was part of an international economy. Like other colonies, though, it too was affected by the American Revolution (1776–83) and the Napoleonic Wars (1803–15). The former meant a loss of supplies which in turn forced residents to rely on local farming, while the latter ended the migratory fishery but caused fish prices to rise. Newfoundland subsequently experienced a sharp increase in Irish immigration, the growth of the resident fishery, and a supplemental spring seal hunt. However, both fish prices and immigration declined precipitously once the Napoleonic Wars ended.

Newfoundland aside, the vast majority of the goods bought by colonists came from Britain; conversely, the markets for their goods were British ones. Merchants in settler colonies were often the linchpins that helped link local economies to the metropole. Such was the case at the Cape, where economic ties and networks were the filaments that bound the region in the early nineteenth century to Britain, itself becoming a global leader in industry and international commerce. Between 1807 and 1817, the value of Cape exports multiplied tenfold, and the growth in imports, primarily European manufactured goods, was also impressive. In particular, Cape Town played a pivotal role in connecting colonial and metropolitan economies. The port city brought together those who bought, sold, and consumed arable and pastoral produce from the region's southwestern districts and beyond, a process that intensified as the region's urban economy began to focus on exporting wine. Human beings also played a part in these networks, albeit in ways that reflected even more starkly the unequal distribution of power in settler societies. Prior to the abolition of slavery, Cape Town was tied to a rural hinterland through the hiring out and selling of urban slaves to farmers: slaves had long been used as a type of human bank, being sold when masters needed cash, and were accepted as security for loans by money lenders. From 1813 to 1823 the trade in human beings helped underpin the expansion of wine farming at the Cape. By the 1820s a new group of Cape Town merchants, many of whom were from Scotland and brought considerable commercial experience with them, began to set up institutions that would promote their social and economic influence, such as the Commercial Exchange and the Cape of Good Hope Trade Society. The latter set up a formal link with merchants in London and also lobbied the imperial government.

In other colonies, the aftermath of the Napoleonic Wars saw merchants move quite quickly to set up banks. Local banks were vital for local economic growth, as they provided small and medium-sized loans, a lucrative business for local businessmen and merchants. They also allowed regional economies to respond much faster to local demands for credit. Simultaneously, local banks made it possible for local business communities to exercise some discretion and latitude in determining their area's needs and priorities, thus providing a degree of local financial independence. Montreal and Sydney took the lead in 1817, and over the next eight years, other cities in

British America—Quebec City, Kingston, Saint John, York, and Halifax— followed. A number of chartered banks were established in British America between 1832 and 1836. When the Bank of British North America, a London-based institution whose royal charter was designed to regulate banking in all the colonies, appeared in 1837, it found that only Prince Edward Island and Newfoundland did not have a competitive system of local banks; by 1867 British America boasted 33 chartered banks. Prior to 1867 banks in British America tended to operate on a province-by-province basis; however, under Confederation banking fell into the Dominion government's jurisdiction. In 1871 the National Bank Act provided a regulatory framework for Canada's banks. In contrast, in Australia over the course of the nineteenth century, Sydney's importance as a regional metropole can be seen in the dominance of the Bank of New South Wales. Not only did it open branches in the other Australian colonies but it also spread to New Zealand and throughout the Pacific, setting up branches in Fiji and Papua New Guinea.

As London's prominence as the centre of world finance intensified, these ties of imperial commerce and trade became even stronger. Although the end of mercantilism in 1846 and the promotion of free trade in mid-Victorian Britain might have suggested otherwise, imperial trade and financial networks did not diminish but, rather, grew in significance. For example, the Upper Canadian wheat trade boomed after the Corn Laws' repeal, while timber exports from British America increased significantly after the expiration of preferential treatment for colonial timber in 1859. By the late nineteenth century, Australia's and New Zealand's markets in Britain for agricultural produce—wool, beef, mutton, cheese, and butter—were well-established, while Canada continued to export wheat and, with the development of its manufacturing infrastructure, agricultural machinery.

However, these processes were not inevitable or straightforward. Rumour and gossip might also affect imperial trade, as well as growing internal markets within a colony. For example, at the Cape in 1840 rumours of a tariff agreement between England and France that would disadvantage the Cape's wine industry had a direct effect on the colony's exports. Although untrue, these rumours came on the heels of reduced duties on European wine, with the result that Cape merchants became reluctant to ship wine to Britain and the wine market declined. It recovered in the 1850s, although primarily as a result of stronger demand within the Cape itself. Grain farming, the largest sector of the Cape's agricultural economy, also benefited from the region's growth, as did the regional market for meat and draft oxen. Merino wool, which was shipped through Port Elizabeth with its pastoral hinterland in the Eastern Cape, was in demand for Britain's many woollen mills, although it constituted less than half of the value of pastoral production.

Over the course of the nineteenth century, settler societies' markets also became significant outlets for British exports. From 1871 to 1913, British goods sent around the empire rose from 26.8 per cent to 35 per cent, as American and industrial European markets for them shrunk. Furthermore, Australia, Canada, New Zealand, and South Africa saw their consumption of British goods rise in relation to the rest of the Empire, an increase that was most pronounced in the case of Australia, New Zealand, and South Africa. By the 1890s Dominion markets offered preferential tariffs for British goods. The growth in demand in settler societies was more likely spurred by other factors, however, such as imperial subsidies for British shipping lines, trading networks based on family and faith (such as the Quaker-based companies of Cadbury, Fry, Rowntree, and Sturges), imperial exhibitions (to be discussed in more detail in Chapter 5), and the global reach of the Chamber of Commerce. Starting in the 1850s, the latter took root across a number of settler societies and provided venues, such as imperial conferences, in which delegates from both Britain and the Dominions exchanged news and discussed strategies around such matters as tariff policies.

Here, too, differences between imperial and Dominion policy emerged. Canadian delegates strongly endorsed preferential trade that helped the Dominions, with the aim of protecting Canadian manufacturers from German and American competition. Manchester cotton manufacturers who supported free trade opposed such measures, however, as they did not wish to see any restrictions on their right to sell in colonial or semi-colonial regions. As well, Chambers of Commerce remind us that other relationships, most notably those of race and class, structured imperial economic networks. At Cape Town, the local Chamber was predominantly composed of a long-standing white merchant elite, one from which less well-off businessmen, merchants, and retailers, both English and Dutch-Afrikaans, were excluded by virtue of the annual £5 membership fee. Lacking access to credit and transport and more concerned with building up capital in cattle and land, Africans were blocked from mercantile activity, not to mention the metropolitan and colonial contacts that benefited the colony's commercial upper class. In Natal, racially based opposition from white residents and businessmen to the colony's Indian merchant community (itself divided into wealthy Muslim merchant groups and smaller shopkeepers, some of whom were former indentured labourers) and subsequent discriminatory legislation against Indian merchants and storekeepers motivated the latter in 1908 to form their own Indian Chamber of Commerce.

Settler economies also were shaped by British investment. Between 1865 and 1914, London's Stock Exchange and financial houses sent around £4.1 billion to 170 countries; by 1913, Britain's net overseas assets had grown to 32 per cent of its national wealth, as compared to 7 per cent in 1850. Although the United States and Argentina, as well as India, Russia, and Brazil, received significant amounts of capital, Australia, Canada, and South Africa ranked among the top six recipients, with Canada second only to the United States. Settler colonies thus saw a faster increase in British investment than any other country or colony. The timing of these investments varied somewhat, though. Australia received considerable capital between the 1870s and early 1890s, while the bulk of the money that flowed into Canada did so after 1904; in contrast, New Zealand's share was far less significant (2.1 per cent as compared to Canada's 10 per cent). Much of British overseas investment sent to the Dominions went into transportation and communication. Settler societies, with rapidly expanding resource industries, thriving agricultural sectors, and growing urban centres and industrial economies, needed railroads, ports, trams or streetcars, and improved postal and telegraph systems to move goods, people, and information. Railways in particular received the lion's share of these funds, much of which came not from a very well-off few but, rather, from a large swathe of middle-class, small-scale investors. Purchasing stocks in railways became somewhat of a mania, with the stocks' value being inflated. Unfortunately for these investors, though, the "railway bubble" (inevitably) burst.

It would be misleading to assume that transportation and communication in settler colonies were entirely dependent on the British investment boom of the mid-nineteenth century: some projects preceded it. In British America during the 1830s, for example, Upper Canada had raised funds from the British bond market to finance the building of canals. After the union of the Canadas in 1841 the imperial government guaranteed a loan that allowed the United Province of Canada to finish the St. Lawrence canal system. Colonial politicians and businessmen also started to discuss railways in the 1830s, discussions that came to greater fruition from the mid-1850s as regional lines, privately owned in Canada but financed by governments in the Maritimes, were built in Ontario, Quebec, New Brunswick, and Nova Scotia. Imperial investment in Canadian railways became even more significant from the 1870s on, as the Dominion government raised funds for the Intercolonial Railroad to the Atlantic. It then provided backing for the privately owned Canadian Pacific Railroad (CPR), which supplied British Columbia with its long-promised link to the rest of the country. Other colonies followed somewhat different practices. In Queensland, Western Australia, New Zealand, and South Africa, Crown Agents (appointed by an administrative agency based in London) supervised public works such as railway construction. They supplied materials and equipment, usually from British manufacturers, and appointed British engineers, inspectors, and staff to design and supervise projects.

Railways played a critically important role in settler societies—as they did elsewhere around the globe—in linking industry, commerce, agricultural production, and resources extraction to markets, internal and imperial. Yet railways also had social, cultural, and political significance and meaning. For one, they were important symbols of modernity, indicating that, like Britain, western Europe, and the United States, settler colonies were indeed making progress through their development of such an infrastructure, one called by historians the "core technology" of the age. Railways and their maritime counterpart, steamships, also linked settler colonies' culture to other parts of the world, both the metropole and elsewhere; they helped engender the increased movement of various forms of culture and popular leisure, both performers (theatrical, musical, and circus troupes, and popular lecturers, for example) and material culture (books, periodicals, sheet music, musical instruments, and home decor). Railways might also play a role in the strengthening of family and kin networks, making it easier for people to see each other. For example, the large, extended Hamilton-Jarvis family of Queenston, Ontario—descendants of Upper Canada's Loyalist and mercantile elite—was able to travel around the province and across the United States border to Buffalo and the Midwestern states, mobility that would have been far more difficult without rail. The railroad also made it possible for them to maintain family ties through letter writing, as their letters were often delivered by family members travelling on southern Ontario's and the United States' railroads.

Yet railways, steamships, and telegraphs were not always benign or innocent of the relations of power that structured settler colonies, for they also reflected and helped shape and reinforce them. At the Cape, railway building in the 1870s relied heavily on imported white British workers, who were brought in through an emigration service based in London and who worked as skilled artisans and in heavy labouring jobs, such as rock cutting. They also were paid more than black railway workers, an inequality explained partly because of their skill and speed but also because colonists wished to suppress black wages and increase the white population. In Canada, Chinese railway workers, brought in to work on the most difficult and dangerous section of the CPR, suffered injuries and diseases that resulted in many deaths; moreover, at the end of their contracts the repatriation to China that they had been promised did not materialize. Forced to remain in Canada, they became the target of organized labour's and the general public's racism and violence. For Indigenous people railways, telegraphs, and steamships were implicated in the spread of settler and imperial warfare, as they made it faster and easier for authorities to move troops, armaments, and information. Such was the case in Canada in 1885, when the Dominion government sent militia by rail from Ontario to the west to suppress the second Riel Rebellion, or in South Africa, when by the early 1850s steamship travel around the coast significantly cut the time it took imperial troops to reach the interior.

### Land and Labour

Capital, markets, and infrastructure thus played an important role in linking these settler economies to Britain. Such ties brought together a range of activities that encompassed agriculture (mixed farming, monoculture, and pastoral), resource extraction, and, over the nineteenth century, industrial production. While, as previously mentioned, the ideal form of settlement for British emigration to these colonies was that of the small, independent yeoman farmer, this model was not achieved in every society—or at least not in its idealized version. In some contexts, climate and topography made it far from feasible. Pastoral agriculture and a greater reliance on livestock, such as sheep and cattle, was far more common in a number of Australian colonies than the mixed farming of crops—frequently wheat—and smaller-scale livestock rearing that marked much of the St. Lawrence Valley and southern Upper Canada. Furthermore, the seigneurial system of New France, in which tenant farmers or *habitants* paid rent in cash or kind to a seigneur and fees for the right to fish, pasture livestock, and grind grain, was by far the most common form of landholding in Lower Canada. Although abolished in 1854, vestiges of the seigneurial system persisted over the course of the century.

Moreover, although freehold ownership of land was far more common in nineteenth-century Ontario, in the first half of that century between one-quarter and one-half of those living on farms were tenants. While it often went unremarked, tenancy in the colony did not resemble its counterpart in

Britain, Ireland, or Prince Edward Island, where extremely unequal relationships between tenants and landlords were common. In Upper Canada, tenancy was a strategy that could allow farming families to purchase land over time. By the 1870s, tenants benefited from a legal structure that provided greater order and regulation of landlord-tenant relations, such as written agreements and the clarification of customary rights. As well, the colonial government was the largest landlord, and its goals were to quicken the pace of settlement and maintain a loyal group of tenants. It therefore tended to be lenient in collecting rents and arrears.

Agriculture also might exist alongside other ways of making a living. While sheep farming came to dominate New Zealand's economy by the late nineteenth century, the colony also had a long history of whaling. The whaling industry involved a range of workers from a variety of ethnic and racial backgrounds, primarily from the Pacific but at times from North America, which also helped create mixed-race communities. In a similar manner, the Canadian Northwestern fur trade tied British traders and workers, many from Scotland and the Orkneys, to Rupert's Land and to Montreal's financial institutions; the meetings of Indigenous women and white men helped found Métis communities throughout the prairies. Nova Scotia's Annapolis Valley and its former Acadian settlement provided fertile soil for farming, but fishing was also significant, while logging and fishing were central to the economies of colonies such as New Brunswick and Newfoundland. Furthermore, in places such as Victoria, South Australia, British Columbia, Nova Scotia, and the Cape Colony, mining—whether gold, coal, diamond, or other minerals—played a role in tying settler economies to imperial and transnational markets, reshaping the landscape, and influencing the contours of local society, particularly demographic patterns.

All these economies drew in labour in a variety of ways. Despite the rhetoric of manly independence or, in Lister's case, the language of the male breadwinner, farms were worked by families. The labour of wives and, in particular, adult children was often invaluable, particularly in frontier settings. (Settler societies in which the number of women was more or less equal to that of men were more likely to be stable and successful, at least so far as the ideals of British settlers were concerned.) Agricultural households were not unique in their reliance on the combined labour of husbands, wives, and adult children, though. On the Avalon peninsula in nineteenth-century Newfoundland, for example, women's contributions to the drying of fish were recognized as significant labour and helped bolster their status in fishing villages. Although lumber camps tended to be homo-social communities, "shantymen," as they were often called in British America, might well be husbands and fathers whose work in the woods was undertaken to support wives and children on an (often marginal) family farm. Mining, particularly the gold rushes that were ubiquitous in the mid-nineteenth century, was known for attracting men who arrived on their own. To be sure, a number were indeed married, with families left "at home" to whom they planned to return once they had made a profit from Castlemaine or the Cariboo, British Columbia, gold fields (see Figure 3.1). Others may well have been fleeing domesticity, with no plans to return to families and home communities. In South Africa, male migrants from rural villages worked on larger, white-owned farms, plantations, railway works, and mines; these workers sold their labour for a limited time before returning home for good or moving to more distant work sites. The cash they brought back to their villages, along with exposure to different norms and practices, brought changes to places ostensibly untouched by global economies.

Settler colonies were often promoted as bastions of individual liberty and of British justice and benevolence; settlers contrasted their societies to other European colonies in which chattel slavery continued. Nevertheless, unfree or coerced labour could be found at the Cape Colony, Natal, and throughout Australia. The questions that surrounded such labour were

**FIGURE 3.1** "The Gold Escort Leaving Castlemaine Camp, Victoria, for Melbourne"

Source: C. Rudston Read, *What I Heard, Saw, and Did at the Australian Goldfields* (London, 1853). Mary Evans Picture Library, Picture Number 10006504.

complicated ones. At the Cape, in the decades between the abolition of the slave trade (1807) and slave emancipation (1833–38), the experiences of slaves held by Afrikaners were shaped by a mixture of paternalist rhetoric and practice. In rural areas, smaller households and small-scale slaveholding, not large plantations, prevailed: the average number of slaves per household was fewer than six, and few masters had enough resources to build separate slave quarters. As well, mistresses, who did not perform field labour and rarely worked outside the household, supervised slaves' and servants' domestic labour; in poorer households mistresses worked alongside slaves in such tasks. Slaves thus lived and worked within the context of their master's family, in which income and resources were shared— although unequally—between the master and mistress, their children, servants, and slaves. In order to maintain the overall social hierarchy on which the Cape depended, the conditions of daily life and work were governed by certain rituals meant to inculcate lessons about the correct relationship between slaves and masters. These teachings would have been learned by both parties as children and included violent punishments, meted out by both masters and mistresses. Nevertheless, the intimacy of the household helped subvert paternalistic order, at least to a certain extent. Complaints that slaves lodged with the Protectors' offices demonstrate the extent to which they used both physical and ideological resistance, underpinned by their own world views, which prized defending their families, taking pride in their work and skill, and using certain aspects of religious and liberal beliefs to counter slaveowners' dominance. Enslaved women were particularly vociferous in using the Protectors' offices in attempts to protect their children from their masters' abuse or neglect.

Urban slavery in Cape Town provides an even more complex picture of the relationship between unfree labour, the growth of urban and industrial economies, and links between local and global markets. As the Cape's ties to Britain's industrial and commercial powers intensified in the early nineteenth century and the value of its exports increased by tenfold between 1807 and 1817, Cape Town's urban economy and, in particular, its craft production also grew. Between 1816 and 1834, around one-quarter of urban slaves were artisans, working in crafts such as silversmithing and sail-, hat-, watch-, and wagon-making. However, the abolition of the slave trade within the British Empire also resulted in a decline in adult slaves in the town's population. By the early 1830s, more than 35 per cent of Cape Town's slaves were under 18, with 20 per cent being 50 years of age or older. Moreover, the British Navy's 1806–16 campaign against the international slave trade brought in "Prize

Negroes," those men, women, and children who were taken from other countries' slave ships captured by naval patrols and arrived in Cape Town during this period. Around 1,000 "Prize Negroes" came to the colony; they were followed by hundreds of European indentured labourers, many of them skilled artisans, who came between 1817 and 1823. In the 1830s, several hundred European children, many of them offenders under the age of 14 who had been apprenticed in the "Children's Friend Scheme," also joined the colony's labour market. High rates of manumission for urban slaves, as well as the end of apprenticeship for Prize Negroes, helped contribute to an urban community of free blacks that by 1834 numbered 4,000.

As well, Cape Town's slaveowners frequently hired out their slaves, a practice that allowed greater interactions between slaves and other members of the community in spaces such as the town's market square. The nature of many urban slaves' work—on building sites as masons, thatchers, brick makers, and painters or in the streets as coachmen, woodcutters, hawkers, and boatmen—brought them into contact with others on a daily basis. Cape Town's slaves, then, were likely to socialize with free blacks, Prize Negroes, and Khoisan and European apprentices, away from their masters' scrutiny. Some slaves also found new networks of support in the city's Muslim community, as Islam permitted marriages between slave converts and offered religious festivals, opportunities to become literate, and medical and economic assistance. In this context slaves helped create a thriving urban subculture, one that undercut the power and paternalism of their masters' households even more directly than at the rural Cape.

After emancipation, the distinctions between those in urban areas, on mission stations, and on farms became starker over time. In the immediate aftermath of the end of apprenticeship the latter were, at least, guaranteed a minimum of support and a degree of stability. Africans who migrated to towns faced an uncertain labour market and economic future, while those on the stations were subject to increasingly strict discipline and paternalistic surveillance. Yet over the next few decades urban dwellers and mission residents—or their children—were able to obtain higher levels of education and greater economic opportunities. In contrast, those who stayed in rural areas were often trapped in cycles of debt bondage that mimicked, even if they did not exactly replicate, slavery. However, urban Africans at the Cape still faced multiple forms of racial discrimination and segregation. Education at non-denominational government schools, generally of a higher quality than at mission schools, favoured light-skinned people, so that by 1875 69 per cent of black Capetonians over 15 were unable to read or write (in comparison to only 9 per cent white illiteracy). The Masters and Servants Acts, passed from the 1840s on, also kept black workers tied to white employers. Moreover, black women faced a gendered and racially divided labour market in which employment in domestic service was over-whelmingly their only option. Working in white households, black female servants were poorly paid, given scant food, and provided with deplor-able sleeping and washing quarters. Unlike those white Canadian servants whose independence so troubled Caroline Boultbee, black women in Cape Town's urban domestic service saw their freedoms strictly curtailed, often living like prisoners in their employers' homes. Although engravings such as Figure 3.2 were meant to illustrate the difficulties Englishwomen in the Cape experienced in hiring suitable servants, such representations failed to portray the oppressive conditions African female servants endured.

Transported convicts' labour fell between that of slaves and "free" workers. Convict transportation in the British Empire was not confined to Australia and Van Diemen's Land (Tasmania). Britain sent convicts to the Caribbean, West Africa, Mauritius, southeast Asia, Bermuda, and

**FIGURE 3.2** "African Servants, No. Eight"

8. " Now Sarah, we are going to spend the afternoon out ; take care of the house, there's a good girl."—" Yes'm, me take bery good care ob eberyting."

Source: *The Graphic,* 3 October 1885. Mary Evans Picture Library, Picture Number 10126228.

Gibraltar; furthermore, penal transportation was not confined to or invented by Britain, as its history can be traced to Portugal's 1415 invasion of North Africa. Although the transportation of 160,000 convicts to the Antipodes between 1788 and 1868 is one of the best documented and analyzed forms of the practice, Britain's use of this punishment did not formally end until 1945, when it closed its settlement on the Bay of Bengal's Andaman Islands. Moreover, although transportation between colonies has not been as well-studied as the outward flow from Britain, not all convicts in Australia and Van Diemen's Land were from the metropole. Prisoners of European, African, Māori, Aboriginal, and South Asian origin were sent from the Caribbean, Canada, the Cape Colony, Mauritius, India, and Hong Kong to Bermuda, Van Diemen's Land, New South Wales, and Western Australia. Convicts were at one time thought of as being unskilled, since those sent from Britain tended to be recidivists transported for petty theft and thus were assumed to lack the skills needed to make a living in an industrializing economy. More detailed research into their backgrounds, though, has demonstrated that they came from a wider swathe of the British and Irish working classes.

Unlike seventeenth- and eighteenth-century transportation to America, which had been run as a private trade, convict transport to Australia and Van Diemen's Land involved much greater oversight and regulation by the colonial state. Convicts' work—making and transporting bricks and tiles, unloading ships, building roads, gardening, and gathering timber—was initially performed collectively; by the late 1790s the word "gang" was in common use. Between 1788 and 1830, a gang might consist of between 40 and 60 men, with a small core of skilled workers supplemented and supported by a larger group of unskilled labour. The end of the Napoleonic Wars saw an expansion of transportation and the arrival of Governor Macquarie, who wished to expand public works projects in the colony (under his time in office, roads were set out and building regulations were formulated in Sydney, which influence the city's central core to this day). These developments resulted in a growth in the number of convicts employed on gangs, which reached a high of 2,843 in 1821. It was not until the arrival of Governor Darling in 1826 that gangs became much smaller and more closely supervised. Macquarie's approach, which had emphasized the need to use convicts as productive labour, was downplayed in favour of collective labour as a form of punishment. Moreover, while male convicts always worked under the threat of brutal punishment in the form of flogging—women were more likely to be punished by having their heads shaved, a form of shaming—it seems that the larger gang system had given them the means to exercise degrees of agency. In late eighteenth-century agricultural gangs, for example, which carried out set tasks, convict workers were able to negotiate with their supervisors and control the hours they worked, something that workers in Britain were finding more difficult. During Macquarie's regime, individual convicts managed to manipulate the kind of gang to which they were assigned, either by concealing skills or by claiming skills they did not have. Convict workers rarely challenged the state's power over them directly, though, and those that did found themselves dealt with brutally. Such was the fate of a group of sawyers who went on a three-week strike in 1817 over changes in their work and their food rations. Nevertheless, even after being punished the sawyers continued to deliberately restrict their productivity. Although the gang system became more tightly controlled and punitive, those who worked on them were still able to negotiate with overseers around matters such as work attendance and performance of their tasks.

Not all convicts, though, worked on public, state-run projects. Convicts were also assigned to individual settlers. Furthermore, in the first few years of New South Wales's existence, colonial authorities often shortened sentences to keep costs down and gave freed convicts small plots of land in order to encourage self-sufficiency. However, after 1817, in a strategy designed to encourage the spread of pastoralism, the British government decided to restrict access to land to free immigrants with capital and extend the assignment system, making the settler responsible for clothing, housing, and feeding convict workers. They were not allowed to mete out punishment, but could send the convict to appear before a magistrates' bench for sentencing. By the early 1820s, a tiered structure developed, ranging from penal stations and chain gangs to private assignment, tickets-of-leave awarded for good conduct, conditional pardons, and full pardons.

The treatment of convicts, like that of slaves, was also gendered in its design and practice. For one, women were not sent to road parties, nor to penal stations. Instead, they were incarcerated in female factories, where they were categorized according to their offence. Moreover, although colonial authorities had encouraged convict marriages in the first few decades—nearly 45 per cent of convict women were married in 1822—it began to place convict women as domestic servants in the homes of wealthy free settlers. By 1842 just over 7 per cent of convict women were married. Accompanying that shift were punishments that made it difficult for convicts to form stable unions. Women who became pregnant, for example, were sent to the factory to give birth. After their children were weaned mothers were given six-month punishments that usually involved doing laundry for the state and private homes, while their children were sent to "orphan schools." Convict factories both disciplined women and provided labour for middle-class settler households. In many ways the treatment of convict women presaged that of other carceral institutions, such as Ireland's twentieth-century religious-run "Magdalene Laundries" to which single mothers were sent.

As well as such gendered forms of punishment, female convicts' work not only differed from that of men's, it might also be critical to settler society's growth, particularly the creation of a settler middle class. In Van Diemen's Land between 1820 and 1840, rapid economic growth fuelled a demand for convict labour and, in particular, for female servants, so much so that the convict department was at times unable to satisfy settlers eager to be assigned a woman convict. Women who could cook, wash, sew, iron, and take care of children according to the settlers' standards were highly sought. Moreover, as Hobart became a significant commercial, mercantile, and financial centre, demand grew for skilled dressmakers, tailoresses, shoemakers, confectioners, victuallers, and servants; the colonial state also sent women to work in its convict nurseries, orphan schools, and hospitals. Yet unlike the situation at the Cape, convict women did not experience a greater degree of freedom or escape from employers' surveillance through their labour in urban settings. Earlier forms of work, performed in the 1820s for small landowners, involved labouring alongside masters and, in some cases, resulted in female convicts' marriages to them. However, work in urban commercial and retail establishments or in wealthier middle-class households involved greater levels of state scrutiny. Middle-class employers' demands for specialized skills meant that the colonial state assessed convict women's qualifications and work experiences more stringently. As well, women found themselves in more hierarchical places of employment, where boundaries between employers and servants were much more clearly drawn. Although convict women's labour was valued and important, their experiences differed according to both time and place.

Indentured workers also represented links between imperial policies, different colonies, and networks of migration. After British emigration, the movement of South Asians, Africans, Chinese, and Pacific Islanders around the nineteenth-century British Empire was a most significant and marked form of labour mobility. While the majority of these workers went to places such as Mauritius, the Caribbean, and Malaya, replacing slave labour in the wake of abolition, they also arrived in Natal and Queensland, colonies without a history of formal slavery, to work on sugar plantations. Natal began to bring in indentured labourers from India in 1861, to a total of 152,184 between then and 1911, while Queensland's recruitment from the South Pacific and China, starting in 1863 and ending in 1904, numbered 62,542 and 5,130, respectively. (Sydney's Colonial Sugar Refining Company also brought indentured labourers from Pacific islands to its plantations in Fiji in 1864 and then turned to India in 1879.) In addition to these workers, Chinese labourers from Hong Kong, usually recruited through a type of debt bondage called the "credit-ticket system," migrated around the world. Between 1854 and 1880, around 118,543 of these workers went to Australia, while 2,394 arrived in Canada between 1865 and 1880.

Humanitarians and British officials often compared indenture to slavery, not least because indentured workers performed similar work to that done by slaves under similarly bad conditions, work that British immigrants did not undertake. As well, deception and coercion marked the recruitment of a number of these workers. The first wave of indentured workers to arrive in Queensland, for example, was poorly informed and had often been kidnapped; the latter practice was outlawed by both Britain and Queensland in 1872 and policed (minimally) by the Royal Navy. To see indentured workers as victims on the same level of slaves, though, overlooks these workers' choice to migrate and create a better, or at least less dire, life abroad. Some indentured workers returned to their birthplace once their contract had expired and, in the case of Pacific Islanders in Queensland, did so forcibly. However, in Natal, as we have seen, approximately three-quarters of indentured Indians remained, forming a large and vibrant community. Furthermore, although indentured workers in Queensland were primarily male, as only six women per 1,000 men migrated there, in Natal one-third were women.

Natal's recruitment has been studied in some detail and provides important insights into the process. W.M. Collins, the colony's postmaster general, was appointed as special agent for recruitment. Using Mauritius (which he toured) as a model, Collins was an important linchpin between Natal and the various agents he contacted in Calcutta and Madras who were already recruiting workers for British Guiana, Mauritius, and Trinidad. Over time Natal's recruiters had the most success in southern India, as two-thirds came from that region and the rest came from Hindi-speaking areas in the Ganges valley. Attracting workers was not a straightforward process, though, as at times recruitment numbers dropped below Collins's and his successor's projections. Tea plantations and railway construction in India offered competition; agents vied with each other to fill labour requirements around the empire; and levels of government banned the recruitment of certain groups, such as Nepalis, or the direct recruitment of workers from the Ganjam district, located in the Madras Presidency. Natal's employers were also less enthusiastic about some groups, particularly Brahmins and Muslims. The former were seen as troublemakers and stereotyped as unsuitable for plantation labour, while Natal's residents objected to the latter's presence in the colony in general. However, in 1896 Muslim women, provided they were "'hard handed,'" had worked as labourers, were not "'beggars, devotees, or dancing girls,'" and were over the age of 18, were officially welcome. Not until 1903 did the Natal government allow Muslim men to enter as indentured workers. Even then it permitted only those from labouring backgrounds "'with hard hands [who] … have worked always in the fields'" to come into the colony.[3] Not surprisingly, such restrictions were not warmly received by hard-pressed agents in India. Moreover, although Natal's recruitment strategy involved hiring a number of subagents in northern India from Hindu, Muslim, Bengali, and Jewish backgrounds, the harshness of local economic conditions, rather than the recruiters themselves, were the main reasons why workers agreed to leave their homes. As yearly fluctuations in recruitment figures demonstrate, the state of the harvest, or the end of work on a district's railway construction, provided incentives for migrants, as did the imperial government's encouragement of recruitment from districts it considered overpopulated.

After their voyage across the Indian Ocean, one that was better-regulated by the last quarter of the nineteenth century and resulted in fewer deaths from disease, Indian workers arrived in Natal to serve a five-year period of indenture. Workers signed on to labour for a single employer at a fixed wage, usually ten shillings per month for men and five for women, and lived in quarters provided by employers. Although indentured workers were not a homogeneous group, they were seen as "coolies" and were treated accordingly. Their living and working conditions were harsh, and their mobility in Natal was severely restricted through the provisions of Natal's Masters and Servants Act. After responsible government was granted in 1893, their employers, the colony's planter class, were able to strengthen their control to an even greater degree over the work force through discriminatory legislation. Moreover, those Indians who had finished their indentures and had established themselves as successful small-scale farmers also encountered anti-Indian sentiments from African tenant farmers. The latter, experiencing land shortages and exhortations from white landlords to not be outdone by the "coolies," also saw that Indians were not subjected to the same kinds of laws and levels of taxation as themselves. Missionaries also played a role in stirring up anti-Indian feelings among African residents on mission stations, feelings that were based in concerns about the availability of land and in religious prejudices against "heathens." Over time Indians and Africans in Natal would realize their common opponents were the colonial state and white planters; solidarity across racial lines was the best route to abolishing racism. Nevertheless, the divisions created by the powerful in Natal during this period were both damaging and long-lasting.

As Chapter 1 has demonstrated, settler colonies' incorporation of Indigenous people into waged labour varied, being shaped by the needs of local economies, state policies, and Indigenous peoples' own needs and desires. In some areas, such as Canada's prairie provinces, restrictions on their mobility and confinement to reserves resulted in a *de facto* form of exclusion of Indigenous adults. In other places Indigenous people themselves actively sought waged work in nearby resource-based industries: fish processing and commercial hop picking on North America's northwest Pacific coast, for example. In mid-nineteenth-century North America, the burgeoning sector of wilderness tourism offered employment for Indigenous guides, whose knowledge of hunting, fishing, canoeing, and "Native lore" in areas such as northern Ontario and the interior of British Columbia was sought by white, urban, middle-class men, eager to rejuvenate themselves by experiencing the continent's "wild" spaces. In the American Adirondack region, Indigenous people moved back and forth across the Canada–US border to work in the tourist industry. Australia's large pastoral sector, particularly in the Northern Territory, drew in Aboriginal men who worked as stockmen; Aboriginal people also worked diving for pearls and *bêche-de-mer* (sea cucumber) along Queensland's coast. As well, Aboriginal women in particular had a long history of domestic work in settler homes, one that dates back to the early days of colonial contact. By the 1880s the government of Victoria province began to develop state-run domestic labour schemes that placed mixed-race girls and young women in white homes in Australia's growing suburbs, particularly around Adelaide. Such schemes would expand in the early twentieth century under the aegis of the new federal government and persist into the latter half of the twentieth century.

Like those historians who study convicts and indentured labourers, scholars have debated the extent to which Indigenous and Aboriginal people's waged work can be described as "free," given the conditions of dispossession and marginalization under which they lived. Such a debate has been particularly intense in Australia. Historians have attempted to uncover Aboriginal workers' motivations and perspectives for engaging with a labour market that did not treat them as white workers' equals and that did so, moreover, with the support and collusion of various levels of government. Such debates are complicated in the case of adult workers: the state, as we have seen, saw itself as a "Protector" of Aboriginal people, including workers, in ways that were both humanitarian and oppressive. For Aboriginal children, though, matters were more clear-cut. In Queensland, for example, their history as workers encompassed not just domestic service but also included the pastoral industry, coastal diving, guiding, and interpreting. All this labour took place under conditions that were much closer to slavery than that performed by convicts or indentured workers, partly because nineteenth-century labouring children in general had little control or choice over their labour and, too, because of their Aboriginal status in colonial society. From the early 1840s until 1897, Aboriginal children were kidnapped and bartered to work for Europeans, their treatment justified on the grounds of settlers' economic needs and the belief that forcing them to engage in "productive" labour would ensure their assimilation. Although the Aborigines Protection Act of 1897 did not regulate Aboriginal children's work, confining itself to that of adults, amendments to it in 1901 gave Queensland's Protector legal recourse to collect wages owed to child workers. Yet from 1842 until the end of World War II, Aboriginal children in rural workforces were particularly susceptible to their employers' abuse. Their position stood in marked contrast to that of non-Indigenous children, whose paid labour was seen not as beneficial but as a social problem, one opposed by trade unions and social reformers in both Australia and British settler societies in general.

## Manufacturing, Mining, and the Labour Movement

Although the economies of the settler societies were predominantly rural and resource-based, by the end of the nineteenth century they had also developed centres of manufacturing and displayed the influences of industrial capitalism. In Canada, for example, manufacturing was the fastest growing economic activity throughout the nineteenth century, a development that persisted into the twentieth century. Although it took different shapes and forms, depending on the location and the particular type of goods produced, manufacturing was a significant aspect of urban life in Montreal, Toronto, Saint John, and Hamilton. It might involve smaller-scale workshops that turned out consumer goods (cigars, clothing, and shoes, for example), or larger foundries that supplied railway companies with rolling stock, or steel mills. Although settler societies' manufacturing sectors did not pose serious competition to those of Britain, western Europe, and the United States, nevertheless by the late nineteenth century the economies of cities such as Toronto and Melbourne employed tens of thousands of artisans and labourers and produced millions of dollars' worth of goods. The industrialization that underpinned the spread of nineteenth-century manufacturing also brought changes to both economic structures and workers' lives. As manufacturing became more concentrated and centralized, in order to increase profits it also demanded faster and more intensified production, greater surveillance of work and workers, increased mechanization and specialization, and the undermining of craft skills through both the subdivision of labour and the use of cheaper, less skilled workers. These changes varied in their timing and intensity, as industrialization was often a protracted and uneven process. Nevertheless, workers in these colonies, as in Britain, western Europe, and the United States, began to share experiences that transcended national or colonial boundaries, as the discipline and rhythms of factory work began to replace those of rural life.

Settler societies also shared and were shaped by workers' migration. While movement between Britain and her colonies and, at times, between colonies marked the nineteenth century, migration within settler societies for work also took place on an increasingly larger scale. In some instances such mobility was from countryside to city. Toronto, for example, owed part of its late nineteenth- and early twentieth-century growth to young, single men and women seeking new economic and social opportunities that could not be found on Ontario's farms or in its small towns. Even though mining in South Africa overshadowed manufacturing, by virtue of mining's size and methods of organization it became an industrial work site. Mining also, though, resembled indentured labourers' work; for example, it involved large-scale migration of workers from rural villages and farms. Migration for work was not new, as it had long been a feature of the Eastern Cape's economy. Men and women from the Ciskei district had moved in and out of work on white farms and the region's small towns. By the 1890s, men from the Peddie district were migrating north to Kimberley's diamonds and then to the gold mines. Labour recruiters arrived in the Transkei in 1904, and 48,000 labourers worked in the Cape's gold mines by 1909. By 1911, the vast majority of labourers in Thembuland were employed in Transvaal's mines.

South Africa's industrial growth—the rapid expansion of diamond mining in the early 1870s and gold in the late 1880s—was also underpinned by colonial conquest of the Transkei region; a combination of race and class relations shaped the industry. The reorganization of diamond mining at Kimberley, the result of European diggers bringing in state oversight to keep out African holders of small claims, also meant that mining became dominated by large-scale capitalists. Yet for African miners, the path from life in a village or on a small farm to that of a migrant labourer was not a straightforward one, nor was it a downward slide into penury from peasant prosperity and rural stability. For one, unlike European miners in the area who were primarily dependent on mining for their survival and, too, were also more dependent on consumer goods, in the 1870s and 1880s many African diamond miners were still tied to village life. Its rhythms and its network of social and economic support, not the demands of mine owners and overseers, shaped miners' lives. Income from mining was used to purchase clothes, liquor, and (at Kimberley) guns, the latter used to hunt game and defend independence: the Bapedi and Basotho people, for example, used guns to protect themselves from Boer aggression.

Changes did arrive, though, with greater amalgamation of companies in the early 1880s, a collapse in the price of diamonds, and huge rises in the cost of technology used at Kimberley. Mine owners introduced a range of surveillance and discipline over black miners: strip searching, courts set up to try workers for diamond thefts, and enclosed compounds that prevented miners from diamond smuggling, drinking, or deserting. They also began to use white workers to supervise black labour, a practice that cut off white miners from African workers and deepened the former's sense of class and racial privilege. Once De Beers assumed possession of the mines, it put in place paternalistic schemes that privileged white workers and intensified racial segregation. As well, the compounds cut off African miners from women and village life for longer periods of time, while in the villages women had to adapt to life without young men. Simultaneously, though, rural economies were strengthened by the growth of urban markets for maize and cattle. During the early 1880s a small black middle class grew up around Kimberley, educated at mission schools or at the mines; its members worked as clerks, supervisors, and translators for the mining companies, traders, and telegraph office. Miners themselves might be changed by their time at Kimberley, as they came into contact with the missionaries who evangelized around the diggings, learned about Christianity, and became literate. Kimberley was not just a place where capital was accumulated: it also was a space in which men learned new skills, accumulated different kinds of knowledge, and forged new identities, ones marked by hierarchies of race and class.

The spread of manufacturing and industrial capitalism also meant the spread of both craft and then industrial unions to settler societies. Such a development should not, of course, be overly surprising. British artisans brought their histories and traditions of craft organizing along with skills such as printing, coopering, and shoemaking; it was no accident, for example, that many leaders of Canada's early labour movement had British backgrounds. In the Canadian case, international links ran not just across the Atlantic but also across the Canada–US border. By the mid-nineteenth century many craft unions started to join larger, "international" unions in the United States and eventually affiliated with the American Federation of Labour. Labour unions were linked between Britain and settler societies through other kinds of networks. Although not overly fond of emigration, British unions worked to assist their members with migration to other parts of the Empire. In the 1840s a number of unions founded emigration funds that helped craftsmen move to New Zealand; the London Typographical Society wrote to its counterparts in Australia to provide typographers in the metropole with information on the trade and possibilities for employment there. Unions also worked with colonial emigration agents in the late nineteenth century to help their members emigrate, particularly to New Zealand. As well, in the early twentieth century British-based unions helped found branches overseas: the Amalgamated Society of Engineers, for example, had more than 5,000 colonial members in 1907 (and more than 3,000 American members). Members of this union were highly mobile, as they went between mines, plantations, railways, and ports; 30 per cent of the Canadian Pacific Railroad's artisans were brought in from Britain through the Society's recruiting.

Unions' imperial networks also helped disseminate certain ideals of masculinity, whiteness, and imperial identity. As Samuel Lister's newspaper article suggests, by the late nineteenth century the concept of the breadwinner wage—a sum sufficient for a male worker to support a dependent wife and children—was part of the discourse of male labour leaders, particularly that of skilled workers. Just as workers in Britain or the United States called for such a wage in order to shore up their claims as male citizens and heads of households, so too did labour organizations and individual men in Australia, Canada, and New Zealand. Their arguments for such a wage (which until the mid-twentieth century was more an ideal than a reality) were predicated on conceptions of their skill. The arguments also were based on their status as white men, not unlike the ways in which calls for responsible government and male enfranchisement often assumed the disenfranchisement of Indigenous people and white women. In settler societies, white male citizenship and the promise of masculine independence had both economic and political dimensions.

Moreover, by the early twentieth century the British working class in both Britain and the colonies tended to see themselves as members of the Empire, not as part of an international community of workers; their identification as white imperial subjects took precedence over cross-racial solidarity. In the Transvaal, labour leaders opposed the 1903 importation of Chinese labourers, brought in by mine owners unhappy with the low supply of black workers. South Africa, union representatives declared, was a country for white men, a statement that echoed similar ones made in Australia and by British Columbia's labour leaders who had also called for Chinese exclusion. Appeals to Britishness as a form of racial solidarity also were heard in 1914 and resonated in both South Africa and England. The summary deportation of nine white South African labour leaders for their role in rail and coal strikes in Natal by a government determined to break unions in the Dominion was met with outrage by the labour movement in Hull, at that time the third largest port in the United Kingdom. As well, the British Trades Union Congress and the Labour Party organized support for the unionists. Yet while the city's labour press invoked the legacy of British liberty, including the well-known name of English abolitionist William Wilberforce, it said little about the plight of black workers. The latter were already working under conditions of white supremacy, including that of the loss of their right to vote in the Transvaal and the Orange Free State. Just as Chinese workers were assumed to be too passive and docile to organize, white-led labour unions did not consider that black workers also should be included in organizing drives. To be sure, recent studies of South Africa's labour movement have pointed to those radical Scottish voices, ones from the international socialist and revolutionary syndicalist movements, that expressed solidarity with black workers and challenged segregation and labour's racially based protectionism. Such voices, though, were in the minority, as the labour movement's espousal of white solidarity was not confined to the situation in South Africa. Unions in North America, for example, were slow to organize workers from ethnic and racialized communities, not to mention from the ranks of women workers. It was not until well into the twentieth century that organized labour in settler societies challenged racism at a deeper and more profound level.

## Conclusion

Economies, and the people who helped fashion them, were important linchpins that tied settler worlds to the metropole, to other transnational networks, and, at times, to each other. The ideals of white masculine independence, whether expressed in the language of the yeoman farmer or the male breadwinner that Samuel Lister wished to achieve, helped link settler societies. It provided a common language and set of cultural idioms that many settlers could readily recognize as intelligible and familiar (even if they might not always agree with them). Settler economies also offered British immigrants, such as the female servant whose independence vexed Caroline Boultbee, fresh opportunities and new forms of mobility. Such was not the case, though—or at least not to the same degree—for Indigenous people and non-European migrants. In a similar fashion, just as railroads, telegraphs, and steamships helped create critically important material ties, the language of private property also provided a shared set of assumptions that linked these societies; eventually it would have significant effects on those communities that were not structured by such a concept. It is important, though, not to lose sight of important distinctions between such sites. Just as those political structures and institutions that "travelled" around British settler worlds were adapted and refashioned, so too were economic beliefs and practices. Nevertheless, such modifications took place within a context in which certain concepts and certain principles predominated. In a similar fashion, the creation of civil society within the settler colonies owed much to British networks and developments in the metropole, ones that then were reworked in dynamic ways within settler societies, as we shall see in Chapter 4.

## Notes

1 Caroline Boultbee to Hannah Jarvis Hamilton, 7 December 1875, John Macintosh Duff Collection, Manuscripts and Archives Collection, University of Guelph Library.

2 Annabel Cooper, "Poor Men in the Land of Promises: Settler Masculinity and the Male Breadwinner Economy in Late Nineteenth-Century New Zealand," *Australian Historical Studies* 39, 2 (2008): 260.

3 Thomas R. Metcalf, "'Hard Hands and Sound Healthy Bodies': Recruiting 'Coolies' for Natal, 1860–1911," *Journal of Imperial and Commonwealth History* 30, 3 (2002): 10.

# 4 | Creating Civil Society

*I shall endeavour to put some restraint in my pen. This is one of the*
*defects of epistolary intercourse. When together hand in hand watching the*
*same setting sun, marking the clouds sailing across the moon, or listen-*
*ing to the howling wind & pelting shower moved by one impulse, we are*
*in no danger of becoming ridiculous or unintelligible to each other—but*
*just conceive of reading a letter full of moonlight sentiments & breath-*
*ing the fragrance of spring while cooking in a Cape kitchen why it does*
*not harmonize well, even with mending Trowsers or darning stockings.*
*But cleaning fish, & saucepans and candlesticks now & then have a sad*
*tendency to destroy the fine polish of our feelings. There is a sad feeling of stern*
*reality creeps over me sometimes as I ask myself—is this the all of life.*
—Eliza Fairbairn, 1839[1]

*There, right on the beach, in a well ventilated, if unscientifically lighted,*
*building, he had collected about thirty boys and girls, whom he instructed*
*in the elements of school learning as then understood. In summer, boots*
*were not very plentiful amongst the youthful students, and it is to be feared*
*that Grace's young aristocrats at Kumutoto looked rather askance at the*
*poorly clad and insufficiently-booted pupils of Rule and Edwards.*
—G. Macmorran, 1900[2]

The daughter of a prominent missionary, John Philip, and the wife of one of
the Cape Colony's most well-known residents, Scottish newspaper editor

John Fairbairn, Eliza Fairbairn wrote to her English friend Mary Ann Smith in 1839. She left historians a rare—and poignant—glimpse of the loneliness and depression experienced by this middle-class white woman living in the colony. Fairbairn's state of mind was quite different from that of Susannah Wall, whose letter from New Zealand opens Chapter 2. However, like Wall's, Fairbairn's letter also tells us of the importance of letter writing, a form of "intercourse" that allowed British settlers to maintain important networks and sustain ties across the empire. It also suggests that mid-nineteenth-century concepts of domesticity might not measure up to the realities of middle-class settler women's lived experiences. For their part, the working-class immigrant children in early 1840s' New Zealand who gathered on the beach to learn their lessons remind us that education was one of the fundamental values brought by settlers to create civil society in the colonies. The children's makeshift school also suggests how colonial conditions shaped the ways in which those ideas were put into practice.

While previous chapters explored the creation of colonial legal systems, forms of political governance, and settler economies, the family, both as a concept and as a set of relationships, played an equally vital role in British settler colonies. So, too, did the institutions of religion and education. Just as colonial governors and judiciaries attempted to replicate British norms, values, and practices, those responsible for founding churches and setting up schools and universities also hoped to reproduce that which they had left behind. Furthermore, they often believed that in creating these institutions they had an opportunity to create a "better Britain" (not to mention better Britons). Entwined with churches and schools were voluntary associations. Some of these groups—temperance societies, Sunday school associations, benevolent groups, and missionary societies—developed out of the churches and maintained close ties to a number of denominations. Others, such as the Masonic Lodge and fraternal organizations, were more firmly rooted in secular society. No matter what their degree of denominational affiliation, though, these organizations helped shape colonial civil societies that were inspired by British models and values; they implemented them, though, in local circumstances that might differ greatly from those left behind. Moreover, just as concepts of land, law, and the economy were shaped by relationships of gender, class, ethnicity, and race, the creation of civil society or the public sphere was also informed by notions of who was—and who was not—fit to participate in settler society. These lines of demarcation were more obvious and marked in areas such as the regulation of leisure, public space, and disease, processes that involved an interplay among voluntary societies, metropolitan governments, and colonial states.

## Family Matters: Domesticity and Intimacy

Despite the importance of schools, churches, lodges, and associations, it was the family that, for many settlers, provided the central foundation for their lives, emotionally and socially. As Chapter 1 points out, family and kin networks were the central means whereby Indigenous people organized their society's political and social structures. Although concepts of the family were differently figured for non-Indigenous society, nevertheless concerns about the family as an institution, one that would provide the necessary foundation for settler societies' stability and order, were often on the minds of colonial administrators, religious leaders, and middle-class commentators. While they may not have shared the elite's anxieties, less powerful colonists also placed a great deal of importance in maintaining, wherever possible, existing familial relationships and creating new ones.

The desire to promote monogamous, heterosexual marriages underpinned visions of settler colonies in a variety of ways. For one, the Colonial Office and colonial legislatures permitted various Christian denominations to perform marriages in order to promote it within these societies. At the Cape, colonial authorities hoped that British migrants would intermarry, forge British identities, and thus shore up boundaries between themselves and Indigenous peoples. In Australia, political leaders believed that encouraging freed convicts to form legal, heterosexual unions would erase New South Wales's and Van Diemen's Land's disreputable image. Emigration schemes that helped single British women to move to these locations would, colonial elites hoped, provide settler employers with a larger pool of domestic servants and, ultimately, settler bachelors with a larger pool of potential wives. Just as missionaries exhorted Indigenous men to abandon hunting for a "settled," European-style agrarian way of life, single male colonists were encouraged by emigration promoters, religious leaders, journalists, and voluntary societies to become husbands and fathers within monogamous, heterosexual marriages, ones in which they would become heads of households. These unions were seen by colonial elites as the necessary foundation for colonial order and prosperity. In turn, settler women learned that it was their examples of domesticity and superior moral conduct within the home that would inspire their menfolk to lead morally upright lives. As virtuous wives, mothers, daughters, and sisters, they would keep their husbands, sons, and brothers from falling into dissolute habits, such as drinking, gambling, brawling, and duelling, and abusing their "natural" power over their dependents. The latter group ranged from the vulnerable in their households to those in society at large. Such advice was frequently offered by temperance advocates, who believed that women were especially susceptible to abuses of masculine authority, whether it took the form of squandering much-needed wages on drink or outbursts of physical violence. Other commentators, writing from both religious and more secular stances, held very similar convictions about the importance of women's "moral mission."

In Britain, the ideals of middle-class domesticity were often juxtaposed against the decadence of the aristocracy. Their sexual profligacy, irreligion, lack of discipline, and extravagant lifestyles were seen as the antithesis of the moral restraint, work ethic, piety, and sexual purity that defined the English middle class (that such virtues might be more idealized than actual was another question). Middle-class domesticity was also increasingly compared to the home lives of working-class men, women, and children. They too were seen as leading morally deficient lives, being susceptible to the temptations of alcohol, crime, and violence, not least because of shortcomings in the working-class home and wives' and mothers' involvement in paid labour. This ideal was meant—theoretically—to apply to all Christian women as a way of life to which all women might aspire. However, writings about the value of domestic life targeted middle-class women very specifically. Such works assumed that they were able to (and should) withdraw from the realms of paid labour and devote their time and energy to creating domestic havens, free from the stresses and strains of the public realm.

It did not take long for settler colonies to create their own versions of the ideology of domesticity (in the case of British America, writings from the United States also played an important role). At times the concept of aristocratic decadence might be used to target those upper-class British men whose financial straits, troubles with the law, or general inability to support themselves had motivated their emigration to British colonies. Supported by their families, these men were seen by settler commentators as lacking the manual and agricultural skills to look after themselves and become heads of households: the figure of the "remittance man," as targeted by writers Mark Twain and Robert Service, became a kind of shorthand for metropolitan weaknesses. Conversely, as Chapter 2 has discussed, the independence that settler societies promised to working-class men, in both the economic and political spheres, was also tied to their positions as husbands and fathers.

Settler colonies also developed codes of conduct and manners for men, women, and children in other ways that spoke to anxieties about local contexts. In colonial Australia, for example, establishing norms of gentility and ideals of "civilization" was a way of establishing racial superiority over so-called Aboriginal savagery. As well, advice about the proper way to behave oneself in both private and public was also shaped by a colonial desire to elevate oneself over the thuggish and brutal behaviour of convicts, the coarseness and ill manners of gold diggers, or the drunken violence of isolated farmers and urban slum dwellers—not to mention those members of the colonial elite who distinguished themselves in front of imperial officials with their uncouth, vulgar, and (especially for women) pretentious behaviour. In the Cape Colony, early to mid-nineteenth-century notions of middle-class respectability were directly related to the struggle to establish British norms and British status in a territory recently controlled by the Dutch that also had a notable Indigenous presence. English-style housing, clothing, education, and Christianity—all of these infused with gendered notions of proper middle-class conduct—were key components of attempts to impose an English identity at the Cape.

Moreover, class distinctions shaped discussions of settler domesticity in other ways. In particular, a number of middle-class British women found themselves engaged in household labour, work that "at home" had been performed by servants. As we have seen, from their potential employers' perspectives servants were always in short supply; those who could be found were frequently deemed wanting in skills, experience, and deference. Because the management of domestic servants had become the domain of middle-class women, the latter's correspondence frequently included discussions of them. Their descriptions ranged from anecdotes that mixed humour with condescension, complaints about their shortcomings, and—consequently—detailed discussions of the work their employers had been obliged to undertake. For some, such as Upper Canada's Anne Langton who lived in the colony's backwoods, learning new domestic skills became a source of pride; working alongside her servants brought her a degree of companionship and camaraderie. Langton, though, was single and had emigrated to join her brother and his family; over time she also moved from the bush into town, where her life more closely resembled the English household of her childhood and youth. Eliza Fairbairn, on the other hand, was not just married, her life thus tied to her husband's fortunes: she also bore five children within nine years. As she told her friend Mary Ann Smith, her many pregnancies, combined with the need to supervise a household while also performing much of the cooking, mending, and cleaning, had "'a sad tendency to destroy the fine polish of our feelings.'" Clearly the kind of refinement and sensitivity that were seen as being fundamental to Englishwomen's gentility were qualities sorely tested by the exigencies of settler conditions. Such was the case suggested by the sketch "Emigrant's Cottage, Otago" (Figure 4.1), which used a familiar concept—the English rural cottage—while simultaneously suggesting how different such a building might be in a colonial context. Of course, constructs of middle-class domesticity were more an ideal than reality in English society, too.

Yet if middle-class settler women found it difficult to maintain the norms and practices of idealized domesticity, other women were faced with the sheer difficulty of simply keeping their families intact. As in the Caribbean and the United States, slaveholders at the Cape held a particular type of power over slave families. Such power included the threat of breaking them up by selling them, since until the 1820s the colony's legal system did not recognize marriages between slaves. While in the northwestern Cape permanent relationships between Khoi slave women and white masters were common, the children born of those unions, known as bastards, took their status from their mother. Although at times white fathers were known to assist their children's mothers to manumit their offspring, kinship ties were no guarantee the children would be recognized by their fathers, let alone be

**FIGURE 4.1.** "An Emigrant's Cottage, Otago, New Zealand"

Source: *Illustrated London News*, 1881. Mary Evans Picture Library, Picture Number 10425167.

allowed to enter white society. Moreover, the acts of the 1820s to the 1840s that either ameliorated slavery or replaced it with apprenticeship promoted a very particular type of marriage, one that stressed both the special power of motherhood and men's dominance over women. Characterizing marriage as having a "civilizing" potential for former slaves, the statutes recognized slave marriages and forbade the separation of mothers and children through sale. However, the colony's governor tied such provisions to men's and women's acceptance of Christianity. It decreed that only converted slaves could marry (and only with their master's permission) and that only children born of Christian marriages, conducted in churches, were protected by the ban on separation.

Apprenticeship did not mean an end to other methods of coercion. Employers attempted to extract as much labour as possible from former slaves by manipulating children's contracts in ways that also gave them access to their mother's labour. Although the mothers usually refused to leave their children, they also complained to the colony's Special Justices about employers' treatment. While the magistrates insisted that mothers prove their fitness to look after their children, the legacy of slavery and its assignment of children to their mothers meant that the latter had more rights than did fathers. With the end of apprenticeship, marriage for African men and women took on distinctly gendered meanings. For men, it meant they could claim ties of blood and lineage denied them by slavery and could also claim power over their wives and children. For women, marriage could offer them protection against a colonial racist discourse that saw them as inherently sexually immoral and thus "fair game" for sexual violence. Yet, despite missionaries' exhortations to wed, many of the rural, poor Africans at the Cape did not marry. Although networks of family and kin might be important, many men had to live apart from their families in order to earn a living, their residence a single-sex dormitory, not the private homes enjoyed by the colony's white families.

Convict women in New South Wales and Van Diemen's Land also faced particular challenges and obstacles in their desire to form nuclear, heterosexual families. The latter colony, which saw its first boatload of convicts in the early 1800s (almost 20 years after the First Fleet's arrival at Botany Bay), was marked by the state's shifting policies toward convicts' families and households. The first governor of Van Diemen's Land, David Collins, believed in particular forms of patriarchal order and authority and encouraged convict marriage and the establishment of households. Although such practices reinforced men's power over convict women, they also spoke to women's own demands that they be permitted to marry and have children. Because transported men vastly outnumbered women, the latter were able to take advantage of the imbalance in the colony's demographics. Furthermore, the need for their skills and contributions to household labour allowed them to negotiate some degree of independence, if not outright freedom. Matters changed, though, in the 1820s and 1830s, as convict labour became the subject of growing scrutiny and regulation by the state. Instead of living in their own households, convict women were moved into the homes of free settlers. There they performed unpaid labour and saw their ability to shape their own domestic lives strictly curtailed, particularly when it came to creating families with convict men. The household and family took on different meanings by the end of the 1830s: instead of being a space where convict women might assert autonomy, it became a place of discipline and control.

If colonial authorities changed their stance on convicts' family relationships, believing that they did not warrant the privilege of their own households, in other contexts imperial and national authorities fretted over the persistence of some kinds of households, ones they believed were quite unsuitable for a settler society's cohesion. On the Canadian prairies during the late nineteenth century the tendency of various communities, such as Mormons, Indigenous, and Doukhobor, to permit either polygamy or divorce (or both), worried both the Dominion government and missionaries. Such customs, they thought, threatened to undermine the prospects of social stability in the newly settled territories, ones that had already seen considerable political unrest and strife. Over time some officials changed their perspectives on these matters. Indian agents, for example, realized that separation and divorce could help keep communities peaceful, as quarrelling couples disrupted communal harmony, a perspective that missionaries did not share. Polygamy in Indigenous communities raised settlers' ire, not least because it suggested to the newly arrived Mormons (who had left their homes in Utah over their refusal to stop practising polygamy) that their marriage practices might continue. In order to promote nuclear, monogamous, patriarchal households in Indigenous communities, such as the Kainai (Blackfoot), missionaries and the Dominion government attempted to bribe, threaten, and coerce Indigenous men to abandon polygamy. While not all Canadian authorities' anxieties around marriage and household formation stemmed from Indigenous peoples' traditions, nevertheless on the prairies this sparked the most severe reactions on the part of the state.

However, for some time Indigenous people were able to maintain their customary forms of marriage. Indian agents and missionaries were often outnumbered and could not exert control over populations that, even though confined to reserves, were still dispersed over large swathes of territory. Moreover, Indigenous leaders also saw customary marriages as a way of countering other attempts to assimilate their people: the early marriage of young women, for example, was a way of keeping them out of residential schools. Polygamy also bothered missionaries in South Africa, as did the practice of bride wealth, in which a groom's family provided his new wife's kin with money, goods, or livestock. While outsiders saw bride wealth as the purchase of a wife and thus equated it to female slavery, bride wealth might serve to bind the two families together and create social ties. As we shall see, racially charged concerns about polygamy in Natal helped fuel other kinds of colonial policies.

Other forms of intimacy and the new types of families these created evoked a range of responses from missionaries and colonial officials. Of course, interracial sex was nothing new in colonial contexts: European men's sexual abuse of African women had a long history within transatlantic slavery. In the North American fur trade, interracial relationships, usually between Indigenous women and European men, might result in either long-lasting partnerships recognized by Indigenous and local communities or, less frequently, marriages solemnized in Christian churches and granted official status under colonial law. A few British fathers acknowledged their offspring and took responsibility for their education. They attempted to find their sons suitable positions in the trade and to ensure their daughters were supported in marriage. Yet race and gender differences were often apparent in colonial society's treatment of fur-trade children. Even with British education, mixed-race sons frequently found it difficult to advance in the fur trade or find suitable employment elsewhere. Mixed-race daughters could—and did—marry British men, in some cases helping to create a new colonial elite in British Columbia's new capital of Victoria. Some exceptions to these patterns existed, though. Alexander Isbister, whose father was an Orkney-born clerk in the fur trade and whose mother was both Cree and Scottish, moved to Britain in 1842 and became a teacher, author, and prominent advocate for the rights of Indigenous and Métis people at Red River. Matilda Davis, the daughter of a Cree woman and an English fur trader, was taken in the early 1820s as a very young child to London by her father, where she lived with English relatives and trained as a governess. On her return to Red River she and her sister opened a successful school and taught a number of fur-trade children. Other fathers, though, did not see their children in the same light as did those of Isbister or Davis. They had little or no contact with them after they retired from the trade and either returned to Britain or settled in the Canadas.

Interracial marriages were not always frowned upon; colonial officials, for example, saw them as a positive development, as such relationships would suit the Colonial Office's policy of racial amalgamation. In mid-nineteenth century New Zealand's South Island, intimate relationships between white men and Ngai Tahu women had a history rooted in the late eighteenth-century sealing industry, practices that continued in the nineteenth century with the development of whaling along the shoreline. Similar to the attitudes expressed by Indigenous chiefs in the fur trade, Ngai Tahu chiefs encouraged these alliances. They perceived them as central to the integration of newcomers into their communities and believed intermarriage would bring wealth and status. Yet over time these women migrated away from their communities, taking their children with them, as their partners searched for new economic opportunities. By the late nineteenth century, interracial marriage was seen as far less desirable, and such relationships became, for many, the source of stigma and shame. At the same time, government concerns about a steep decline in the Māori population resulted in its encouragement of interracial marriage. However, such unions were seen as desirable only as they involved Indigenous women and white men. While Indigenous women also created domestic unions with South Asian, East Asian, Middle Eastern, and European men, the government did not wish to encourage such unions, particularly with Chinese men.

In some places, such as colonial British Columbia, missionaries actively discouraged such racial mixing. They argued that it was best if Indigenous people and Europeans did not intermingle and that mixed-race children could only pose a problem to settler society. Generally, though, missionaries preferred to encourage mixed-race couples to marry in the rites of the Christian church, as they saw Indigenous marriage practices as little better than concubinage or prostitution. However, in settler societies Christian marriages did not guarantee that interracial couples and their children could integrate easily; local white communities often treated them with hostility and suspicion. Moreover, by the early twentieth century children born to unmarried Australian Aboriginal women and European men were forcibly taken from their families and communities and placed into training programs. Such policies intensified in their scope over the course of the twentieth century.

Intimate relationships between Indigenous women and white men were the most common forms of cross-racial intimacy in these societies and, as we have seen in the case of New Zealand, were the most likely interracial unions to be encouraged. However, a small minority of white women married Indigenous men. While not formally forbidden, as British imperial authorities did not tend to legislate against interracial unions, these relationships might be seen by contemporaries as scandalous and degrading to the women involved. Such was the case when in 1833 Englishwoman Eliza Field married the Upper Canadian Mississauga Methodist missionary Kahkewaquonaby/Peter Jones. The press in New York City and Upper Canada published articles full of prurient fascination with the couple's attraction for each other, describing their marriage as resembling that of Desdemona and Othello. Their marriage was followed in 1840 by that of Kahgegagahbowh/George Copway, also a Mississauga missionary, and Elizabeth Howell, a young Englishwoman who was a friend of Eliza Field's. Unlike the Field-Jones union, theirs was not as long-lasting nor as happy a marriage. In 1853 George Johnson, a member of the Six Nations, married Englishwoman Emily Howells; their daughter, Emily Pauline Johnson, would become a well-known Mohawk-English poet and performer. Although the Johnson-Howells marriage was a more stable and happier relationship than that of Copway and Howell—ending only with Johnson's death in 1884—the couple also experienced their share of social criticism. The Anglican missionary at Six Nations refused to marry them, members of the Six Nations were displeased at the prospect of a white woman having access to the community's annuities, and Howell's family claimed to be scandalized by their union.

While relatively rare in the context of nineteenth-century British America, these marriages were more than historical curiosities. Significantly, they exposed the extent to which white women were charged with maintaining racial boundaries: in fact, the paucity of such marriages suggests how heavily settler societies were invested in such concepts. Moreover, the fact that Jones, Copway, and Johnson were educated and familiar with many of the important institutions of white settler society, such as the colonial state and Christian missions (Johnson was an interpreter for both church and state), also played a role in linking these men to white women. These British American marriages stand in sharp contrast to those between Indigenous men and white women in Australia, where a lack of an educated group of Indigenous men meant that Australian marriages took place between working-class white women and Indigenous men.

As well as racially charged tensions around marriages, settler societies grappled with other challenges, particularly the rights of married women to their property and the question of divorce. For many settlers and, in particular, their governments, Christian marriage was key to a stable, respectable, and secure society: it was both a means of civilizing a society and a measure of its civilized state. Colonial governments preferred that the Anglican Church be the only denomination to solemnize marriages, though they already had made an exception in the case of British America, where the Roman Catholic church was allowed to stay on after the conquest of 1763. In a similar manner, conditions in New South Wales and Van Diemen's Land compelled the authorities to reconsider their stance that the Anglican Church alone officiate marriages. For one, the colonial government's desire that white settlers should marry each other was coupled with an equally strong desire that they be kept apart from Indigenous people. As well, officials hoped both sites would shed their reputation as penal colonies in which sexual promiscuity was rife. Such concerns resulted in the Colonial Office and colonial legislatures granting a number of Christian denominations the power to marry settlers.

Moreover, although access to divorce was far from being uniform, a number of settler colonies began to make divorce more accessible. Eighteenth-century Nova Scotia and New Brunswick permitted judicial divorce, unlike England's strictures that permitted divorce only by an act of Parliament. By the time of Confederation in 1867, Prince Edward Island and British Columbia had established their own divorce courts; at Confederation the Dominion government assumed responsibility for divorce, although existing provincial divorce courts were allowed to continue functioning (estranged couples living in provinces without such courts, such as Ontario and Quebec, were forced to petition the federal parliament for private legislation, a lengthy and inconvenient process). Although modifications to divorce were made in the aftermath of World War I, Canada did not have a comprehensive national divorce act until 1968. In Australia, the English Divorce Act of 1857 provided an impetus for divorce laws, as prior to the English legislation Australian colonies did not have divorce courts. In a manner somewhat similar to the situation in Canada, all six Australian colonies set up their own courts between 1858 and 1873, with New Zealand establishing divorce courts in 1867. Not all the colonies followed the metropolitan example completely, though, as New South Wales and Victoria abolished discrimination between men and women in cases of adultery.

With the exception of Lower Canada/Quebec and South Africa, where English common law did not determine wives' status, in the early 1850s settler governments also began to discuss granting married women greater control of their property. New Brunswick breached the common law doctrine of the unity of person, or coverture, in 1851. Eight years later Upper Canada passed a Married Women's Property Act; Prince Edward Island followed suit in 1860. While debates over preventing deserting husbands from returning and absconding with their wives' earnings and property had taken place in the Antipodean colonies as early as the 1840s, it was the passage of England's 1882 Married Women's Property Act that prompted state legislatures to catch up. (While England had passed an 1870 act that gave married women possession of their own earnings, the 1882 act gave married women rights to property that they had brought to the marriage.) Mindful of their reputation as "better Britains," worried that British women would not emigrate if they discovered they had fewer rights in marriage in the Antipodes than at home, and concerned that colonial governments needed to treat women fairly, New Zealand, New South Wales, South Australia, and Queensland passed Married Women's Property Bills in the early 1880s. Colonial governments in the Antipodes feared that they would be surpassed by the metropole on issues of women's equality. They also looked to the examples of other countries and colonies, such as France, the United States, Canada, and India, and saw that these places had passed married women's property laws without the breakdown of the social order.

Family inheritances were also affected by changes in the colonial laws, particularly around primogeniture (the right of a firstborn son to inherit the bulk of a parent's estate) and married women's dower. In many instances, such as in the Maritimes and Upper Canada, the abolition of primogeniture was brought about by a desire to liberalize land law and give landowners the ability to sell or bequeath their property as they saw fit. Similarly, in New South Wales inheritance laws became particularly contentious after the passage of manhood suffrage in 1858. Four years later the colony ended primogeniture, a practice that appeared ill-suited to a colony in which far more land was held by the Crown than in the freehold system for which primogeniture had been designed. Partible inheritance, its supporters argued, was a much better fit for a colony in which land appeared to be open to all; it was not something that would be passed down and controlled by a few elite families. Furthermore, in a society in which unemployed men could vote, rejecting the relations of deference and paternalism embodied by primogeniture was an important step. While a number of colonies moved toward freeing up property by changing laws around land, as Chapter 2 has discussed, British American colonies retained wives' dower.

Families and households around the world were—albeit in widely differing ways—the basic structure or "backbone" of society, their formation and composition the subject of political, religious, social, and legal surveillance and supervision. They also held significance for settlers in other ways. For one, early to mid-nineteenth-century migration to these colonies was often a "family affair," as families went together to Upper Canada, New Zealand, the Cape, and the Australian colonies. Although a number of single men and women left Britain for settler colonies, many did so either to set up households for family members who they hoped would join them or with the expectation of being reunited with family members who had already set up homes. While churches, voluntary organizations, and local communities helped new arrivals with the problems they faced as they attempted to build homes, find work, and establish themselves, people tended to first look to family and kin to help ease them into their new surroundings when possible. Family networks and connections were also an important means of maintaining ties between Britain and the colonies, ties sustained through the medium of letter-writing and, for some, sharing of diaries and journals about life in new places. Although writers such as Eliza Fairbairn often complained that "epistolary intercourse" was no substitute for direct human contact, letters between family and friends provided considerable emotional support for new settlers, helping to mitigate loneliness and isolation. It also might alert those "at home" in Britain about colonial conditions in more realistic and practical ways that literature promoting emigration, which often stressed only the positive aspects, did not. As well, correspondence with family and friends was a powerful means for some migrants to maintain cultural identities, whether local, regional, national, or imperial.

### Religion in Settler Colonies

Settler societies were also linked to Britain and, in multiple ways, to each other through the spread of Christianity. Although it would be an exaggeration to claim that all those who arrived in the colonies possessed deep and abiding religious commitments and beliefs, nevertheless the arrival of British settlers also brought churches and related associations that shaped the physical, social, and cultural landscapes of these societies. Moreover, religion was an important linchpin that helped to bind settler societies to the metropole, each other, and, in many cases, other colonies, such as Jamaica or India.

The spread of beliefs, people, and artifacts—Bibles, tracts, newspapers, and other forms of material culture—were important in helping to constitute the imperial worlds of settler colonies.

Although the imperial government preferred that the Church of England become the official established denomination in its settler colonies, it was confronted in those colonies with just as many religious tensions and heterogeneity as in Britain. Loyalists who arrived in Quebec and the Maritime colonies in the 1780s belonged to a range of Christian denominations, ones that included pietistic sects such as German Mennonites and Quakers. In turn, British immigrants of the early nineteenth century were members of denominations ranging from the established Churches of England and Scotland to the Roman Catholic Church and, too, to those linked to seventeenth- and eighteenth-century dissent and religious enthusiasm, such as the Methodists and Baptists. Furthermore, in both the Cape and British America colonial authorities were faced with the long-standing existence of other, well-established Christian churches: the Dutch Reformed Church (DRC) and the Roman Catholic Church. In both contexts religious identities were tied to those of ethnicity, and in both contexts British authorities chose not to challenge the situation directly. At the Cape, the DRC remained the established church and received support from a number of newly arrived Scottish Presbyterians. In Lower Canada/Quebec, the government pursued a policy of religious toleration.

The American Revolution (1776–83) changed things, as the imperial authorities took steps to bolster the imperial tie by supporting the Church of England in the colonies. With that aim in mind, the Crown established clergy reserves in Nova Scotia in the 1780s and Upper Canada in 1791. In both Upper and Lower Canada, the colonial government set aside one-seventh of all Crown lands in large blocks, often some of the best agricultural properties in the colonies, and then rented them out. The income derived from these rents was earmarked for the support of one established church: the Church of England. The imperial government also saw the reserves as a means of generating revenue within the colony—a way of transferring the costs of colonial administration to the colonists themselves. In the 1820s, clergy reserves were also set up in New South Wales. In both that colony and at the Cape, the Anglican Church sought to create a stronger presence. The arrival of 4,000 settlers at the Cape in the early 1820s spurred the church to extend its parish system, for fear that new arrivals would drift away and join either dissenting Protestant denominations or Roman Catholicism. Furthermore, in a number of colonies—British America, the Caribbean, and New South Wales—education was (at least initially) dominated by the Anglican Church's National Schools.

Clergy reserves, though, became an increasingly sore spot in Upper Canada. In the 1820s and 1830s, other denominations mounted a number of challenges to them. The Church of Scotland successfully lobbied the imperial government to divide the reserves' revenue among other groups, while those who supported religious voluntarism (the separation of church and state) called for their secularization and the distribution of the funds to—for example—public education (other colonists had cited them as an impediment to the development of transportation, particularly better roads). In 1826 the imperial government named a Commissioner of Crown Lands, whose duties included sales of the clergy reserves. Settlers were eager to purchase good land, buying up 130,000 acres of the reserves from the late 1820s until 1832; sales remained steady until well into the 1830s. During this time the colonial government also began to see the reserves as an albatross, as they provoked considerable political controversy and did not promote loyalty to Britain but instead threatened to undermine the colony's connection to the Empire. In 1854 the reserves were secularized. While those members of the clergy whose salaries had been paid out of them continued to receive support, the reserves' revenues were used to fund municipal development and improvements and railway building. The presence of Whig leadership in the imperial government during the 1830s, a group committed to voluntarism and pluralism, also undermined special treatment for the Anglican Church. In 1836 New South Wales passed a Church Act that ended the Church's privileges and granted state aid to the colony's four main Christian denominations. By no means did Anglicanism disappear from settler colonies, though. For example, the Anglican Church played a significant role in founding theological colleges and early universities. The introduction of voluntarism, though, meant that it was obliged to compete with other denominations.

The spread of Christianity in settler colonies was also a manifestation of the larger global missionary movement. As Chapter 1 pointed out, in the context of these colonies the movement had a direct, if at times complicated, effect on the lives and well-being of Indigenous people. As part of their "civilizing mission," Protestant missionaries might work to assimilate Indigenous people to the norms, beliefs, and practices of settler society. On the other hand, missionaries, acting in concert with Indigenous communities and secular humanitarian organizations, could offer strong and influential critiques of colonial governments' actions and of settler violence toward Indigenous people. Moreover, missionary work in settler societies had multiple dimensions, as it also was focused on the "civilization" and religious needs of settlers. Single men employed in mining or logging, for example, were seen as needing religion, living as they did in all-male communities and lacking the "civilizing" influence of white women's moral guidance. These men stirred up missionaries' fears that they would seek companionship with Indigenous women, forswear the sacrament of Christian marriage, and raise mixed-race, unbaptized children. A number of Christian churches also became concerned about the spiritual, moral, and physical welfare of newly arrived immigrants. In 1832 the Catholic Church in both Lower and Upper Canada, for example, offered medical assistance to immigrants stricken with cholera and to those Irish migrants fleeing famine in the mid-1840s. In nineteenth-century Quebec, the Catholic Church assumed a range of responsibilities in the fields of education, health, and social welfare. By the end of the nineteenth century a number of Christian churches were active as missionaries in urban centres. They offered both the possibility of religious conversion and philanthropic aid to working-class and immigrant populations through city missions and the settlement house movement.

However, Christianity was not the only religion that played a role in these colonies. As Chapter 1 pointed out, Indigenous people had their own spiritual beliefs and practices, ones that might persist even after the establishment of missionary churches and Indigenous conversions. Furthermore, the Muslim population at the Cape formed a noticeable and significant religious minority, one tied to its origins in the Malay archipelago. Many of those brought to Cape Town from the area had been slaves; along with many free blacks, this group and their descendants constituted the colony's Muslim population. Islam proved to be a powerful way of creating community, as a number of former slaves—primarily male—converted to the religion from the 1820s to the 1870s. By the 1850s, Cape Town's white population saw Malay and Muslim as synonymous; by the 1870s, when the Muslim population reached 2,656, they began using "Malay" to describe themselves. To a great extent, conversion to Islam was a means of affirming one's status as a freed person, a way of claiming a different identity than that of the master's or mistress's Christianity. Attending mosques and madrasas (religious schools), practising different rituals, wearing distinctive dress, eating other kinds of food, and using different medicines helped contribute to psychological, spiritual, social, and cultural independence. Moreover, belonging to a community of fellow-Muslims, one in which charity was seen as a fundamental tenet, offered material support for its poorer members. It also might afford respect and social status for wealthier Muslims that were unavailable in white society.

## Voluntary Societies

While not coterminous or synonymous with the missionary movement, voluntary associations were often linked to or rooted in particular denominations or, more broadly, religious movements. Over the course of the nineteenth century Sunday schools, benevolent and philanthropic organizations, and groups dedicated to social reform and welfare appeared in a number of colonies. Such organizations and institutions were in many ways multifaceted, as their goals and motivations encompassed a range of purposes. Sunday schools, for example, helped contribute to European settlers' literacy. In the case of British America they were an important force in the development of the transatlantic book trade and print culture, since tracts, newspapers, periodicals, and books were sent overseas from the metropole in order to promote Christianity and literacy. Institutions devoted to the care of infants and children, the indigent, the ill and disabled, widows, and the aged might be organized by a specific church, as in the case of Catholic hospitals, orphanages, and asylums founded and run by nuns in Quebec. While Protestant philanthropy might be organized by a particular denomination, interdenominational organizations became increasingly common over the course of the century. In many ways philanthropy in settler societies closely resembled similar initiatives in Britain; it was either initiated by newly arrived British immigrants or was influenced by developments in the metropole.

Local conditions might mean that philanthropic work took a different direction from British models; moreover, differences between colonies existed. Not all settler societies adopted the Poor Law, for example. Although Nova Scotia and New Brunswick passed such legislation, mandating the state to provide a bare minimum of relief, Victoria, Upper Canada, and the Cape did not. Although New Zealand had a number of philanthropic and benevolent organizations, its smaller white (or *Pakeha*) community meant that these groups turned to the colonial government for financial support to carry out their work. Such organizations justified their existence by emphasizing their moral influence and ability to provide more personalized care to recipients.

Despite these variations, philanthropic work across these colonial sites was marked by a number of similarities, ones also shared with Britain (and, in many cases, the United States). With the exception of those fraternal organizations that aimed to provide working-class men with insurance in case of disease, accident, or death, philanthropy was largely organized and directed by members of the colonies' middle class toward their societies' working class and poor. As well, such work was almost invariably marked by distinctions of gender. Middle-class men were often the official leaders and directors of philanthropic societies, overseeing their legal and financial affairs, but it was middle-class women who carried out much of the work of visiting those who received assistance. At Cape Town, for example, the Ladies' Benevolent Society, formed in 1822 to promote religion, morality, and industry among the colony's poor, established a School of Industry for girls whose parents could not afford to provide them with any formal education. The school provided close surveillance of both its pupils and their parents but was forced to close in 1840 when the Society decided to shift its attention to poor relief. For the rest of the nineteenth century the Society was devoted to fundraising and visiting the recipients of its aid.

Colonial conditions might change patterns developed in England, though. In Melbourne, for example, those members of the Melbourne Ladies' Benevolent Society (the city's largest provider of outdoor relief) who undertook home visits were older, married women. Unlike the situation in Britain, where visiting tended to be the province of single women who often found a vocation in philanthropy, the greater number of married Australian women (the result of the colonies' gender imbalance) changed the face of female philanthropy. Women also played significant roles in fundraising for such societies. Their labour was crucial in helping to organize society and church bazaars, as they sewed, knitted, and embroidered the items sold at these events and also provided food and decorations.

Like their counterparts in Britain and elsewhere, those who received assistance were far from passive in their relationship with middle-class philanthropists. Evidence of their perspectives is less plentiful and must be interpreted with caution, since it was filtered through the lens of their benefactors' notions of "deserving" and "undeserving," the "respectable" versus the "dissolute" poor. Nevertheless, recipients of philanthropy across the colonies had their own concepts of useful assistance and appropriate behaviour. When possible, they presented philanthropists with narratives designed to elicit sympathy while simultaneously attempting to maintain their own values and practices (spending money on sugar, for example, or buying clothes that visitors deemed overly luxurious). Moreover, in the colony of Victoria poor white women demanded that the state, not private charities, should take responsibility for the support of their families. Such women visited magistrates demanding money, food, clothing, or references for employment that would allow them to keep their families together. By the late 1850s, the colony's magistrates campaigned actively for legislation establishing state-funded homes for neglected and "criminal" children, a major initiative in state welfare.

In Cape Town, despite the efforts of groups such as the Cape Town Ladies' Benevolent Society, the Free Dispensary (established in the 1850s), and the Salvation Army, and the (admittedly small) amounts of government relief offered to the city's European immigrant poor, by the early twentieth century the city's poor had developed their own strategies for survival, ones that were shaped by religious and linguistic lines of affiliation. As we have seen, Muslims could turn to community organizations that provided formal assistance and to those rituals and festivities that provided both work and food. Newly arrived Jewish immigrants looked to an older, Anglo-Jewish community that was integrated into Cape Town's establishment. Poorer Jewish immigrants benefited from religious beliefs in the importance of charity and from the fears of the older segment of the Jewish community that the new arrivals' poverty would stir up anti-Semitism (around the same time, a similar process took place in Montreal). Unlike Christian charities, though, the Cape Town Philanthropic Society preferred to find applicants work with other Jewish businesses instead of relying on relief. Other churches, such as Dutch-speaking mission churches, the Wesleyan Forward Movement (which did not discriminate on the basis of class or colour), and the African Methodist Episcopal Church, also promoted independent self-help instead of paternalism. Moreover, those seeking food and shelter might be aided by kin and neighbours. The very poor—generally those African migrant workers who were vulnerable to downturns in the economy and who lived on the city's outskirts—might have to turn to petty crime as a means of survival.

Other organizations, although not strictly or exclusively philanthropic in nature, also combined forms of assistance with a desire to either reshape colonists' identities or reaffirm those already forged in the metropole. Like the evangelical churches with which many of them were associated, temperance societies made much of the great changes that renouncing alcohol—or at least moderating one's drinking—would bring, not just to individuals but to families and communities. Controlling drinking, these groups thought, would result in a decrease in domestic violence in working-class families and an increase in household budgets. Temperance organizations in settler colonies were rooted in the movement in Britain and the United States; the American-based Women's Christian Temperance Union (WCTU), in particular, spread to Canada and Australia in the 1880s and 1890s. Unlike its parent body in the United States, the WCTU in the Dominions had only limited success in persuading settler legislatures to ban the sale of alcohol. Nevertheless, the WCTU played an important role in bringing women together across national boundaries. For some, their activism in moral reform groups such as the WCTU helped propel them into the women's suffrage movement, both within their own societies and at an international level. Furthermore, fraternal organizations, groups that ranged from mutual aid societies to insurance companies to societies organized around ethnic identities—the St. Andrew's, St. George's, the Orange Order, and St. Patrick's societies, for example—also provided settlers with a range of support and linked them to international and imperial networks. English, Scottish, Welsh, and Irish societies, with their banquets, parades, and other commemorative events, helped perpetuate their members' identification with "home." While belonging to such organizations did not preclude feeling connected to the British Empire, the strength and persistence of these groups also reminds us that being "British" was not a homogeneous or uncomplicated position.

### Moral and Medical Regulation

Voluntary organizations and associations both provided material benefits and helped shape settler identities, assisting in defining lines of belonging and lines of exclusion. Other ways of providing such definitions existed, ones in which monitoring certain spaces and places was crucial. Vagrancy laws, for one, served to regulate civil society in a number of ways. Such laws had a lengthy history in England; by the mid-sixteenth century they were being used to enforce social order. The English Vagrancy Act of 1824 was used as a model for a number of colonial statutes; one of its most significant features, particularly in colonial settings, was the amount of discretion with which it could be applied. From 1824 until 1930, vagrancy laws were passed throughout Australia. Their intent included policing ex-convicts' movements and maintaining order, helping to enforce the Masters and Servants Acts' provisions by jailing workers deemed to be vagrants, preventing interracial liaisons, and controlling prostitution. While in many ways these acts were used in very similar ways in England, in Australia they also were used to patrol racial boundaries through attempts to restrict Indigenous people's use of public spaces.

In colonial Natal the Vagrancy Act of 1869 was used to address a moral panic about urban African men's sexuality. As they were already seen by white settlers as undisciplined, idle, itinerant, and prone to living off women, these stereotypes intersected with a growing number of black migrant labourers, an increase in firearms, and African communities that refused to accept whites' control. Like moral panics around Indigenous men's sexuality in other colonial contexts, the spectre of black men raping white women was raised as a reason to pass a law that permitted the conviction of those found trespassing, loitering, indecently exposing themselves, or behaving in a riotous manner. Significantly, it also allowed municipalities to impose a curfew for black people and to convict those who were found wandering after nightfall. Natal's legislation presaged measures used to enforce racial segregation in twentieth-century South African cities.

Public health ordinances were also far from being neutral, particularly so far as the dynamics of race, gender, and class were concerned. The Contagious Diseases Acts, initially passed in England between 1864 and 1869 as a means of controlling the spread of venereal disease in port cities and military encampments to British troops, were—like the Vagrancy Act—imported to a number of colonies, particularly India and Hong Kong. From 1868 until the late 1870s, versions of these acts were passed in the Cape Colony, Natal, New Zealand, Queensland, Victoria, and Tasmania. The acts were meant not to eradicate prostitution but, rather, to provide continuous inspection of women suspected of being prostitutes and prevent them from infecting British soldiers and sailors. Those women who were found to be infected with venereal diseases were incarcerated in lock hospitals, where they were kept until they had recovered and were deemed to no longer be infectious. If they remained in the area, such women were then subject to periodic inspections by the medical authorities. The Tasmania legislature passed its version of the act when the Royal Navy threatened to end its visits to Hobart if contagious diseases legislation was not put into effect. In Queensland the legislation was extended to civilians in towns that did not host British garrisons, the intent being to control new immigrants and visitors from abroad. Victoria's legislation, though, was not followed by the foundation of lock hospitals. Their absence rendered the legislation ineffective, and prostitution continued to be controlled through vagrancy laws and informal collaboration between magistrates and the police. At the Cape, the acts were introduced not because of local demand but because the War Office called for action to be taken against the rates of venereal disease suffered by imperial troops stationed in the colony. As in Tasmania, the threat of the troops' withdrawal spurred the legislature to action.

As in other settler societies—and the metropole—working-class female prostitutes were the focus of legislators' concerns. In Natal, though, the structure of domestic service also worried authorities and the medical profession. The latter (incorrectly) raised the spectre of male domestic servants—"houseboys" or "nurseboys"—spreading sexual disease through non-sexual contact with children, theories that were picked up by settlers who then accused African men of sexually assaulting white children. Here, too, very little evidence backed up such accusations. Although Natal attempted to introduce contagious diseases legislation between 1886 and 1890, the bill that eventually passed in 1890 was disallowed by the Secretary of State for the Colonies, a reminder that not all settler legislatures controlled their internal affairs. Moreover, as in the case of the Vagrancy Act, the controversy over contagious diseases demonstrates the ways in which different configurations of race and gender shaped Natal's discourses around disease and contagion.

The acts did not go uncontested, however. In Britain, a vigorous campaign led by the National Anti-Contagious Diseases Acts Association and the Ladies National Association attacked the acts for their ineffectiveness, their immorality, and their enforcement of a double standard, as well as their stigmatization of women, usually working-class, who frequented public spaces. Similar objections were raised in New Zealand and at the Cape, which abolished its act in 1871. In the latter colony, though, public support for the acts' repeal was limited to white, middle-class men. This group included a number of Dutch Reformed ministers who objected to the acts' sanctioning of immorality, not their abuse of women's civil liberties. The voices of middle-class women—who had formed an important part of the British campaign—were not heard. In 1888 the Cape passed a new act that applied to the seaports of Cape Town, Port Elizabeth, East London, and King William's Town. In the Australian colonies, the laws stayed on the books and were supplemented from the 1890s on with other kinds of regulatory legislation.

Although venereal disease attracted the attention of imperial and military authorities, those authorities also were faced with the threat of other infectious diseases. Epidemics of cholera and, in particular, smallpox arrived with British and European immigrants. Cholera first came to Quebec in 1832, part of a global spread of the disease from India. It then moved rapidly to major centres along the St. Lawrence River, Lake Ontario, and Lake Erie, its virulence and rapid growth resulting in approximately 6,000 deaths in Canada (there were subsequent outbreaks in port cities from 1834 to 1871). The colonial authorities' method of controlling the disease involved crowding all new arrivals, sick and healthy, into small sheds close to the docks, where often those who were not infected soon fell ill. Such an approach was based on the perspective that the arrivals were dirty, poverty-stricken, and thus prone to spreading contagion.

While cholera was certainly a serious threat to settler societies, the smallpox virus proved deadly to Indigenous people. Between 1788 and 1870, three major smallpox epidemics made their way through Indigenous communities in Australia, starting on the eastern coast and spreading further inland, to the northwest coast, and to South Australia. Children under ten were extremely susceptible to the disease's effects, while those adults who survived might suffer extreme disfigurement or blindness. In some cases settlers, along with missionaries and the NorthWest Territory's Protector, P.M. Wood, provided vaccines for Indigenous people; Wood also set up quarantines for those who were infected. In British Columbia, where 20,000 Indigenous people died in 1862–63 alone and the Northwest Coast population suffered losses overall of approximately 90 per cent, smallpox was devastating. Yet like their counterparts in Natal, the colonial authorities in British Columbia saw the presence of smallpox as embodying not just disease but also racial contagion. After creating a reserve outside the town limits to which they hoped Indigenous people would be confined, the city council of New Westminster then burned their homes in the town. Prior to the outbreak of smallpox, the British Columbia city of Victoria also imposed methods aimed at racially segregating the local Lekwammen people from white settlers, imposing curfews and burning Indigenous homes in the city. Indigenous women, in particular, were frequently targeted as settlers' anxieties about interracial sex grew. When smallpox struck in 1862, the local police first pressured and then forced Indigenous people to leave, burning their homes and moving them out by gunboat to coastal communities, thereby spreading smallpox to other Indigenous villages.

Other forms of regulation were implemented over the course of the nineteenth century. As we have seen, controlling the sale and consumption of liquor was a concern for the temperance movement; throughout the nineteenth century municipal authorities and colonial legislatures also sought to regulate and control liquor sales. To some extent this was done through the licensing of taverns and other commercial establishments that sold liquor, a process that controlled taverns' hours of operation and the kinds of activities that could be conducted alongside drinking. Beginning in the 1790s, for instance, Upper Canada banned gambling in public houses, although the injunction tended to be ignored if gamblers behaved themselves and did not become violent (billiards, however, were permitted under a separate licence). By the end of the nineteenth century, though, the temperance movement's influence in Ontario resulted in more stringent conditions around licensing and taxes on liquor sales. These regulations tended to target and affect working-class and immigrant communities. Like other ordinances, rules around drinking in settler societies also were shaped by discourses of race. By 1901 Cape Town's black urban poor were unable to buy liquor, since the colony's temperance movement pressured the city to adopt the Innes Liquor Act, which prohibited its sale to Africans. It was followed by the 1902 Morality Act, which banned betting, gaming, and brothel-keeping. Canada's 1876 Indian Act forbade Indians from drinking alcohol, a prohibition meant to safeguard Indigenous people from themselves since they were perceived as developmentally unable to guard against moral turpitude. Furthermore, the Chinese population of British Columbia, seen as fundamentally unassimilable by both colonial officials and missionaries, were targeted in the 1890s by religious and secular writers. They believed Chinese immigrants were responsible for plying Indigenous people with alcohol and contributing to their racial downfall. Such concerns were expressed in the language of protecting Indigenous people but were underpinned by fears of racial mixing between Chinese, Indigenous, and mixed-race communities. Legislation controlling the sale and consumption of alcohol thus helped contribute to racial segregation and exclusion in settler societies.

### The Movement for Settler Self-Improvement

Nineteenth-century liberal ideologies of self-improvement, part of a broader transnational movement linked to middle-class formation in Britain and the United States, also spread to settler societies. It was also one of the means whereby various groups of working men—and, to a lesser extent, women—legitimized their claims to respectability. Mechanics' Institutes, for example, which had originated in Britain in the 1820s, soon spread to British North America, with the first Institute opening in 1828 in Montreal.

The Institutes offered a mixture of evening lectures, lending libraries, and reading rooms. By 1900, Ontario had more than 300 Institutes with a membership of more than 31,000 (the Mechanics' Institute also became popular in British Columbia's Cariboo gold fields). In Australia, from the late 1850s on the Institutes—also known as Schools of Arts—spread to various towns in New South Wales, often through the work of the colony's Presbyterian clergy. While the Institutes and Schools were founded by men, by 1856 the *Sydney Morning Herald* told its readers that the city's Mechanics' School of Arts was offering classes to women in subjects such as French and music. In Newcastle, the local School of Arts targeted female members from its inception. The School's founders argued that it would be a place where women could improve their social life, and compete with men in the acquisition of art and science; the School also could help them with their important work of childrearing. Not all of these organizations attracted mixed-sex audiences, though. In the colony's mining districts Mechanics' and Miners' Institutes were predominantly masculine institutions.

Mechanics' Institutes were aimed at a particular sector of settler society; lending libraries, though, reached a wide range of different groups and regions. Like the Institutes and other voluntary associations, libraries in the colonies were inspired by developments in Britain. By the early nineteenth century the publisher and bookseller William Lane had established a national network of commercial circulating libraries; they were followed by 500 proprietary circulating libraries and 6,500 middle-class cooperative book societies and clubs. The great wave of British emigrants who arrived in settler colonies from the 1820s on came as readers, with a keen interest in reading for moral instruction and improvement, for critical analysis and debate, or for the pleasure of entertainment (or possibly a mixture of all three). Reading on board emigrant ships, for example, was a common practice for middle-class men; women of all classes, it seems, often had both domestic labour and childcare to occupy their time en route to their new homes. For example, in 1855 cleric George Holditch Mason described his journey from England to Natal as being made more pleasant by the regular reading group he and his fellow-passengers formed, in which they read aloud popular works drawn from a fellow-passenger's library. Once settlers arrived in, for example, Natal, the Cape, New South Wales, or New Zealand, they quickly organized lending libraries, supplied by the imperial and transatlantic book trades. Often these became public libraries, since the fees for commercial libraries were frequently beyond the reach of rural settlers or those who lived in resource-based communities, such as mining camps.

In a number of colonial cities public libraries and galleries also flourished and helped mark and shape civic space, not least for a growing colonial middle class. At the Cape in 1877, King William's Town's public library, founded in 1861, acquired a two-storey building constructed in the neoclassical style. Supported by the Cape government as well as by members' fees, the library sat at one of the town's main intersections, close to the magistrates' court and other public buildings. Yet although libraries held out the promise of creating a better-educated, literate society through greater access to books, periodicals, and newspapers, their practices remind us such access was in fact more of an ideal than a reality. Just as the absence of a large community of skilled white workers meant that Mechanics' Institutes did not flourish at the Cape, popular libraries also lacked a strong popular base of support. King William's Town's library, for example, was controlled by the local white male elite, and membership in it was classified according to the amount of subscription fees paid by a member. While the government insisted that its support was contingent upon the public having daily public access to the reading and reference collections (although not to newspapers), only subscribers could sign out books or periodicals and read newspapers. Moreover, although by the end of the century King William's Town was home to an active and educated black community, the library's membership remained all-white.

Other forms of hierarchies shaped public libraries. Melbourne's Public Library, opened in 1856, promised democratic, open access to all readers that, as the artist who sketched its Picture Gallery noted, also included women (Figure 4.2). Nevertheless, at the urging of those who were uneasy about women's presence in this public space, in the early 1860s the Library established a "Ladies'" reading room. Just as women's use of the British Museum's reading room in London was a source of unease, over the next 20 years Melbourne's female library patrons were still controversial subjects, particularly those female members who refused the seclusion of the Ladies' reading room and insisted on circulating throughout the building.

### Formal Education

Colonial schools and universities also reflected settler colonists' desire for education. Prior to the introduction of state-regulated, primary-level education, colonists had set up their own schools. They ranged from small, private ones, frequently headed by women and run out of their proprietors' homes, to larger institutions. The latter were typically single-sex, founded

**FIGURE 4.2** "The National Picture Gallery at the Public Library, Melbourne"

THE NATIONAL PICTURE GALLERY AT THE PUBLIC LIBRARY, MELBOURNE.—See Page 7.

Source: *Australian News for Home Readers*, 25 January 1863. Latrobe Picture Collection, State Library of Victoria.

and staffed by religious bodies, either Roman Catholic or Protestant. In some cases, such as Upper Canada's grammar schools for boys, schools received grants from the colonial government, eager to see an educated and elite class of colonists develop but less enthusiastic about setting up state-run, taxpayer-supported education. A number of these institutions survived well into the twentieth century. In British America, colonial reformers began to argue for compulsory, state-regulated education in the 1830s. Those interested in state-sponsored education were frequently inspired by developments elsewhere. In 1844–45, for example, the prominent Upper Canadian education reformer and first superintendent of the colony's common schools, Egerton Ryerson, toured Europe to gather ideas for public education. He was particularly interested in Ireland's curriculum, most notably its non-sectarian textbooks.

Colonial education reformers also had to contend with local conditions that shaped the colonies' educational policies and structures. In both British America and New South Wales, the Anglican Church's dominance in education and preferential status was challenged: in British North America by political reformers and in New South Wales by Governor Bourke.

Like Ryerson, Bourke looked to Ireland's education system as a model; although Christian, Irish schools attempted to downplay denominational differences. However, the colony's 1836 Church Act gave Protestant churches the bulk of state funds and by 1847 two forms of education had been established in New South Wales. Technically non-denominational, the public system favoured Protestantism, while the private system was heavily weighted toward schools with clear religious ties, primarily to the Catholic Church. Although legislation was passed in a number of colonies—Victoria in 1872, Queensland and South Australia in 1875, and New South Wales in 1880—that called for public education to be free, compulsory, and secular, nevertheless the term "secular" was not clearly defined. Schools continued to infuse their curriculum with Christian precepts.

Religion was not the only point of contention, though. In Canada, provisions for the protection of linguistic minorities guaranteed in the British North America Act came under attack in the latter part of the nineteenth century. Events such as the Riel Uprising of 1885, the payment of compensation to the Jesuit order in Canada for its losses in the Conquest, and the arrival of non-British immigrants in the Canadian west created an atmosphere of acute racial and religious anxiety. Accordingly, between 1890 and 1916 Anglo-Protestants in Canada lobbied to ensure that education reinforced children's loyalty to the Empire. In 1890, for example, Manitoba's government replaced a dual Protestant-Catholic school system with one that promoted English Protestantism; the ensuing court battle resulted in a ruling that favoured the province over minority rights. Similar attacks took place in Ontario and New Brunswick.

In addition to debates over religion and language, establishing a teaching workforce also preoccupied colonial educators. In some jurisdictions, colonial governments founded schools for teacher training. Ryerson, for example, set up Normal Schools in Ontario designed to impart both academic knowledge and moral lessons and character development. Officials in Australia took to heart, it seems, the advice of English educational reformer James Kay-Shuttleworth, who advocated setting up the kind of teacher training colleges he pioneered in the metropole. Such institutions, Kay-Shuttleworth believed, should keep character formation foremost in teachers' education. Indeed, Sydney's Fort Street Model School, established in 1851, was set up by the Englishman William Wilkins, who had attended Battersea Training College in London and was an advocate of Kay-Shuttleworth's approach to teacher training. However, despite Kay-Shuttleworth's belief in character development, when it came to staffing the common schools the overriding concern of colonial governments—in both Australia and British America—was economic. Their desire for a cheap teaching force tended to override other considerations, such as college-level education for primary-school teachers. This problem was particularly acute in Australia (as it was in the metropole), and it was not until the early twentieth century that teachers' colleges were established in Western Australia (1902), Tasmania (1906), and Queensland (1914). In British America the desire for a cheaper teaching workforce also led to a distinctly gendered one, as young women predominated at the elementary-school level.

As they did in Britain, secular, state-regulated schools coexisted with a range of both religious and private institutions. As well as missionary schools founded to educate Indigenous children, denominationally based schools also offered colonists the chance to maintain their religious identity. While Protestant churches were active in this regard, the work of Catholic teaching orders was notable, not least because they could be found in a number of colonies and because their schools might reach students from a range of class backgrounds. This was particularly the case in Lower Canada/Quebec, where the church provided education for Catholic children and young adults of both genders. Its work was not limited to Quebec, however, as teaching orders of both priests and nuns established schools in other provinces and territories. Catholic education in Australia represented a complex, transnational network. Irish female religious teachers from the Dominican Order and the Sisters of Mercy, as well as the English Dominican Sisters, brought Irish, French, English, and Argentinean influences to the education of upper- and middle-class girls and young women in South Australia. These influences were manifested in the curriculum taught in the classroom and, more generally, rules concerning pupils' conduct.

Other educational institutions, both secular and denominational, were important sites for the transmission of "Britishness" and loyalty to the Empire, particularly in the late nineteenth and early twentieth century when imperial sentiment pervaded many forms of popular culture. The use of textbooks (often imported from Britain) that either focused on British—or, more likely, English—history and literature or saw colonial developments as part of a larger story of the spread of Empire; maps that emphasized the reach of the Empire; and material culture, such as portraits of the monarchy: these genres and artifacts helped tie generations of settler students to Britain. As well, although exchanges of teachers between Britain and the Dominions became more common after World War I, in 1909 a party of teachers from Manitoba travelled to Britain to, in the words of the trip's organizers, facilitate their task in their home province. The teachers were charged with making "British the thousands of children of foreign birth ... who are peopling the Western prairies ... (a) great National and Imperial task."[3] Trips to the "motherland" would help the teachers decide "whether the British nation was still to be their ideal and first love."[4]

As well as being shaped by gender and class relations, education in the settler colonies took on a distinctly racial nature. As discussed in Chapter 1, Indigenous children's education was generally dealt with separately from that of their white contemporaries, particularly for those who lived on reserves. Asian and black children often faced discriminatory practices and policies in places such as British Columbia, Nova Scotia, and Upper Canada. In the latter colony, although formal segregation based on race was banned in provincial Education Acts, white communities nevertheless succeeded in obtaining a *de facto* form of segregation and excluding black children from local public schools. While black parents protested such discrimination, many African-Canadian students found that obtaining secondary education, let alone college or university training, was a difficult struggle well into the twentieth century, particularly in rural areas. At the Cape, racial distinctions and discrimination in education were even more firmly entrenched and prevalent. Missionary-run church schools received only small amounts of government assistance and tended to serve poorer communities. In contrast, more affluent whites were served by public education that excluded poor whites and most blacks by virtue of the high fees charged by schools (the system required parents to contribute to half the costs of running schools). By the late nineteenth century the Education Department began to call for more explicitly racially based policies as a means of upholding white supremacy and maintaining a poorly educated—and thus poorly paid—pool of black labour. Such policies saw success after the South African War (1899–1902). The 1905 School Board Act, for example, provided white children with compulsory public education to the age of 14, while making such education available to only a small number of black children. Over the course of the twentieth century, racism in South African education would be persistent and prevalent; in the 1970s and 1980s, it became a flashpoint for students' political activism against the apartheid regime.

Elementary and secondary education, then, was shaped by both metropolitan ideologies and institutions and by the particular conditions of settler societies' histories, economies, and political structures, formal and informal. Universities in settler colonies also were influenced by a similar interplay of metropolitan currents and local conditions. In British America, starting with the foundation of all-male seminaries and classical colleges in seventeenth-century New France, religion played a central and significant role in the founding of the colonies' first universities. The first university in British America to grant degrees, Nova Scotia's King's College, was founded in 1789. Based on Oxford University, King's was meant to train Anglican clergymen who would serve as moral and religious leaders in the colony. Over the course of the nineteenth century it was followed by other institutions with religious foundations, such as Quebec City's Laval, Halifax's Dalhousie, Montreal's McGill, and Toronto's King's College (the University of Toronto was founded in 1850 as a non-denominational institution). Colonial elites hoped that the classical education provided by these universities would help create a suitable class of "gentlemen" who would provide the colonies with doctors, lawyers, and clergy. Perhaps not surprisingly, the number of male students who attended these institutions was low. By 1871 only 1,561 students were enrolled in Canadian universities; some campuses had as few as 50 students.

South African College, founded at the Cape in 1829, was envisioned in somewhat different ways. The College was intended to fulfill two goals: to anglicize rural Afrikaner youth who would then return to their home districts as magistrates and ministers and to provide training for English settlers' sons. The latter would then go on to work in Cape Town's merchant houses and as lower-level government officials. Unlike British America's universities, the College was not intended to equip either group of young men with the cultural and social capital to become powerful leaders in the colony. Such an elite would, the Cape's politicians thought, come from England to run colonial affairs. By mid-century, the advent of responsible government at the Cape; the development of a diamond-mining economy that required expertise in commerce, engineering, and law; and the spread of state-supported schools for the colony's white population meant that a new class of "home-grown" male leaders was needed. Consequently the College shifted its focus to training professionals and "gentlemen" who could become political, commercial, and professional authorities.

In Australia and New Zealand, higher education differed from its counterparts elsewhere in the Empire. The University of Sydney (1850) and the University of Melbourne were state supported, secular, non-residential, and urban. Moreover, they were intended to be open to, in the words of university advocate and politician William Charles Wentworth, "'the child of every class,'" regardless of social standing and background.[5] These universities, along with New Zealand's University of Otago in Dunedin, founded in 1869, rejected the religious tests still in use in English and Scottish institutions that excluded Protestant dissenters and Catholic applicants. They also promised a secular curriculum; furthermore, both Sydney and Melbourne took in a substantial number of scholarship students. However, the ideal of a completely inclusive university was not always realized. Both colonies lacked a comprehensive public education system that would prepare students for university entrance examinations: poor children, those who lived outside metropolitan areas, and Aboriginal children were unable to qualify for university. As it was elsewhere, university in Australia was predominantly a masculine domain, as opposition to girls' education was widespread. Nevertheless, a more inclusive conception of the student body, particularly in contrast to universities in Britain and North America, meant that Australia's universities did not simply recruit from the ranks of the established elite in creating their student bodies. Instead, these institutions helped create a new colonial elite. Furthermore, by the 1870s public education began to expand, so that those who had previously been cut off from university—students from rural areas and girls, for example—were increasingly able to acquire the necessary qualifications for entrance examinations.

Although colonial ideologies and conditions played an important role in shaping Australia's universities, the latter were tied to the metropole in a number of ways. At times they reacted to problems in British institutes of higher education and searched for ways to avoid them in the Australian context. For example, Australia's and New Zealand's institutions were set up in the aftermath of a movement to reform British universities, one that inspired many Antipodean educators to look beyond the models of Oxford and Cambridge for structures better suited to the local context. Conversely, they continued to see Britain as a source of academic expertise. University governors in Australia and New Zealand looked to Britain for advice in appointing professors. Sydney, for example, recruited its faculty from Oxford and Cambridge, while Melbourne drew its professoriate from Dublin's Trinity College. By the early twentieth century, it was quite common for Australian-born academics to further their careers in Britain and then return home as full professors. Such mobility helped shape academic networks that would persist well into the twentieth century.

## Conclusion

Settler societies, then, strove to recreate the values, practices, and structures their members had left behind and to maintain those ties and networks that linked them to Britain: witness, for example, those children seated on the New Zealand beach. In many ways their efforts bore fruit in the spread of the missionary movement, educational institutions, or philanthropic organizations. However, creating civil institutions within settler societies was by no means a smooth transfer of metropolitan institutions and sensibilities, something that Eliza Fairbairn knew all too well. Instead, attempts to create a "better Britain" and "better Britons" were shaped by local conditions that involved a range of different demographies, geographies, and, significantly, histories, not least those of Indigenous peoples. The schools, charities, family relationships, and churches of settler societies thus resembled in many ways their British counterparts but were not carbon copies of the latter, not least because settlers' identities, the subject of Chapter 5, shifted and changed over the course of the nineteenth society.

## Notes

1 Kirsten McKenzie, "'My Own Mind Dying within Me': Eliza Fairbairn and the Reinvention of Colonial Middle-Class Domesticity in Cape Town," *South African Historical Journal* 36 (May 1997): 3–23. 17.

2 Sue Middleton, "Schooling the Labouring Classes: Children, Families, and Learning in Wellington, 1840–1845," *International Studies in Sociology of Education* 18, 2 (2008): 139.

3 Frederick J. Ney, *Britishers in Britain. Being the Record of the Official Visit of Teachers from Manitoba to the Old Country, Summer, 1910* (London: Times Book Club, 1911), 4.

4 Ibid., 5.

5 Julia Horne and Geoffrey Sherington, "Extending the Educational Franchise: The Social Contract of Australia's Public Universities, 1850–1990," *Paedagogica Historica* 46, 1 (2010): 210.

# 5 | Creating Settler Identities

*We felt that we were returning home ... we rejoiced to see again the
ancient landmarks of England and the monuments that mark the resting place of many of its famous men. We felt proud that we, too, were
Britishers and that we also had a share in the great and glorious part of
that country. Seeing other lands had made our own dearer to us, and we
thanked Providence that we lived under the dear old Union Jack.*

—Margaret Dickie, 1911[1]

*We are all New Zealanders and now we are away from our own coun-
try we all stick together like glue.... We do not work and are fed and
trained up to think that we are just it and fear nothing and nobody.*

—Rod McCandish, c. 1914[2]

Winnipeg resident Margaret Dickie wrote of her great pride in being a
"Britisher" during a 1910 tour of Britain and parts of Europe, one that she
shared with a number of fellow-teachers from Manitoba. Organized by
the writer and future executive secretary of Canada's National Council on
Education Frederick J. Ney, the trip was intended to display the Canadian
teachers' love of the Empire to British audiences and to deepen the teachers' ties to Britain by exposing them to historical sites and institutions. In
contrast, New Zealand trooper Rod McCandish, stationed in Hobart during World War I as part of the New Zealand Expeditionary Force, viewed
himself and his fellow soldiers with no little pride in their distinct, if rather

isolated, position (New Zealand's soldiers had had little contact with other armies since the South African War [1899–1902]). His sentiments were partly echoed by his British commander, Sir Alexander Godley, who believed that his men "joined up with the Australians ... compare most favourably in appearances, and I think from what I hear also in discipline ... [the Australians] have the usual trouble with venereal, and are rather worse than us."[3]

Dickie's and McCandish's writings demonstrate that by the early twentieth century different, sometimes diametrically opposed, attitudes toward the British Empire and the settler nation existed within early settler societies. Furthermore, between Dickie's identification as a staunch champion of Canada's tie to the Empire and McCandish's declaration of being a "New Zealander" was a range of positions and sensibilities. Many settler colonists thought of themselves as members of the Empire. Their identification as imperial subjects, though, might include both the broader concept of "Britain" and the British monarchy and particular countries—England, Ireland, Scotland, and Wales—or even particular regions within the latter, such as Yorkshire or the Scottish Highlands. Furthermore, over the course of the nineteenth century and into the early twentieth, British settlers' sense of themselves as being located within a "British world" might also be mediated by being Australian, Canadian, a New Zealander, or South African. Such national identities were themselves complicated by concepts such as region, race, ethnicity, gender, religion, and language.

Settlers expressed their sense of who they were in a number of genres. Not surprisingly, they used cultural forms brought from Britain and Europe, such as novels, poetry, painting, sketching, and children's literature to explore their relationships to their new homes. The growth of the press over the nineteenth century provided settler colonists with a forum in which to discuss and debate both colonial affairs and their ties to imperial and international worlds. Different forms of popular culture, ranging from circuses to Shakespeare, circulated around imperial and colonial networks and circuits, linking settlers to the metropole as well as to other contexts (most notably the United States). Exhibitions—industrial, colonial, imperial, and international—allowed settler colonists to promote their societies' progress and imagine their future: they were also active in creating historical narratives and public forms of commemoration. Finally, participation in war, whether internal conflicts, the South African War, or World War I, also led to the creation of narratives, monuments, prose and poetry, and other forms of representation. These genres valourized the Dominions' participation in such conflicts; they also suggested that such experiences were not only important testimonies to imperial devotion and loyalty but also were part of the process of nation-building.

Yet the creation of such identities was not a neutral process, devoid of relationships of power. For one, it was profoundly gendered. Although white, middle-class women often were keen participants in many of these processes, their relationships to both nation and empire were frequently mediated through their capacity for motherhood, not through the "manly" independence claimed by white settler men. Class also is a complicated question here, since although there is evidence of working-class support for imperial and nationalistic ventures, working-class men and women often were excluded from the groups and processes that produced the most dominant narratives of empire and nation. While at times other Europeans, people of colour, and Indigenous people claimed a space for themselves and their histories in settler colonies, in general they were excluded from British settlers' imagined national and imperial communities.

## Settler Colonies and the British Monarchy

The British monarchy played an important role in settler identity throughout these colonies. However, feelings of connection to, let alone affection for, the institution could not be taken for granted. Representations of the Crown underwent a number of changes over the course of the nineteenth century, ones that culminated in large imperial celebrations of Queen Victoria in 1887 and 1897. However, long before these Jubilees, for some colonists the figure of George III served as an inspiration, one evoked to strengthen transatlantic ties of patriotism and loyal devotion. Such sentiments were clearly at work in Upper Canadian Anglican rector John Strachan's 1810 *Discourse on the Character of George the Third*. Written for the King's birthday, the *Discourse* celebrated the monarch for his personification of virtues both public and intimate. George was a good father to his people, as he ruled over them with solicitous and beneficent authority, and he also was a good husband and father to Queen Charlotte and their many children. Indeed, in Strachan's eyes the two roles were deeply intertwined. Of course, Strachan's *Discourse* was not only about the monarch. It was written by a member of an elite worried that the colony, itself established out of the upheaval of the American Revolution (1776–83), might succumb to the dangers of republicanism that lurked both south of the border and across the ocean in France. The reigning monarch, then, could remind Upper Canadians that their stability would be best secured by maintaining the imperial tie. Such warnings intensified as the colony was threatened by the spectre, and then the reality, of American invasion during the War of 1812.

Royal tours also became an important way of reminding colonists of their relationship to the Crown. In 1860, the Prince of Wales's tour of British America (he also travelled to the United States as a private citizen) was the first state visit: the 18-year-old prince was met with a great deal of enthusiasm and celebration. While the tour was not without its complications, as the Orange Order's determination to gain royal recognition was not welcomed by imperial authorities, nevertheless it was marked by numerous well-attended parades, receptions, and balls. Other royal visits followed. In 1868–69 the Prince's younger brother, Alfred, travelled to Australia where, as Figure 5.1 demonstrates, he received a (mostly) warm welcome. In 1901, after being urged by Prime Minister Lord Salisbury and Arthur Balfour, the Government Leader in the House of Commons, King Edward VII agreed to allow another royal tour, that of the Duke and Duchess of Cornwall and York. The future King George V and Queen Mary undertook the longest and one of the most costly royal tours. Their eight-month itinerary took them to Australia, Canada, New Zealand, and South Africa; it also included shorter stops in Aden, Gibraltar, Ceylon (Sri Lanka), Malta, Mauritius, and Singapore. The 1901 trip was touted by the media—which by that time included not just the press but also film—as being an event of great ceremonial significance. Royalists in the Dominions argued that it demonstrated the late Queen's desire to show her appreciation of their role in the South African War. Subsequent analysis of the 1901 tour, though, suggests that the event's overall tone was militaristic and jingoistic. In South Africa, for example, the royal visit helped shore up support for the Empire but it also was aimed at promoting South African identity, one that moderate Afrikaner nationalists could also share. Members of the royal family continued to visit Commonwealth countries well into the twentieth and twenty-first centuries. The 1939 tour of King George VI and Queen Elizabeth was the grandest and, perhaps, most notable of them; it was undertaken as a distraction from the miseries of the Depression and the threat of another world war.

Although accessible to a far smaller group of colonial subjects than royal tours, Victoria's Golden and Diamond Jubilees attracted those with the means and desire to travel to London. The Golden Jubilee, held in June 1887, drew hundreds of thousands of spectators from across Britain, Europe, the United States, and the colonies (similar events took place

FIGURE 5.1  "Welcome Alfred." The classical female figures seen here were common nineteenth-century representations of colonies and nation-states.

WELCOME ALFRED.

Source: *The Illustrated Sydney News*, 25 March 1868. National Library of Australia.

10 years later at the Diamond Jubilee). Colonial politicians and members of the military participated in the various public events surrounding the Jubilee, including parades and processions through London's streets. Not only might colonial visitors catch a glimpse of royalty at the Jubilee, they also had the opportunity to see and sometimes meet fellow "colonials." As well, the large number of souvenirs that were sold at both events, such as souvenir programs, biographies of Victoria, teacups, teapots, plates, spoons, and medals, made their way home across the ocean in colonial visitors' luggage, while companies that advertised around the Empire were eager to display the Queen's image on their products. Moreover, if George III was thought of by John Strachan as a benevolent husband and father, those who crafted Victoria's image in the late nineteenth century also focused on her morality and domesticity. "The dear, faded little mother ... Queen of our hearts" was one English-Canadian woman's impression of Victoria when she caught a glimpse of the Queen.[4] Victoria's image was very purposefully crafted to be that of a good woman who had experienced domestic bliss with her husband, Albert, only to be left a widow, charged with the care of a large family—not to mention an empire—at the age of 40.

The Jubilees occurred during a period of significant political debate over the Empire and its settler societies. During the 1870s British imperialists engaged in a discussion of the concept of "Greater Britain," an entity they imagined would unite the metropole and the colonies in one political community. Motivated by concerns over democratic political reforms in Britain and by fears of economic and political competition at the international level, metropolitan proponents of imperial federation pinned their hopes on a range of strategies, such as the creation of a cadre of imperial patriots who would then emigrate to Australia, Canada, New Zealand, and parts of South Africa. While there were different conceptions of Greater Britain—radical politician and writer Charles Dilke called for a recognition of the United States in it, while historian J.R. Seeley suggested that India could constitute a Greater Britain, separate from the settlement colonies—the majority of discussions focused on tying the settler colonies closer to Britain, thus creating an Anglo-Saxon polity. The movement for imperial federation resulted in the 1884 formation of the Imperial Federation League. Created in London, branches of the League also spread to Australia, Barbados, British Guiana, English Canada, and New Zealand.

In Canada, the League's membership consisted of urban, middle-class men drawn from the ranks of Protestant clergy, educators, intellectuals, and journalists. English-Canadian supporters of federation included the Conservative magistrate George T. Denison, who linked federation to the United Empire Loyalist legacy and declared the Loyalists to be the first imperialists. He was joined by George Grant, principal of Ontario's Queen's University, who saw British imperialism as a means of promoting global progress and moral uplift. George Parkin, the headmaster of Toronto's Upper Canada College (an elite all-male school), suggested in his 1892 book *Imperial Federation* that the Anglo-Saxon "race" was particularly well-suited for self-government and human progress—attributes that the Dominion government of the time believed were not within the reach of Indigenous or Asian communities within Canada. In the aftermath of the South African War, promoters of imperial federation in Britain included a number of prominent Liberal politicians and thinkers, a wide-ranging group whose interests also included various aspects of social reform. Their influence spread to Australia and, most notably, to Melbourne (at that time the federal capital), where a group of Liberal imperialists centred around prominent Australian politician Alfred Deakin. Deakin's circle discussed the possibilities of an imperial system that could develop into that of a commonwealth, presaging developments of the twentieth century. Others went even further. Journalist Leonard Biggs proposed a radical plan that involved the harmonization of pensions, industrial conditions, and immigration;

other members of this group supported tariff protection and a racially based exclusionary policy for immigration.

While those directly involved with the Imperial Federation League—not to mention the frequent Imperial Conferences held in London—were male, elite women also became involved in imperial promotion during the early twentieth century. Their political activity was not new, though. Such women had been members of female emigration societies and the Primrose League, an extra-parliamentary organization dedicated to promoting Conservative principles in Britain. The aftermath of the South African War saw the growth of female membership in groups such as the League of the Empire, the Navy League, and the Imperial Maritime League. The Victoria League, formed in 1901, was the sole imperial propaganda organization that was chiefly female, although it admitted male members. Spurred on by the contributions of Australia and Canada to the war, the Victoria League saw itself as an important linchpin that would bind the settler Dominions to Britain, a goal its members felt was critically important in the face of growing colonial nationalism. Many who joined the League had been to South Africa, either just before or after the war, and their experiences had convinced them of the need for renewed imperial sentiment around the Empire. The League organized charitable war work aimed at providing relief in South Africa and simultaneously anglicizing the new Dominion, imperial education (directed to children and the working class), hospitality for colonial visitors to Britain, the dissemination of literature and art to colonies, and social reform.

While influential, the Victoria League was by no means the first female imperial organization. In 1900 the Guild of Loyal Women of South Africa was created by elite colonial women who wished to play a public role in political life, specifically in the context of the war, without alienating their male counterparts with discussions of suffrage. The Guild called for closer ties between South Africa and the Empire, British supremacy throughout South Africa, and the preservation of the Cape as a British colony. Spreading across the Cape Colony, Natal, and the Orange River and Transvaal colonies, the Guild initially dedicated itself to maintaining war graves at sites such as Bloemfontein, Magersfontein, and Paardeberg. Its work led it to correspond with families in Britain and the colonies whose relatives had died in the war. In many ways it set an example for the post-World War I Commonwealth Graves Commission. As political union became more feasible in the aftermath of the South African War, the Guild also began to approach the question of reconciliation. Instead of depicting the Boers as enemies, the Guild represented them as sharing British colonists' history of fighting for civilization and freedom. Its members also embarked on a program of political education that, although it still steered clear of the contentious issue of woman's suffrage, encouraged all white South African women to think of themselves as loyal citizens. Despite its rhetoric of unity in a new South Africa, the Guild did not succeed in attracting Afrikaner women; it also had little to say about black women's involvement in either its activities or in South Africa in general. By March 1911, the Guild decided to hand its work over to a newly formed South African Victoria League.

The Guild was encouraged and supported by other colonial women's organizations, most notably in Canada. In 1900 the Federation of Daughters of the British Empire was founded in Montreal by Margaret Clark Murray, a journalist and philanthropist. Like the women involved in the Victoria League, Murray had visited South Africa and was motivated by a similar sentiment to bring British women around the Empire together. She hoped to found an Empire-wide organization but was thwarted by the Victoria League, which demanded that she restrict her work to Canada. The organization, renamed Imperial Order Daughters of the Empire (IODE), moved to Toronto in 1901; while chapters were formed in the Bahamas, Bermuda, India, Newfoundland, and the United States, its greatest success was in Canada, particularly in Ontario. Adopting the motto "One flag, one throne, one Empire" and dedicating itself to promoting patriotism, imperial unity among women and children, charitable work for military dependents, and commemoration, the IODE saw its greatest growth during World War I, with a membership of 50,000. Similar organizations were founded in Australia and New Zealand; independent branches of the Victoria League appeared in Tasmania in 1903 and in Otago in 1905. While in many ways the work of these Leagues resembled the goals and activities of the British organization and the IODE, New Zealand's League was notable for the presence of Māori women, since Indigenous women in Canada and Australia were not included in such groups.

While support for the Crown was often strong, not all settlers believed that Victoria, the monarchy, and the imperial tie were desirable. Throughout the nineteenth century some colonists saw the Crown as a hindrance to settler democracy. In the 1837 Rebellion in the Canadas, reformers in both provinces impugned the Queen's virtue and portrayed her as being indifferent to her subjects' suffering at the hands of colonial governments. At times attacks took a more direct, physical form. During his 1868 tour of Australia, Prince Alfred was shot in the back by a would-be Fenian agent,

Henry James O'Farrell. Although the wound was a minor one, the assassination attempt shocked the prince's colonial hosts, and the rest of Alfred's travels in the Antipodes were cancelled (the tour took in the Cape of Good Hope, India, and New Zealand). While this was an extreme and, insofar as the monarchy's reception in the colonies was concerned, rare example of physical opposition to the Crown, a range of attitudes toward the monarch existed. In discussions about imperial federation and realignments of colonies' relationships to Britain, British intellectuals and politicians, for example, believed that the monarchy as an institution could be a significant representation of continuity and tradition. They saw Victoria as an important symbol that would bind the metropole and settler societies more tightly.

In mid-nineteenth-century Australia, where the influence of British radical movements, such as the Chartists, was strong, the Queen was claimed as an icon of popular constitutionalism, liberty, and opposition to injustice and despotism. The 1880s and 1890s saw a surge of republican attacks on the monarchy; it was perceived as representing corruption and class privilege and being a parasitical drain on the public purse, sentiments that also were expressed in Britain. By the end of the 1890s, however, the weakening of Australian republicanism meant these attitudes became muted in favour of more pragmatic acceptance of the monarchy. They were not eradicated, as Labor figures who were either locally born or came from Ireland continued to disparage the Crown. They called, for example, for coins to be minted in Australia and demanded that postage stamps feature Australia's name more clearly; they also denounced imperialism, militarism, and global capital's desire for cheap labour. In particular, the Dominion's labour press castigated Britain for not being honest about its reasons for waging war in South Africa; the press believed that the metropole only wished to extract the colony's resources using poorly paid African workers.

In other colonies, settlers who were not British held attitudes toward the Crown and the Empire in general that were either nuanced or ambivalent. For the most part, other European immigrants in Canada's western provinces did not demonstrate outright hostility toward the monarchy. They did express strong and continuing ties to their homelands, marking the landscapes in which they settled with names, particularly of churches, that reminded them of places left behind in Eastern Europe. French Canada was a somewhat different matter. As a result of a number of historical developments, such as the relative weakness of British colonial institutions in Lower Canada, the persistence of the French language, and the great deal of autonomy enjoyed by the Catholic church in the colony, French Canadians were able to deploy the link to Britain and the Crown in ways that helped them integrate—but not assimilate—into English Canada. While a small number of elite families were Anglophiles, the British Empire and the Crown did not hold the same cultural meaning for French Canadians as they did for their counterparts in English Canada. The latter's route to higher education in Britain, which often meant Oxford or Cambridge, was not one chosen by many French Canadians. Nor did they occupy high ranks in the military or (for the most part) serve as imperial administrators in other parts of the Empire. When such French Canadians looked outside of Canada for cultural links and ties, they tended to focus on France.

Indigenous peoples' perspectives on the monarchy were no less a product of their historical relationships with colonial and imperial governments. In British America, Indigenous nations' roles as military allies and trading partners, coupled with the Royal Proclamation of 1763, led to Indigenous perceptions of a relationship to the Crown that was greater than that of dependent subjects, a belief and political stance that would persist over time. At times the Dominion government invoked the Crown in its negotiations with Indigenous people; it claimed to represent the Queen directly, its actions and words following her express instructions. During the negotiations for Treaty 6 at Fort Carlton in Saskatchewan, for example, Lieutenant-Governor Alexander Morris stated that all parties involved were the Queen's children. In turn, Aboriginal negotiators also invoked kinship ties, depicting Victoria as their mother from whom they expected generosity and support. Moreover, in the face of settler encroachments on their lands and resources and settler governments' desire to assimilate Indigenous people, Indigenous nations turned to the Crown for support, travelling to provincial capitals, to Ottawa, and, at times, to London to ask the imperial government's representatives to intervene on their behalf. These visits had a long history: members of the Haudenosaunee confederacy had travelled to London in 1710, appearing at Queen Anne's court in an attempt to forge an alliance between their people and England. The "Four Indian Kings," as they were (incorrectly) known, were followed by other Haudenosaunee members: Joseph Brant in the 1770s and 1780s and his protegé, Haudenosaunee adoptee John Norton, in 1804. Over the course of the nineteenth century and into the twentieth, Indigenous leaders from a range of other communities met with the Crown in attempts to resolve problems with land and resources encountered at the hands of settler governments. Their numbers included Joseph Brant's son John Brant (1821–22), Mississauga Kahkewaquonaby/Peter Jones (1837–38),

Mississauga Nahnebahwequa/Catherine Sutton in 1860 (se Figure 5.2) and, in 1906, British Columbia chiefs Charlie Isipaymilt (Cowichan), Joseph Capilano (Squamish), and Basil David (Shuswap), accompanied by Stó:lõ interpreter Simon Pierre. Although such visits met with varying degrees of success—John Brant was unable to resolve Haudenosaunee land claims, while Nahnebahwequa's appeal for the return of her lands was granted—Indigenous people continued to remind the Crown of its historical promises to their communities when settler governments broke those promises.

Māori people also travelled to Britain and met with the monarch. Earlier in the nineteenth century these visits occurred as part of more general travels to England and did not raise political questions about colonial governance. However, beginning in 1882 Māori leaders, supported by the Aborigines' Friend Society, petitioned Victoria and sought audiences with her in order to redress a raft of grievances. Unlike Indigenous petitioners from Canada, they were thwarted by imperial officials and returned to New Zealand without having met the Queen in person. In 1914 Māori King Te Rahata was able to meet with King George V and Queen Mary. Despite it being the first meeting between Māori and British royalty, imperial authorities forbade Te Rahata from presenting his peoples' grievances to the British monarch.

**FIGURE 5.2** Nahnebahwequa/Catherine Sutton, c. mid-1860s

Source: Image courtesy of the Grey Roots Archival Collections, Owen Sound, Ontario.

In South Africa, Indigenous chiefs met the Duke of Cornwall during the latter's 1901 tour. Lerothodi, principal chief of the Basutos, was presented to the Duke because of his aid to the British during the South African War. As well, Natal's Indian and coloured communities addressed the Duke, praising the British Crown's commitment to "'impartial and enlightened government'" and expressing their "'confidence'" that a "'happy reign of justice, equality, and freedom'" would prevail "'throughout the length and breadth of [the] vast territory of South Africa.'"[5] The coloured community at the Cape, however, was somewhat more pessimistic in their evaluation of their situation. They told Lord Milner, the Crown's representative, that they viewed "'with much sorrow and grave apprehension the efforts being made in certain quarters to enact laws, which are inimical to our welfare.'"[6] Although they perceived Milner as a "'staunch friend,'"[7] their hopes would be dashed when Milner approved segregation and, overall, was not much interested in securing their hoped-for equality, justice, and freedom in post-war South Africa.

## Culture in Settler Societies

It was not just settlers' relationships to the Crown that played a role in shaping a sense of self, one both linked to and, over time, distinct from that of the metropole. Settlers brought multiple forms of cultural genres and representations with them, such as visual art, fiction, poetry, and drama, all of which they used to create representations of the colonies from the late eighteenth century on. At times first impressions of new landscapes placed Indigenous people at the centre of the images. Indigenous Australians' resistance to Captain Cook's 1770 landing at Botany Bay, for example, was recorded by the voyage's artist, Sydney Parkinson; his sketch of two "warriors" was then repeated in a number of Australian paintings throughout the nineteenth century. Perhaps one of the best-known Indigenous figures to be painted during the early years of contact was that of Mathinna, a young Indigenous girl who had been taken into Lady Jane Franklin's care at Government House in Van Diemen's Land. This skilled and empathetic portrait, commissioned in 1842 by Lady Franklin and created by convict artist Thomas Bock, helped spark a number of stories. They carried a range of meanings about childhood and Indigenous peoples' relationships to settler Australians, ones that are still being told today.

As well as creating portraits and sketches of Indigenous people, amateur artists in Australia struggled to depict a landscape that not only was very different from European scenery but that also displayed, in very short order, signs of Europeans' destruction of it. In contrast, professional artists tended to focus on established settlements, creating representations of colonies that demonstrated signs of order, hierarchy, and commercial development. By the 1880s and 1890s, a group of painters based in Melbourne was creating paintings of rural Australian landscapes. Inspired by European Impressionism, this Heidelberg School (its name taken from the Heidelberg area east of Melbourne painted by many of these artists) sought to evoke and recreate the intense, often harsh light of that part of Australia. Their paintings, along with the short stories of Henry Lawson and the folk ballads of Banjo Paterson, were seen by cultural commentators and critics as constituting an "authentic" Australian culture. At the Cape, painters at first tried to make the unfamiliar landscape familiar, turning the terrain of Africa into the Scottish or Cornish countryside. However, over time they began to recognize the beauty of the colony and to emphasize its specificity. This development was probably shaped by the influence of surveyors and naturalists who also were rendering very detailed documentation of the Cape's topography.

In British America, a range of both professional and amateur artists—the latter included those military officers sent as surveyors and mapmakers—depicted Indigenous people in their drawings and paintings, either in their own communities or as part of the colonies' markets and streetscapes. They also recorded their visual impressions of the landscape. From 1791 to 1796 Elizabeth Simcoe, the wife of Lieutenant-Governor John Graves Simcoe, kept a diary that detailed her travel across the Atlantic to, first, Quebec and then Upper Canada. She also recorded her impressions of the landscape and people in the form of watercolours and sketches, ones that provide some of the earliest European representations of the new colony. In Lower Canada, Cornelius Krieghoff, who was born in Holland and moved to Montreal and then Quebec City via the United States, specialized in scenes of daily life among the province's *habitant* communities. He also was known for his paintings of Indigenous people, most notably from the Kahnawake reserve near Montreal. While Krieghoff's choice of subject matter was not initially to the taste of those commercial elites who bought art—they preferred paintings of English horses, for example—by the 1860s his work became popular with British officers searching for souvenirs of their time in Lower Canada. In 1893 English-Canadian critic John-George Bourinot heralded Krieghoff as the first painter to recognize the aesthetic value of Canadian scenes. However, other settlers attempted to impose their own conceptions of landscape on the places they recorded, replicating, for example, the English countryside in their paintings of Lower Canadian seigneuries and ignoring those elements—such as habitant farms and pine trees—that differed from it. Another artistic genre, though, became popular in French Canada, that of the historical painting (it was not, of course, a new form of art or unique to Lower Canada). Artists such as Théophile Hamel (1817–70), Joseph Légaré (1795–1855), and Antoine Plamondon (1804–95) painted events such as the deaths of Jesuit priests Jean Brébeuf and Gabriel Lalement, the "massacre" of the Hurons by the Iroquois, Jacques Cartier's meeting with the Stadaconans, and the battle of Sainte-Foy. These paintings demonstrated that the province's urban middle class had a taste for its history; they also provided a basis for the late nineteenth-century historical paintings that would become very popular in Quebec. Such art created a pantheon of heroism, both secular and sacred.

As well as art, settlers also turned to the written word to express their thoughts, hopes, and fears about their new homes. While, as Chapter 4 points out, settlers' literary tastes had been shaped by British genres and forms, from a relatively early period colonial authors also began to publish fiction set in their new homes. In the case of Henry Savery, transported from Bristol to Van Diemen's Land for forgery, such fiction was highly autobiographical. Savery's *Quintus Servinton: A Tale Founded upon Incidents of Real Occurrence* (1830) recounted many of the events of Savery's journey from England to Hobart. Published in Tasmania, his novel was followed by popular works such as Marcus Clarke's *For the Term of His Natural Life* (1874), and Joseph Furphy's *Tom Collins*. These and other novels were set in both the penal colonies and early rural settlements. Australian women novelists also placed their work in the colony; in 1838 Anna Maria Murray Bunn published her Gothic romance, *The Guardian: A Tale*, in Sydney. Others followed: Catherine Spence, Matilda Evans, and Catherine Martin published work between the 1850s and the early 1920s that explored a range of themes about Australia, including the gold rush and the situation of Aboriginal people, particularly Aboriginal mothers.

British American writers, influenced by Walter Scott's historical romances of eighteenth-century Scotland, turned to the historical novel. Niagara-born John Richardson, a major in the British army who had served in the War of 1812, Europe, and the West Indies, published a number of such works: 1832's *Wacousta*, a story of the Odawa chief Pontiac's 1763 uprising on the Detroit frontier and, in 1840, *The Canadian Brothers; or, the Prophecy*

*Fulfilled*, which explored the War of 1812 from a Canadian perspective. Other writers addressed eighteenth-century colonial history through the genre of historical romance. Eliza Lanesford Foster, for example, originally from Massachusetts, wrote historical romances of the American Revolution (*Saratoga* and *Yorktown*) before moving to Montreal in 1840 with her husband, Dr. Frederick Cushing. Between 1838 and 1851, she wrote short stories, poetry, and historical romances for the magazine *Literary Garland of Montreal* (she also became its editor), as well as articles for magazines in the United States. The best-known female Canadian historical novelist, though, was Rosanna Eleanora Mullins Leprohon. Born in Montreal in 1829, Leprohon first wrote poetry inspired by religious, domestic, and Canadian themes, as well as a small number of poems that featured Aboriginal Canadians. Published between 1859 and 1868, Leprohon's historical novels dealt primarily with the domestic and romantic lives of French and English Canadians before or just following the Conquest. Her work attempted to resolve historical conflicts between the "two nations" by explaining the feelings and intentions of each to the other.

Proximity to the rapidly growing American market and the need to be published in either London or New York made earning a living a struggle for Canadian writers. Nevertheless, during the early twentieth century a number of writers—L.M. Montgomery, Sara Jeanette Duncan, Stephen Leacock, Marshall Saunders, to name a few—published work that was set in Canada and recognizable to a number of English-Canadians, whether the place was Montgomery's Cavendish (Prince Edward Island), Duncan's Brantford, Leacock's Orillia, or Saunders's Halifax. These authors also engaged with questions that their Canadian contemporaries might recognize, whether they be the foibles of small-town Ontario, adoption in the Maritimes, or the question of imperial federation. Duncan also published *Cousin Cinderella, or, a Canadian Girl in London*, which dealt quite explicitly with the metropolitan experiences of two English-Canadian "colonials" navigating upper-middle-class English society (a number of Duncan's other novels were set in India, where she met her husband and lived from 1894 to 1897).

Literature for children, whether published in the format of novels, magazine and newspaper articles, or didactic religious material, also told its readers many stories about their respective homes and their location within the British world of imperial expansion. Some of this material fell within the genre of adventure stories, ones that featured brave deeds (primarily by boys but, in a few cases, girls) that took place in remote bush or frontier settings. Such tales might also feature Indigenous people, who played the role of either threatening or exotic others over whom white children might exercise moral, intellectual, and cultural superiority. Missionary publications, both the religious press and books aimed at children and youth, told white children in settler societies about their membership in the wider world of the Empire with stories about the heroism and dedication of figures such as David Livingstone or the benefits of Christianity for children in Africa, China, and India. In late nineteenth- and early twentieth-century Australia and New Zealand, missionary and Sunday School publications also became increasingly focused on teaching children about the Pacific world and missionaries' work in places such as Fiji, New Guinea, Samoa, Tonga, and the Torres Strait. At times, though, missionary writers also set their work in settler societies. Eliza Jones, wife of the Indigenous Methodist missionary Kahkewaquonaby/Peter Jones, told the story of the inspirational life and death of her niece, Elizabeth Jones, in her 1838 *Memoir of Elizabeth Jones a Little Indian Girl Who Lived at the River-Credit Mission, Upper Canada*. Although marked by the images and tropes of the period's religious writing, not least the need to be prepared for an unexpected death, Jones's short book differed from those of her contemporaries. Elizabeth was not an anonymous or generic "heathen" child converted to Christianity: instead, she had a very specific family history and identity and was herself both pious and intelligent, a quick learner of lessons both sacred and secular.

Fictional representations of settler colonies also were crafted in the metropole. A number of British writers set their tales of imperial expansion and adventure in Australia, Canada, and South Africa. An early example, Mrs. R. Lee's 1851 *Adventures in Australia; or the Wanderings of Captain Spencer in the Bush and the Wilds*, was written by an Englishwoman, Sarah Wallis, who did not visit Australia (although she travelled to parts of Africa). *Adventures in Australia* went through three printings in London, was republished in the United States under a slightly different title, and was reviewed in the Hobart and Sydney newspapers. South Africa particularly fascinated those British authors who published stories of romance and imperial adventure in the colony. Their numbers included writers of juvenile fiction, such as Bessie Merchant, G.A. Henty, W.G.A. Kingston, and Mary Wynne, who—like Mrs. Lee—did not venture there. In contrast, John Buchan and H. Rider Haggard, whose novels included the well-known *Prester John*, *King Solomon's Mines*, and *She*, were government administrators. Their books differed in their depictions of the imperial government's role vis-à-vis Indigenous South Africans, though. *King Solomon's Mines* portrays the imperial authorities assisting the "true" Zulu king to take his kingdom from a usurper. In contrast, *Prester John*'s main character, a university-educated and ordained Zulu minister Reverend Laputa, attempts to overthrow British rule and is driven by his failure to commit suicide. Nevertheless, theirs' and other, similar novels, written during a period of large-scale expansion of industrial mining, depicted South Africa for both international and local audiences as a place in which fortunes could be made by white men with sufficient pluck and ambition, not to mention the will and ability to dominate the local Indigenous population.

A number of late-Victorian and Edwardian English authors—Martin Allerdale Grainger, John Mackie, and Argyll Saxby—chose the Canadian west as a place in which their middle-class British heroes could maintain their gentlemanly status while simultaneously performing manual labour. Such a feat helped address British concerns about such men, as social commentators in the metropole grappled with anxieties about their physical, social, and cultural status; by 1913 middle-class men were emigrating to Canada in ever-growing numbers. These books were first published in London for British readers; if they sold well, they then would find an audience in Toronto or New York.

Colonial newspapers also played their part in helping to create settler societies' sense of self and connections to a number of worlds. Not only did they print fiction that ranged from Dickens's serialized novels to home-grown tales of the colonies: in historian Benedict Anderson's famous phrase, they also helped shape "imagined communities." In the newspapers, settlers were invited to think of themselves as members of the same colonial community, as they pored over accounts of colonial legislative debates, agricultural product prices, and the social and cultural goings-on in their areas (the times of church services or the opening of a new school, hospital, or asylum). Such articles created opportunities for settlers—even if they were geographically removed from the places discussed—to make connections with other members of their society. The newspapers' coverage of imperial developments, whether those that took place in the metropole (the death of a monarch, for example, or the discussions underway at an imperial conference) or in other colonies (the 1857 Indian Uprising, the South African War) also helped contribute to settlers' sense of belonging to a widespread imperial community. Being aware of how the latter would perceive them might influence the way in which the settler press represented colonial developments, particularly where settler-Indigenous relationships were concerned. During the 1860 Taranaki War in New Zealand, for example, Auckland politician and newspaper editor Hugh Carleton consistently downplayed settlers' anxiety about Māori violence and characterized settlers as being sympathetic and displaying a humanitarian attitude toward the Māori in the pages of his newspaper, *Southern Cross*. Mindful of the paper's circulation in Britain and being an advocate for responsible government, Cameron wished to paint a portrait of New Zealand settler society that would not raise metropolitan concerns. In South Africa, British journalists' fascination with the colony in the 1870s was observed by newspaper editors at the Cape. The metropole's interest in "South Africa" prompted editors in Cape Town to start deploying the term themselves, even if its meaning was ambiguous.

As well as mainstream secular publications, edited and published by white, male middle-class politicians and journalists, the colonial press also included religious newspapers and those of various ethnic and racial groups. During the 1850s, for example, African Canadians in southern Ontario founded newspapers—*The Voice of the Fugitive* and *Provincial Freedman*—which called attention to the situation of former slaves in the province and demanded an end to slavery. Both newspapers are also notable because of the role of prominent African-Canadian women Mary Bibb and Mary Ann Shadd in their founding and publication. While publishing was a difficult endeavour for Indigenous people, given their lack of access to capital and control by agents and Protectors, a few managed to do so. Motivated by a desire to promote political participation among his fellow-Mississauga and to overcome their isolation in the face of the Canadian government's Indian Act, which had confined people to their reserves, Peter Edmund Jones, a medical doctor and the son of Mississauga Methodist missionary Kahkewaquonaby/Peter Jones, founded *The Indian* in 1885. Although short-lived—lasting only one year—the newspaper represented an attempt to create political solidarity within a number of southern Ontario's Indigenous communities, who had been recently (although temporarily) enfranchised by the Conservative government. Simultaneously, newspapers appeared in the Cape and Natal, founded by educated Africans who were also active in setting up independent black churches and political organizations. Not unlike Jones, they feared the racially charged challenges that were being mounted to the (admittedly limited) liberalism of the Cape and sought ways to protect themselves. Moreover, European communities in settler colonies also established their own press, both as a way of maintaining languages such as German—the German-language press was a distinct presence in nineteenth-century southern Ontario, for instance—and preserving links to homelands in Europe. The existence of newspapers published from spe-cifically Irish or Welsh perspectives and, in the latter's case, in the Welsh language in British America or Australia reminds us that the category "British" was more complicated and heterogeneous than historians some-times assume.

While newspapers catered to a literate public in these societies (which, by the late nineteenth century, included the vast majority of their English-speaking population), other forms of metropolitan and transnational culture also linked settler colonies. Travelling theatre troupes, circuses, compa-nies of musicians, popular lecturers, and other forms of performance and entertainment circulated around the nineteenth-century British Empire. In some cases, British imperial institutions were directly involved in spreading cultural genres and forms. Military garrisons stationed in British America, India, and New South Wales performed some of the earliest amateur theatre witnessed by settler audiences in their new homes, productions that often featured Shakespeare and other English playwrights' work. Moreover, the transatlantic and imperial circuits and networks discussed in Chapter 3, which helped the flow of technology and economic exchange, also brought commercial entertainers to a number of British colonies. Theatre compa-nies, for example, travelled from Britain to British America and the United States, resuming transatlantic circuits that had been interrupted by the American Revolution and the Napoleonic Wars. The development of mass entertainment in the urban northeastern United States, particularly in New York City, also extended into cities such as Halifax, Montreal, Saint John, and Toronto; mid-nineteenth-century railway lines in British America made it possible for a range of performers to reach smaller cities and towns. Such troupes included blackface minstrel shows, a popular entertainment that had originated in the northeastern United States and that involved white performers, their faces blackened, depicting African Americans and their culture in mocking and derogatory ways. Despite the protests of black community members—Toronto's African Canadians, for example, peti-tioned local government to prevent such performances from appearing in the city—this entertainment spread into British America and, by the late nineteenth century, across the Atlantic to Britain.

Over the course of the century, as steamship journeys became more frequent, cheaper, and faster, it became easier for metropolitan culture to reach not just North America but also Australasia. The tour of the paint-ing *Derby Day*, by the English Royal Academician William Powell Frith, suggests the various ways in which British culture circulated and took on particular meanings for a range of colonial audiences. Painted between 1856 and 1858, *Derby Day* depicts a wide spectrum of mid-Victorian society, one that includes men, women, and children, gathered for the Epsom Derby race; it was viewed by Queen Victoria and Prince Albert when it was first shown at the Royal Academy in 1858. Organized by the London art dealer and publisher Ernest Gambart in conjunction with his commercial agent William Shields, from 1865 to 1866 *Derby Day* toured Australia and was shown in Melbourne, New South Wales, South Australia, and Tasmania; in Melbourne it appeared at Victoria's National Gallery alongside an exhibition of European oil paintings. *Derby Day* was viewed by those middle-class Australians who saw themselves as cultural gatekeepers of refined British taste and was heralded as representing Melbourne's ascension to the status of a modern, progressive centre of culture. However, it also received a warm welcome in the gold-rush town of Ballarat, where it arrived via train from Melbourne. The local press saw *Derby Day*'s exhibition in Ballarat as emblematic of the town's enterprising and modern nature. The painting received similar accolades in other Australian cities throughout its tour. *Derby Day* did not inspire colonial artists to emulate Frith's style: for one, those who chose horse racing (by the 1840s a popular form of leisure in the Australian colonies) as their subject focused on elites, not Frith's wide swathe of social classes. Moreover, only a few decades later Australian artists turned to the continent's landscapes, less so Frith's form of narrative style, for their inspiration. Nevertheless, the success of *Derby Day*'s tour suggests yet another way in which colonial audiences were linked to Britain through the medium of visual spectacle.

Places like Ballarat also played a role in other forms of cultural circulation. For performers, the mid-nineteenth-century gold rushes of California, Victoria, and Otago were a powerful inducement to expand the range of territory covered by their tours. George Coppin, for example, seen as the "father" of modern Australian commercial theatre, took advantage of the greater economic opportunities offered by miners with money to spend on entertainment to bring the prominent English actor G. V. Brooke to Australia; Coppin followed his success with Brooke with other theatrical "imports" from the metropole. With the opening of the Suez Canal in 1869 and the completion of the American transcontinental railroad, the Australian colonies were linked to a global theatrical circuit of British actors who appeared before audiences in not just Australia and North America but also Burma, Cairo, China, India, and New Zealand. In the 1870s, as Australia became increasingly part of a Pacific world tied to the United States, it became a major centre for theatrical networks in the Pacific and Indian Oceans that brought American and British performers to the Sydney and Melbourne theatres. In particular, the American-born actor, producer, and manager J.C. Williamson, who settled in Australia with his wife, the actor Maggie Moore, brought international theatrical stars to Australasia and New Zealand, a list that included Canadian-born actor Margaret Anglin. This cultural traffic was not one way, though. A number of white Australians, including many women, travelled to Britain for training in music, acting, and painting, as well as to launch literary careers. The growth of silent film in the early twentieth century also drew actors from both Canada and Australia to the New York City studios of Vitagraph, Biograph, and Thanhouser and then increasingly to Hollywood. Performers such as Mary Pickford, Enid Bennett, Nance O'Neil, Marie Dressler, and Judith Anderson built careers based on mid-nineteenth-century imperial and transnational links.

## Envisioning Settlers' Futures

Conceptions of a glowing and prosperous future, whether that of a "better Britain" or of a promised settler nationalism (or a combination of both), were also important aspects of settlers' identities. These projections of better tomorrows took place in myriad ways. Children, for example, particularly those of British descent, were seen as the bedrock on which settler societies would grow and flourish. Their presence at ceremonies such as the dedication of historical monuments or at Empire Day, an annual celebration of Queen Victoria's birthday created in 1899 by Canadian nationalist and imperialist Clementina Fessenden, was a means of affirming the bright future of settler societies. Organizations such as the Boy Scouts and Girl Guides also promised to mould both British and white settler children into patriotic imperial subjects. The Scouts, formed in 1908 during the aftermath of the South African War by British military officer Robert Baden-Powell, were intended to encourage discipline, loyalty, obedience, and a love of the outdoors in young boys. In urban centres, the Scouts were seen by parents and educators as an antidote to perceived problems of industrialization and urbanization, processes that were removing children (particularly boys) from nature and contributing to boys' effeminacy. Less militaristic than the Scouts, the Guides were formed one year later by Agnes Baden-Powell, Robert's sister, to develop patriotism and provide opportunities for girls to develop a love of the outdoors and be physically active. Over time both the Scouts and Guides would expand their membership, as branches were formed in other colonies (India, for example) and within Indigenous communities in Canada.

As the case of New Zealand suggests, at times the concept of the future was taken even further. New Zealand was frequently framed as a utopia. Nineteenth-century leaders of colonization projects, individual settlers, writers of fiction, and a range of social, economic, and political movements used images of New Zealand as Eden, a land of promise, a middle-class paradise, and "God's own country" to symbolize their hopes and dreams for the colony. No doubt its Māori residents would have seen the colony as having a somewhat different historical trajectory, as settlers' conceptions of Indigenous peoples' future were frequently framed in terms of the assimilation of a dying race.

Future-oriented settler nationalism—while forged within the context of the British Empire—also was expressed through the creation of certain figures who embodied a specific Dominion's ideal qualities, ones synonymous with a newness that would reinvigorate its residents. In the case of Australia and New Zealand, the archetype of the male "Digger" came to represent the Dominions' military contributions in the South African War and World War I, not least because many soldiers had been former miners and their wartime work involved constructing trenches. The term also bore connotations of egalitarianism, male friendship, and loyalty to one's countrymen. In English Canada, the figure of "Miss Canada" appeared in political cartoons of the 1880s, representing a new and virtuous nation being courted by the much older (and far less virtuous) "Uncle Sam," with her mother Britannia offering wise counsel and protection against Uncle Sam's advances. Her male counterpart "Johnny Canuck" became popular even earlier, making his appearances in political cartoons published just after Confederation in 1867. Often depicted as a hardy, wholesome, and vigorous representative of Canada's resource-based economy (as a *habitant*, farmer, logger, or soldier), for 30 years Johnny Canuck was shown resisting the bullying and blandishments of both the United States and Britain, thus embodying a new form of settler nationalism.

Agricultural, industrial, and imperial exhibitions also celebrated settler societies' achievements and future progress. The display of agricultural goods had a lengthy history, being rooted in medieval fairs and market days. Industrial exhibitions' history could be traced to displays mounted in the 1750s and 1760s by London's Society for the Advancement of Arts, Manufacturers and Commerce, as well as similar shows in late eighteenth-century France. Agricultural societies found a home in late eighteenth- and early nineteenth-century British America, their spread motivated by elite concerns about the state of agricultural production in the colonies and by their desire to bolster their own status as progressive "improvers" and educators. By mid-century, though, these exhibitions of crops, livestock, and other forms of material culture had become more democratic; as well, increasing commercialization and the growth of popular culture resulted in displays that focused on entertaining the public as much as educating them. London's Crystal Palace Exhibition of 1851, though, was a turning point in industrial exhibitions. This large display of commercial and industrial prowess inspired similar exhibitions across western Europe and was imitated in a number of British and European colonies. In Australasia, cities such as Sydney (1870 and 1879) and Melbourne (1880 and 1888) used both the Crystal Palace and subsequent displays in Paris, Vienna, and Philadelphia as a model for demonstrating their economic accomplishments, ones that— at least for the exhibitors—symbolized their international stature among modern nations. These exhibitions were copied in smaller centres, such as Adelaide, Christchurch, Dunedin, Hobart, and Perth. In Toronto, the city's Industrial Exhibition, founded in 1879, followed a similar path. Its displays of butter, cheese, cattle, and horses boasted of the province's agricultural prosperity, while demonstrations of new forms of technology (sometimes in the form of agricultural machinery) helped the province's residents to marvel and, ultimately, congratulate themselves on their achievements.

Exhibitions thus told settlers about the advance of "civilization" in their respective societies. Such a narrative was frequently underscored by representations of Indigenous people, whose craftwork was presented as emblematic of the benefits of missionary and state education. In Brisbane, for example, and in other exhibits in Queensland in 1912, a range of crafts and material goods created by Indigenous children in mission schools (samplers, schoolwork, baking, and carving) were set up in "Aboriginal courts." In other contexts, particularly international and imperial exhibitions, Indigenous people might also appear as living ethnographic displays. While missionaries and colonial officials might prefer they demonstrate their "civilized" state, on occasion Indigenous people seized the opportunity to display their own cultures. Much to the dismay of their Indian agent, the northwestern Pacific coast's Kwa'kwaka'waw, who appeared at Chicago's 1893 Columbian Exposition, performed a number of dances that the Dominion government had decided were "primitive" and should be suppressed. Moreover, despite the central buildings' emphasis on order, progress, and rationality, the commercial midways that appeared alongside the main buildings catered to visitors' desire for amusements and thrills that were as much carnivalesque as they were educational. At the midway, audiences might be titillated by Orientalist spectacles of "dancing girls," "freak shows" that featured a range of human disabilities, and displays of so-called primitive people, such as African pygmies or South Sea "savages."

### Celebrating the Past: Settler Histories

Although visions of bright futures stirred settlers' imaginations, they also wished to create narratives of their pasts. At a relatively early period, colonial histories became a popular genre in settler colonies. These accounts frequently included detailed descriptions of colonial topographies and natural histories, as well as narratives of exploration and settlement; they were often aimed at attracting metropolitan investment and providing information for prospective migrants. Watkins Tench, a marine captain on the First Fleet that arrived in Sydney in 1788, wrote about the settlement of Sydney; his work was followed in 1819 by William Wentworth's *A Statistical, Historical, and Political Description of the Colony of New South Wales*. Like many historians of the nineteenth century, Wentworth held multiple roles, those of poet, explorer, journalist, and politician. In British America from the mid-eighteenth century on, colonists of British, Anglo-American, and European origin engaged in highly visible and publicly debated attempts to create a "past" for their communities. Promoters of emigration, journalists, lawyers, and political leaders wrote histories of the Maritime colonies, Lower and Upper Canada, the northwestern Pacific coast, and Vancouver Island that served a range of purposes. They were meant to attract emigrants, mend internal political divisions, celebrate the perceived triumph of British institutions and values, and (particularly in the case of British Columbia) create a British past in an area disputed by Britain and the United States.

By the late nineteenth century, colonial histories became increasingly popular among the white middle class across the settler world. Although a number of historical societies were founded earlier in the nineteenth century—the Literary and Historical Society of Quebec, for example, was established in 1824—from the 1880s on historical organizations were founded in both French and English Canada. They were particularly popular in the Maritimes, Quebec, and Ontario. In some cases the commemoration of certain events, such as the 200th anniversary of the Loyalists' arrival, led to the formation of groups such as the United Empire Loyalist Association, devoted to preserving and celebrating their ancestors' genealogy and history. Forging the Loyalist "myth," as late twentieth-century historians have dubbed it, involved creating a narrative of an elite group of settlers whose dedication to the imperial tie forced them to leave their homeland in the new republic; their superior virtue and preservation of political and social order were the building blocks of Canada. While also interested in the story of the Loyalists, other English-Canadian societies focused on the War of 1812 as an important moment in settlers' demonstration of loyalty to Britain, or on the valuable contributions of pioneers in creating a stable and "settled" society. In the case of French Canada, the golden age of New France was the subject of many avocational and popular histories and was an important part of ethnic, linguistic, and religious identity. Figures such as the explorers Jacques Cartier and Samuel de Champlain, the fur trader and "defender" of the colony Dollard des Ormeaux, and religious leaders such as Bishop Laval or Marie de l'Incarnation were constructed as the "founding fathers" (and at times mothers) responsible for the establishment of a French, Catholic culture that, despite the conquest of 1759, persisted into the late nineteenth century. Historical narratives were thus used to help bolster a range of national and imperial sentiments.

A similar phenomenon occurred in Australia. Although the Historical Society of Australasia was short-lived (1885–86), the years after Federation (1901) saw both national and state historical societies spring up; they also were founded in a number of smaller cities and towns such as Manly, Newcastle, and Paramatta. At the state level, the historical societies were both founded and run by professional male elites, in conjunction with avocational historians, a few university professors of history, and settler descendants. The histories they wrote and the pasts they commemorated were narratives of progress and stability and tended toward antiquarianism; moreover, the Australian past they constructed did not recognize women, Aboriginals, convicts, or workers as having been a significant part of the country's history. While in many ways these histories were similar to those created in Canada, the two countries' popular—or usable—pasts differed in a number of ways. In Canada, narratives of the Loyalists and of the War of 1812 admitted, if at times grudgingly, that the Six Nations had played important roles in both events. Furthermore, while historical societies in Canada certainly had their share of elite male leadership, middle-class women played a significant role, both as prominent figures at the provincial and local levels and as founders of all-women groups in both Ottawa and Toronto. Although interested in many of the same narratives as their male counterparts, they also argued for greater attention to be paid to white middle-class women's history. The historical societies in both countries, though, were united in their lack of interest in working-class and labour histories; they were responsible, then, for an outpouring of written narratives aimed at creating a past—not least a unified story of the progress and prosperity of settler nations—that would serve contemporary national and imperial needs. Significantly, much of their work also influenced the histories that were taught in schools. Members of these organizations and those interested in the past sought to record and preserve colonial histories in other ways. Colonial museums, which often preceded the historical societies, presented a range of histories—settler, Indigenous, and natural. In British America, museums initially were smaller collections, often organized at the local level by particular individuals or organizations, such as Mechanics' Institutions, religious orders or denominations, colleges and universities, scientific societies, and private collectors. It was not until the establishment of Toronto's Royal Ontario Museum (ROM) in 1914 that the Dominion saw a larger (and at least to some extent) state-supported institution. Moreover, the ROM was modelled on the line of the British Museum, dedicated to collecting material from around the world, and was not exclusively focused on Canadian history. In Australia, industrial museums became quite popular and were closely linked to industrial exhibitions. In Victoria and New South Wales, museums of applied sciences and arts were housed in buildings that had served as exhibition spaces, their contents arranged to demonstrate the application of technology to colonial economic and commercial life, such as gold mines, railways, and wheat farms.

Victorians' fascination with natural history also spread to settler colonies. In Australia, British America, and South Africa, collections of natural history and of Indigenous material culture were critically important in bringing both landscapes and peoples under the ambit of European science and colonial knowledge. At the Cape, the South African Museum, founded in 1825 with the intent of classifying the colony's animals, vegetables, and minerals, was heavily influenced by Scots doctor, hunter, ethnographer, and zoological researcher Andrew Smith. Smith made a number of expeditions to the colony's interior; when he left in 1837 for Britain, he took a number of natural history specimens with him and published extensively on its zoology and on the San (Bushman) people. Although Smith's collection went with him, over the course of the nineteenth century the museum continued to develop and expand its collections.

In Australia, such collections were rapidly brought under the aegis of the state. The Colonial (later the Australian) Museum, established in 1827 by Governor Darling, was supported by the Colonial Office, while the Acanthe Museum, founded in 1842 by Sir John and Lady Franklin, became a state institution in 1885. Other Australian museums followed a similar pattern. In British America, organizations such as Montreal's Natural History Society (1827), the Geological Survey of Canada (1842), and Toronto's Canadian Institute (1851) played a central role in helping establish areas such as natural history, archaeology, and ethnography. While the colonial and imperial state played a more prominent role in fostering and promoting Australia's natural history, the content and organizational schema of these museums were, overall, quite similar. Non-Europeans and Indigenous peoples, in particular, tended to be represented in the same way from colony to colony: as part of humankind's early development or as part of a "primitive" and vanishing culture. In neither case were their artifacts and the values they represented seen as having any link with or connection to the superior and more "advanced" progress of settler civilization. Moreover, during this period other European immigrants' cultures in Australia or Canada received scant attention from those who founded and ran museums.

Settler histories also appeared in visual forms, one of the most highly visible being that of the monument. Edifices to British imperial military figures, whether they had fought in North America or not, appeared in the British American colonies as early as 1809, when a statue of Britain's Admiral Nelson was erected in Montreal. One of the first such edifices to the Admiral's memory (others were erected in Glasgow and Edinburgh in 1806 and 1815), it was financed by publicly raised money and organized by a committee that included prominent, wealthy English-speaking members of the city's political and commercial elite. During the 1820s colonial wars were memorialized, as statues were put up to the memory of General Isaac Brock, an acclaimed military figure during the War of 1812, and of the opposing generals of the Battle of the Plains of Abraham, James Wolfe and Louis-Joseph de Montcalm. Over the course of the late nineteenth and early twentieth century, the landscapes of Ontario and Quebec, in particular, were marked with monuments that honoured explorers, religious figures, military leaders, and, in some cases, politicians. Although governments at the Dominion, provincial, and local levels were involved in these efforts, middle-class and secular voluntary organizations, sometimes with the support of religious denominations, often took the initiative in starting campaigns to honour their heroes. Almost all the figures these groups chose for public commemoration were male; with a few important exceptions, such as the statue erected to Six Nations chief Joseph Brant, almost all were of European descent. British monarchy was also honoured, as statues to Queen Victoria (an important exception to the masculinity of Canadian monuments) and then to her successor, King Edward VII, were built in a number of Canadian cities.

In Australia, the most notable marking of public space with monuments took place in the 1830s. A number of statues were put up in Sydney's Domain and Hyde Park as an attempt to create an aesthetically impressive public space in the city. Throughout the nineteenth century others followed: like their counterparts in British America (as well as in Britain, the United States, and Europe), they were intended to nurture patriotism—and future patriots—by venerating heroes such as Captain Cook. As in the case of British America, the late nineteenth- and early twentieth-century period was, as historians have argued, the "heroic age" of Australian public monuments. Hundreds were put up to politicians, the monarchy, imperial generals, and cultural and political figures whose memories were dear to various groups in Australian society, such as the Scottish poet Robbie Burns or the Irish patriot Daniel O'Connell. As well as these figures, early twentieth-century schoolteachers and avocational historians banded together to erect a range of tablets and cairns in sites linked to the early history of Australian "discovery" and exploration.

### Forging Settler Identities through War: South Africa

Identities—national, imperial, and Indigenous—were reaffirmed and, simultaneously, reshaped by the South African War and World War I. Alfred Milner, Britain's High Commissioner to South Africa and a key political leader in postwar reconstruction, envisioned South Africa's anglicization. For one, he wished to promote increased British emigration to South Africa under a state-sponsored settlement scheme. Few took advantage of it, as most preferred to go to Australia, Canada, or the United States. Furthermore, Milner's desire to transplant "British" institutions and attitudes in the Transvaal and Orange Free States backfired: he instead stimulated an Afrikaner political consciousness that became the foundation for Afrikaner political activism after 1904. To be sure, Afrikaners were not a unified group in the years leading up to 1910's Union. Some Afrikaner men, for example, had either deserted or collaborated with British authorities during the war.

Afrikaner political subjectivities were also gendered, as Afrikaner women's wartime experiences were mobilized to craft the group's identity.

General Botha, the country's future leader, evoked images of women and children's suffering and heroism during the "Great Trek" of the 1830s and 1840s. Botha linked their time on the Trek to their wartime experiences, particularly the hardships of the British-run concentration camps; the latter became a central rallying point of Afrikaner national identity. As well, Afrikaner women were active in shaping their own form of nationalism. In the war's aftermath and, too, with the migration of many young Dutch women from farming to urban areas (a phenomenon that occurred in other settler societies, the United States, and Britain), Afrikaner women formed a number of philanthropic organizations, such as the Afrikaner Christian Women's Society. These groups claimed their own public spaces as mothers of the nation, seeing themselves charged with protecting its future through maternalism.

The years leading up to Union also sparked a call among the Afrikaner community for a revision of the vernacular Afrikaans language, a debate that took place amidst great concerns over its usage in schools and the civil service. Proponents of the changes wished to make Afrikaans respectable, purge its associations with lower-class and coloured communities, and ensure that it could compete with English. Afrikaner women became an important part of this process. Both male and female authors also created a literature for Afrikaner women that warned readers of the dangers of urban life and presented them with images of a sanctified home, a place where women could best serve their family and the *volk* by creating and fostering the spirit of a true Afrikaner identity.

Yet while Milner may have failed in his quest to anglicize South Africa, historians point out that many of the structures he put in place provided the foundations for modern South Africa, not least the creation of a state bureaucracy that served capitalist development and helped create white South African identity. Formed in 1903, the South African Native Affairs Commission was key to much of this process. The Commission shifted labour policies away from coercion or forced labour and advocated neither the assimilationist model of the Cape nor the repression of the Afrikaner republics as a way of managing whites' increasingly intense fears of African workers. Instead, the Commission developed policies and practices that foreshadowed the future Union's racially based segregation. Cognizant of the fact that the promises the British had made to them during the war of political equality were being broken, black political leaders mobilized to protest these developments. Like other Indigenous communities had done in the nineteenth century, in 1909 a delegation travelled to London in an unsuccessful attempt to persuade the British Parliament to reject the South Africa Act. Led by W.P. Schreiner, the former premier of the Cape, the delegation also included Abdullah Abdurahman, a prominent spokesperson for the coloured community, and John Tengo Jabavu, the Xhosa activist and newspaper editor. Black and coloured activism was by this point not new. Leaders from both groups had formed associations, congresses, and educational bodies, being brought together through mission conferences, the press, and letter-writing networks. Their activism owed much to missionary networks of educated black South Africans, a number of whom had also studied in the United States and became leading educators and political figures. In 1891 members of these groups came together to found the South African Native Congress at the Cape and were joined by representatives from the Transvaal in 1902. However, British control of black territories in the years after the South African War resulted in black leaders becoming increasingly aware of each other's activism and of developments in their respective regions, ones that did not bode well for racial equality. In 1912 members of both black and coloured communities banded together to form the South African Native National Congress, which would later become the African National Congress.

In Natal, a newly energized Indian community also emerged after the war. While a Natal Indian Congress had existed prior to the war, many of its campaigns had been defeated and the Congress had become less active and publicly visible by 1901. However, by 1903 the Congress had undergone a political revival, one spurred by the British government's treatment of Indians in the Transvaal. Although the British had protested the republic government's policies of racial segregation prior to the war, in their attempts to appease Transvaal politicians they began moving Indians into particular residential and trading locations. In 1906 they then demanded that Indians in the Transvaal be fingerprinted. Angered by these actions, the Congress invited Mahatma Gandhi back to South Africa (after a sojourn in the colony, he had returned to India in 1901). The Indian community's reminders to the British authorities of their loyalty to Britain during the war went unheeded and, with Gandhi's help, the Congress started a campaign that lasted until 1914. Thousands of Indians protested and hundreds, including Gandhi, were jailed for refusing to register with the government. It was during this campaign that Gandhi began to formulate his philosophy and practices of nonviolent resistance that would be put into place in India.

Yet while these campaigns of black, coloured, and Indian activists were significant in mobilizing anti-imperial forms of identity, they did not include all members of these communities. Class, education, and religion (particularly missionary education) played significant roles. Indentured and ex-indentured labourers from India, the coloured proletariat, and African peasants and workers were not included in these protest movements. The vast majority of political mobilization took place among the ranks of the educated: blacks, members of the coloured community, and Indians who protested their exclusion from the new South Africa's definition of who was a "civilized" male citizen.

The South African War also played a role in settler societies, as Australia, Canada, and New Zealand sent 30,000 troops to fight in it. In Canada, supporters of the Empire pushed the Liberal government of Wilfrid Laurier to muster more than 7,000 volunteers for the conflict, the first time the country participated in an official military expedition overseas. A number of British-Canadian women also travelled to South Africa; the majority served as nurses, although some also worked in the concentration camps as teachers. While Canadians were not unanimous in their support for a faraway conflict that for some, particularly those in Quebec, had little direct effect on domestic matters, nevertheless the country's participation took place in a context of growing support for the Empire among British Canadians. Even as the troops boarded ships for South Africa, retailers responded to popular demands for a range of commemorative items, such as postcards, books, maps, buttons, commemorative plates, and khaki handkerchiefs and suspenders. Prominent citizens of Victoria and Montreal and members of the IODE organized committees to put up memorials.

Once the war ended portraits, busts, tablets, and monuments were put up in cities and towns across the country. As well, the Canadian South African Memorial Association, formed in 1902 by Lady Minto (the Governor General's wife), the minister of the militia, and other prominent figures, worked with the IODE (albeit with no small degree of competition) and with the Guild of Loyal Women of South Africa in identifying and marking the grave sites of the 270 Canadians who died in South Africa. Veterans played a significant role in perpetuating the war's public memory, as they relived their experiences through dinners, company reunions, South African Veterans' Association meetings, and the South African Medals Association. Two hundred of them represented Canada at Edward VII's coronation, while others were able to parley their South African War service into public office or military positions of higher rank. Some soldiers became public lecturers on their return to Canada, speaking about their experiences in South Africa; various levels of the Canadian government offered land grants in

Northwest Canada to the veterans. The war also helped raise the visibility and status of the Canadian militia, as its wartime work helped legitimize arguments to increase its size, funding, level of training, and equipment. Like the myth of the loyal militia of 1812, created before the South African War and elaborated during the early twentieth century, narratives of the militia's importance were used to argue for a trained force of citizens, not a standing army.

In Australia and New Zealand, opposition to the war was even less vociferous than in Canada. While socialist and republican Arthur Hill Griffith, the Labor member for Newcastle in the New South Wales Legislative Assembly, spoke out against it, his attacks on British policy were met with public demonstrations of support for the Empire and Australia's involvement in South Africa. More Australians volunteered than could be included in the official contingents incorporated into British units; around 6,000 Australians travelled to South Africa to fight as members of irregular units. Overall, 20,000 Australian men and women, 6,000 New Zealand troops, and a number of New Zealand teachers and nurses went to South Africa. Moreover, while support for the War began to flag in 1900—as it did in Britain—in its aftermath both countries also erected memorials to its memory. Although in numbers alone more war memorials were put up in Australia—518 as compared to New Zealand's 228—once differences in population are taken into account more went up in New Zealand than in Australia, perhaps not surprisingly, as a greater number of New Zealand troops per capita served in South Africa. The tone of memorializing was quite similar and also resembled that of Canada's memorials: the Dominions' contributions to the war were remembered with pride, not mourning for those killed.

Yet there were also some significant differences between Australia's and New Zealand's public memory of the South African War. Soldier-figures predominated in New Zealand, while in Australia obelisks were more popular. Moreover, in New Zealand the war's memorialization also was shaped by a rhetoric of Dominion nationalism. Images such as ferns, the southern cross, and Zealandia (the female figure that had come to represent the Dominion as Britannia's youthful daughter—much like the figure of Miss Canada) appeared. Furthermore, the Ranfurly Veterans' Home in Auckland served as a national memorial, unlike Australia where no national memorial was constructed. New Zealand's commemoration of its participation in South Africa also sparked public interest in memorializing the New Zealand Wars (1845–72); between 1900 and 1915 more than 20 memorials to those who died were erected. Although a number of statues had been put up to honour those wars between 1865 and 1900, including one of a weeping Māori woman erected to the memory of those who had defended Wanganui town against their fellow-Māori, many New Zealanders did not care to remember the New Zealand Wars. For the vast majority of settlers in Australia, the less that was said about armed conflict between Australians and Indigenous people, the better. A few memorials existed to those Europeans killed by Australian Aboriginals; they were, however, remembered as victims of "murder," not of military conflict.

## World War I and the Settler World

The outbreak of World War I led to nationwide commemorations of Dominion contributions on an even larger scale and in multiple genres, much of it built on commemorations of South Africa and, in the case of Canada, the War of 1812. It did not take long for such public efforts to get underway. In December 1914, for example, four months after the first shots were fired and before many Canadian troops had reached Europe, Vancouver's Canadian Club asked the provincial government to designate the city's old Court House Square for a memorial. Other requests for such spaces quickly followed. In Australia, 60 memorials were completed by the end of 1918. In the war's aftermath, many Australians, Canadians, and New Zealanders worked hard to commemorate the "Great War" in ways that were multifaceted in the forms that they took but were remarkably similar in their thematic and didactic unity. One of the most publicly visible means of commemorating World War I survives to the present day: the war memorial. Statues, obelisks, and other memorials became so ubiquitous that they still can be found in a number of public places, ranging from larger urban centres to small towns, throughout Australia, Canada, and New Zealand. Although a number of well-known writers and intellectuals in Britain believed the war to have been a tragic and pointless exercise that should be mourned, not celebrated, public representations depicted World War I quite differently. The monuments unveiled in cities, towns, and villages tended to portray the war and those who fought it as embodying a glorious triumph of manhood, not a deplorable loss. Many of these statues and monuments, moreover, paid tribute to more than officers or generals, as they also commemorated the ordinary soldier, whether the Australian and New Zealand Army Corps' "digger" or the Canadian citizen soldier. This theme would emerge very clearly in veterans' reunions and Remembrance Day ceremonies.

Far from being brutalized or traumatized by his experiences, a common image in postwar writing by novelists and intellectuals, the Dominion soldier in public and popular myths surrounding the war was an inspirational, often Christ-like figure who willingly, one might even say joyfully, sacrificed himself for his home and family, his country, and his empire. Even in Newfoundland, whose troops saw massive losses at Beaumont Hamel in 1916, the war was initially remembered as an affirmation of Newfoundlanders' commitment to their country and to the Empire. Such a commemoration of noble sacrifice was underscored by the fact that the monuments listed the names of the dead, a memorialization that tied the soldiers directly to their communities. In Australia war monuments also listed those who had enlisted, making the monuments a celebration of service and life as well as sacrifice. The location and form of these memorials would prove important in perpetuating that memory. They provided a direct reminder, both for participants in Remembrance Day ceremonies and for those who made their own private, less formal visits to the cenotaph, of who had sacrificed themselves for community and nation (and, equally importantly, who had not).

These dominant forms of remembering the war focused on a masculinity that personified the best qualities of the Dominions and their new status as nations (the fact that all participated because of Britain's, not their own, initiative tended to be glossed over). These were soldiers marked by vigour, courage, moral standing, and youthfulness: men who were frequently depicted as products of unspoiled, natural settings that, in turn, exemplified Australia or Canada in their purity. Moreover, while Dominion women had provided formal and informal support on the home front, and had been the recipients of government propaganda telling them of its great value to the war effort, their contributions received far fewer tributes, even though many commemorative efforts, particularly fundraising for monuments, were spearheaded and run by groups such as the IODE. A few memorials to women's wartime service were erected, such as the Canadian Nurses' Association War Memorial, unveiled in 1926 in Ottawa at Parliament Hill's Centre Block. Moreover, the British nurse Edith Cavell, executed by the Germans in 1915 for helping British prisoners escape from occupied Belgium, received a number of tributes in both Britain and around the Empire: monuments, a mountain in Alberta's Jasper National Park, schools, hospitals, and streets. Like the Christian soldier, Cavell was depicted as a martyr, courageous and self-sacrificing. Despite her physical weakness because of her sex, she provided an example of courage and stoicism.

Yet not everyone remembered the war in such heroic and inspirational terms. In Canada, the vicious attacks levied against French Canadians in debates over conscription exacerbated already-present rifts and were not quickly forgotten: indeed, the "conscription debates" helped shape French-Canadian nationalism in the 1920s. In South Africa, pro-republican Afrikaner opposition to the war erupted in armed rebellion in 1914; the memory of that event, perpetuated in poetry, fiction, and newspaper articles, was used by Afrikaner nationalists to create a memory for political mobilization in the 1940s. White English-speaking South Africans, Anglo-Afrikaner loyalists, members of the Cape Corps (whose members came from rural coloured communities), and those who remembered the South Africa Labour Contingent (600 of whom drowned in 1917 on the English troopship *Mendi* in the English Channel) worked to perpetuate distinct memories of a divided war experience. The *Mendi*, for example, gave rise to a number of memorial days, religious ceremonies, war dances, clubs, and educational scholarships. These forms of memory helped perpetuate a black nationalist depiction of sacrifice and heroism for Allied freedom and self-determination that lasted well into the post-World War II years. In Newfoundland, the memory of Beaumont Hamel shifted as Newfoundland first lost its sovereignty in 1934 and then made the contentious decision in 1949 to join Canadian Confederation. After those events, the battle took on a more tragic meaning, that of the beginning of a long decline in Newfoundland's fortunes, and its anniversary became a day of mourning.

Moreover, although in Australia, Canada, and New Zealand Indigenous men volunteered (in New Zealand, some Māori were conscripted), after the war Indigenous veterans in Canada continued to face a wide range of political and socioeconomic discrimination, including remaining disfranchised. Conversely, the Department of Indian Affairs attempted to enfranchise certain Indigenous leaders in an attempt to remove them from their communities. This does not mean, of course, that Aboriginal communities forgot their members' service. Their leaders were proud of men such as Francis Pegahmagabow, the Ojibwa army sniper who earned a number of medals in the war. Pegahmagabow was inducted into the Indian Hall of Fame at the Woodland Centre on the Six Nations reserve, the Canadian Forces named a building at Camp Borden after him, and in 2005 Métis novelist Joseph Boyden used Pegahmagabow and his story in his award-winning novel *3 Day Road*. Yet for the most part Indigenous veterans' service and contributions to the war have only recently been acknowledged and honoured by the Canadian government and general public. A similar fate befell Australian

Aboriginal veterans. Like their counterparts in Canada they were not expected to serve, but a number did so, although their wartime experiences were rarely recorded on war memorials. Instead, they were memorialized on honour boards on reserves.

The war's memory was also a complex one for other racialized communities in the Dominions, as the case of the decorated veteran Sergeant Masumi Mitsui and the Vancouver Japanese-Canadian War Memorial shows. To honour those Japanese Canadians who had enlisted in the Canadian Expeditionary Force, the Japanese-Canadian community in British Columbia raised funds for a new war memorial in Vancouver. Their efforts were rewarded with a site in Stanley Park; the memorial combined Western and Japanese influences and featured plaques that listed fallen soldiers from the community and returning veterans. The ceremony dedicating the monument was intended both to remember the soldiers' contributions and to call for the enfranchisement of Japanese Canadians. Yet with the outbreak of World War II and the internment and forced removal of Japanese Canadians from the lower mainland, the Japanese-Canadian war memorial was no longer the scene of Remembrance Day or any other types of celebrations: the lantern at the memorial was extinguished. Not until 1985, when the treatment of Japanese Canadians was understood as discriminatory and unjust, did Sergeant Mitsui return to the memorial (he too had been forcibly removed from Vancouver) for a relighting ceremony.

## Conclusion

Settler identities were expressed in multiple genres and forms. While relationships to Britain and, in particular, the monarchy did not fade in their importance to settlers' sense of self over the course of the nineteenth century, they often were complex and interlaced with settlers' own feelings of pride in their particular society (and then nation). For some, ties to the faraway metropole might have to take the form of more abstract symbols and representations, even if settlers experienced such ties as very real and meaningful. Feelings of belonging to the British Empire could be supplemented by connections to the particular places in which settlers lived—connections expressed in poetry, prose, painting, and sculpture. The latter ties might, in some cases, supersede links to Britain, with settler nationalism taking precedence over imperial sentiment. Others, though, found no contradictions in feeling themselves members of both a settler society and the British Empire, as discussions of imperial federation or patriotism during the South African War and World War I, for example, demonstrated.

Yet, as this chapter has shown, settlers' identities were not homogeneous. Being "British" might be important at certain moments but so too was being English, Scottish, Irish, or Welsh. Furthermore, settler colonies were home to other Europeans and people of Asian or African descent, communities whose relationships to Britain were complicated by ethnicity, religion, and race. Indigenous peoples' identities were no less complex. While they might claim a particular and specific relationship to the British Crown, they also felt a keen sense of belonging to their own nations and territories.

## Notes

1 Margaret Dickie, "Continental Tour," in *Britishers in Britain. Being the Record of the Official Visit of Teachers from Manitoba to the Old Country, Summer, 1910*, ed. Fred J. Ney (London: Times Book Club, 1911), 238–39.

2 James Bennett, "'Massey's Sunday School Picnic Party': 'The Other Anzacs' or Honorary Australians?," *War and Society* 21, 2 (2003): 36.

3 Ibid., 35, 36.

4 Emily Murphy, *The Impressions of Janey Canuck Abroad* (Toronto, 1902), 128.

5 Phillip Buckner, "The Royal Tour of 1901 and the Construction of an Imperial Identity in South Africa," *South African Historical Journal* 41 (Nov. 1999): 343.

6 Ibid., 343–45.

7 Ibid.

# Conclusion
## Better Britains?

The growth of British settler colonies in the nineteenth century was shaped by both metropolitan influences and imperial direction and by the historically rooted circumstances and contingencies of regional and local levels. Although imperial authorities and imperial policy played a significant role in these colonies' development, settlers also brought with them their own desires, hopes, and fantasies, ones that did not always mirror or directly follow those of imperial governments. Links to Britain, while critically important, did not always result in a seamless or predictable transfer of British values, institutions, or practices. Furthermore, colonists did not enter "virgin" or unoccupied territory. The presence and persistence of Indigenous communities, other Europeans, and people from other parts of the world meant that these colonies' histories were shaped by interactions with those who, in many cases, also saw these territories as "home." Although settler colonialism was a remarkably long-lasting form of imperial expansion, and much of what occurred in the nineteenth century set the foundation for twentieth-century developments and the formation of settler nations, it was not untouched by the uncertainties and contingencies of empire.

Settler colonialism within the British Empire was a dynamic and ongoing process. Did it result, though, in the formation of "better Britains?" The answer to that question, like so many other historical problems, depends on one's perspective. Some of the individuals we have met in this book, such as mid-nineteenth-century New Zealand settler Susannah Wall or the early twentieth-century Manitoba teacher Margaret Dickie, might well have answered yes. Wall's correspondence depicts the recreation of familiar structures—home, church, and school—within a landscape and climate that, while unfamiliar, promised to be aesthetically and physically appealing. For her part, Dickie celebrated the opportunity to rejuvenate her ties to British culture during her 1910 trip to England. She would then put those cultural lessons to work in instructing new arrivals to Canada on the benefits of being both Canadian and British, as well as reminding those with longer histories of settlement of their "roots." Others were not so optimistic that life in a settler colony both replicated and improved upon the metropole. Eliza Fairbairn, for instance, mourned her loss of genteel society's comforts and sociability at the Cape, while Samuel Lister's life as a skilled worker in 1890s' Otago did not live up to the promises of manly, British independence he thought his "better Britain" promised. For some, the question might not have been so much about "Britishness" as it would have been about economic and social opportunities. Indentured workers in Natal, for example, did not arrive with the intent of creating a "better Britain," and many settlers from Eastern Europe who created communities on Canada's early twentieth-century prairies maintained ties to their ancestral homelands. As well, in the eyes of government officials and many members of these societies' middle class, certain groups—people of Asian and African descent, for example—could not be considered British, even if they acculturated and adopted the dominant society's practices and mores. So far as Indigenous people were concerned, the concept of "better Britains" had even more complicated valences: the creation of settler societies was predicated on Indigenous peoples' dispossession and losses, not least of their homes and ancestral territories. At times, though, they made use of concepts of British justice and fairness in order to contest such processes.

Changes in the 1920s brought different configurations of the networks and relationships that had shaped these societies' ties to Britain. Although British migration to Canada, Australia, New Zealand, and South Africa continued throughout the decade, it dropped off during the Depression. The 1931 Statute of Westminster gave the four Dominions, along with the Irish Free State, full legislative independence if they so wished, abolishing the need for Britain's approval of Dominion legislation and creating the modern Commonwealth. Over the course of the twentieth century more highly visible forms of settler nationalism developed, often expressed in nationalist historiographies that, by the 1960s, tended to emphasize settler societies' distinct qualities, less so their ties to Britain. As well, other forms of European nationalism in settler societies, such as that of Afrikaners or

Quebeçois, challenged the notion that settler societies were homogeneous, English-speaking entities. Moreover, ties to the United States that had already shaped Canada and, by the early twentieth century, Australia, intensified in both quantity and significance. After World War II the United States became increasingly powerful globally, not just at the political and military level but also in the spread of its popular culture, a phenomenon that also had a strong influence on British culture. As well, shifts in post–World War II patterns of immigration, brought about partly through the slow lifting of racially based restrictions on entry, resulted in very different population demographics, especially in larger urban centres.

This is not to argue that links to Britain or the sense of being part of a "British world" vanished or died out in these societies: emigration to Australia, Canada, and New Zealand resumed after World War II, for example. Historians have only recently begun to examine the various ways in which this migration represented both change and continuity in the meaning of "Britishness" in the former Dominions, particularly around questions of identity and culture. In Canada and Australia, a number of publicly funded cultural institutions—radio, television, and the performing and visual arts, for example—were modelled on British examples, while trips to Britain for higher education, training in the arts, and leisure were still considered by many to be essential cultural markers. Those who made them often found a Britain very different from their expectations, although that was not a new phenomenon: such had been the case from at least the late nineteenth century.

Moreover, for Indigenous people in Australia, Canada, New Zealand, and South Africa, the structures, relationships, and practices established in the nineteenth century did not disappear over the course of the twentieth century. In some cases, such as the establishment of apartheid in South Africa or in Canada's growing panoply of restrictions on Indigenous people that were expanded under the Indian Act, racially defined categories of exclusion and rule intensified. As they had in the nineteenth century, but to an even greater extent and with greater visibility, in twentieth-century settler societies Indigenous people protested their marginalization by establishing political organizations of their own. They called for the return of land, languages, and cultures that had been taken from them by settler colonialism, at times linking their activism to that of others who formed decolonization movements in India, Africa, Asia, and the Caribbean. They also forged alliances with sympathetic and humanitarian-minded whites, although such alliances might also be as complex in the twentieth-century context as they had been in the 1830s. The question of decolonization in Australia, Canada, New Zealand, and South Africa is one of the most pressing and complicated legacies of the nineteenth-century desire to create "better Britains."

# Select Bibliography

The bibliography for each chapter represents the historiography that has been synthesized for this book.

## General Works, Texts, and Collections

Bayly, Christopher. *The Birth of the Modern World 1780–1914*. Malden, MA: Blackwell, 2004.

Belich, James. *Replenishing the Earth: The Settler Revolution and the Rise of the Anglo-World, 1783–1939*. Oxford: Oxford University Press, 2009.

Bridge, Carl, and Kent Fedorowich, eds. *The British World: Diaspora, Culture and Identity*. London: Frank Cass, 2003.

Buckner, Phillip, ed. *Canada and the British Empire*. New York: Oxford University Press, 2008.

Buckner, Phillip, and R. Douglas Francis, eds. *Rediscovering the British World*. Calgary: University of Calgary Press, 2005.

Darian-Smith, Kate, Patricia Grimshaw, and Stuart Macintyre, eds. *Britishness Abroad: Transnational Movements and Imperial Cultures*. Carlton, Australia: Melbourne University Press, 2007.

Hamilton, Carolyn, Bernard K. Mbenga, and Robert Ross, eds. *The Cambridge History of South Africa*. Vol. 1, *From Early Times to 1885*. Cambridge: Cambridge University Press, 2010–11.

Levine, Philippa. *The British Empire: Sunrise to Sunset*. Harlow, UK: Pearson, 2007.

MacKenzie, John. "The British Empire: Ramshackle or Rampaging? A Historiographical Reflection." *Journal of Imperial and Commonwealth History* 43, 1 (2015): 99–124.

Porter, Andrew, and Wm. Roger Louis, eds. *The Oxford History of the British Empire*. Vol. 3, *The Nineteenth Century*. Oxford: Oxford University Press, 1999.

Ross, Robert, Anne Mager, and Bill Nasson, eds. *The Cambridge History of South Africa*. Vol. 2, *1885–1994*. Cambridge: Cambridge University Press, 2011.

Weaver, John C. *The Great Land Rush and the Making of the Modern World, 1650–1900*. Montreal: McGill-Queen's University Press, 2003.

Woollacott, Angela. *Gender and Empire*. Basingstoke, UK: Palgrave Macmillan, 2006.

## Chapter 1

Ballantyne, Tony. "Te nAu's Story: A Fragmentary History of Difference and Racialisation in Southern New Zealand." In *Rethinking the Racial Moment: Essays on the Colonial Encounter*, edited by Alison Holland and Barbara Brookes, 49–74. Newcastle, UK: Cambridge Scholars Publishing, 2011.

Belich, James. *The New Zealand Wars and the Victorian Interpretation of Racial Conflict*. Auckland: Auckland University Press, 1986.

Broome, Richard. *Aboriginal Australians: Black Responses to White Dominance, 1788–2001*. Sydney: G. Allen and Unwin, 2002.

Carey, Jane, and Jane Lydon, eds. *Indigenous Networks: Mobility, Connections and Exchange*. New York: Routledge, 2014.

Carter, Sarah. "Aboriginal People of Canada and the British Empire." In *Canada and the British Empire*, edited by Phillip Buckner, 200–19. New York: Oxford University Press, 2008.

Carter, Sarah. *Lost Harvests: Prairie Indian Reserve Farmers and Government Policy*. Montreal: McGill-Queen's University Press, 1990.

Clendinnen, Inga. *Dancing with Strangers*. Melbourne: Text Publishing, 2003.

Crais, Clifton. *Poverty, War, and Violence in South Africa*. Cambridge: Cambridge University Press, 2011.

Dickason, Olive Patricia, with David T. McNab. *Canada's First Nations: A History of Founding Peoples from Earliest Times*. Don Mills, ON: Oxford University Press, 2009.

Elbourne, Elizabeth. *Blood Ground: Colonialism, Missions, and the Contest for Christianity in the Cape Colony and Britain, 1799–1853*. Montreal: McGill-Queen's University Press, 2002.

Elbourne, Elizabeth. "Indigenous Peoples and Imperial Networks in the Early Nineteenth Century." In *Rediscovering the British World*, edited by Phillip Buckner and R. Douglas Francis, 59–85. Calgary: University of Calgary Press, 2005.

Eldridge, Elizabeth, and Fred Morton, eds. *Slavery in South Africa: Captive Labour on the Dutch Frontier*. Boulder, CO: Westview Press, 1994.

Laidlaw, Zoë, and Alan Lester, eds. *Indigenous Communities and Settler Colonialism: Land Holding, Loss and Survival in an Interconnected World*. Basingstoke, UK: Palgrave Macmillan, 2015.

Lester, Alan, and Fae Dussart. *Colonization and the Origins of Humanitarian Governance: Protecting Aborigines Across the Nineteenth-Century British Empire*. Cambridge: Cambridge University Press, 2014.

Miller, J.R. *Compact, Contract, Covenant: Aboriginal Treaty-Making in Canada*. Toronto: University of Toronto Press, 2009.

Reynolds, Henry. *Frontier: Aborigines, Settlers, and Land*. Sydney: Allen and Unwin, 1987.

Reynolds, Henry, and Ann Curthoys, eds. *Contested Ground: Australian Aborigines under the British Crown*. Sydney: Allen and Unwin, 1995.

Ross, Robert. "Khoisan and Immigrants: The Emergence of Colonial Society in the Cape, 1500–1800." In *The Cambridge History of South Africa*. Vol. 1, *From Early Times to 1885*, edited by Carolyn Hamilton, Bernard K. Mbenga, and Robert Ross, 168–210. Cambridge: Cambridge University Press, 2010–11.

Russell, Lynette, ed. *Colonial Frontiers: Indigenous-European Encounters in Settler Societies*. Manchester: Manchester University Press, 2001.

Taylor, Alan. *The Divided Ground: Indians, Settlers, and the Northern Borderlands of the American Revolution*. New York: Vintage, 2006.

Vibert, Elizabeth, and Jennifer Brown, eds. *Reading Beyond Words: Contexts for Native History*. Toronto: University of Toronto, 2003.

White, Richard. *The Middle Ground: Indians, Empires, and Republics in the Great Lakes Region, 1650–1815*. Cambridge: Cambridge University Press, 1991.

Worden, Nigel, and Clifton Crais, eds. *Breaking the Chains: Slavery and Its Legacy in the Nineteenth-Century Cape Colony*. Johannesburg: Witwatersrand University Press, 1994.

## Chapter 2

Banner, Stuart. "Two Properties, One Land: Law and Space in Nineteenth-Century New Zealand." *Law and Social Inquiry* 24, 4 (1999): 805–52.

Bannister, Jerry. *The Rule of the Admirals: Law, Custom, and Naval Government in Newfoundland, 1699–1832*. Toronto: University of Toronto Press, 2003.

Belich, James. *The New Zealand Wars and the Victorian Interpretation of Racial Conflict*. Auckland: Auckland University Press, 1986.

Belich, James. "The Rise of the Angloworld: Settlement in North America and Australasia, 1784–1918." In *Rediscovering the British World*, edited by Phillip Buckner and R. Douglas Francis, 39–57. Calgary: University of Calgary Press, 2005.

Bitterman, Rusty. *Rural Protest on Prince Edward Island: From British Colonization to the Escheat Movement*. Toronto: University of Toronto Press, 2006.

Bosher, J.F. "Vancouver Island in the Empire." *The Journal of Imperial and Commonwealth History* 33, 3 (2005): 349–68.

Boucher, Ellen. *Empire's Children: Child Emigration, Welfare, and the Decline of the British World, 1869–1967*. New York: Cambridge University Press, 2014.

Boucher, Leigh. "Alfred Howitt: Anthropology, Governance, and the Settler Colonial Order of Things." In *Rethinking the Racial Moment: Essays on the Colonial Encounter*, edited by Alison Holland and Barbara Brookes, 97–124. Newcastle, UK: Cambridge Scholars Publishing, 2011.

Breathnach, Caira. "Even 'Wilder Workhouse Girls': The Problem of Institutionalization among Irish Immigrants to New Zealand 1874." *Journal of Imperial and Commonwealth History* 39, 5 (2011): 771–94.

Buck, A.R. "'This Remnant of Feudalism': Primogeniture and Political Culture in Colonial New South Wales, with Some Canadian Comparisons." In John McLaren, A.R. Buck, and Nancy E. Wright, *Despotic Dominion: Property Rights in British Settler Societies*, 169–89. Vancouver: University of British Columbia Press, 2005.

Buckner, Phillip. "The Creation of the Dominion of Canada, 1860–1901." In *Canada and the British Empire*, edited by Phillip Buckner, 66–86. New York: Oxford University Press, 2008.

Chilton, Lisa. *Agents of Empire: British Female Migration to Canada and Australia, 1860s–1930.* Toronto: University of Toronto Press, 2007.

Chilton, Lisa. "Managing Migrants: Toronto, 1820–1880." *Canadian Historical Review* 92, 2 (2011): 231–52.

Clarke, John. *Land, Power, and Economics on the Frontier of Upper Canada.* Montreal: McGill-Queen's University Press, 2001.

Constantine, Stephen. "British Emigration to the Empire-Commonwealth since 1880: From Overseas Settlement to Diaspora?" In *The British World: Diaspora, Culture and Identity*, edited by Carl Bridge and Kent Fedorowich, 16–35. London: Frank Cass, 2003.

Crais, Clifton, ed. *The Culture of Power in Southern Africa: Essays on State Formation and the Political Imagination.* Portsmouth, NH: Heinemann, 2003.

Curthoys, Ann, Ann Genovese, and Alexander Reilly. *Rights and Redemption: History, Law and Indigenous People.* Sydney: University of New South Wales Press, 2008.

Elphick, Richard, and Hermann Gloomy, eds. *The Shaping of South African Society, 1652–1840.* Middletown, CT: Wesleyan University Press, 1988.

Errington, Jane. *Emigrant Worlds and Transatlantic Communities: Migration to Upper Canada in the First Half of the Nineteenth Century.* Montreal: McGill-Queen's University Press, 2007.

Etherington, Norman, Patrick Harries, and Bernard K. Mbenga. "From Colonial Hegemonies to Imperial Conquest, 1840–1880." In *The Cambridge History of South Africa.* Vol. 1, *From Early Times to 1885*, edited by Carolyn Hamilton, Bernard K. Mbenga, and Robert Ross, 319–91. Cambridge: Cambridge University Press, 2010–11.

Evans, Julie, Patricia Grimshaw, David Philips, and Shurlee Swain, *Equal Subjects, Unequal Rights: Indigenous Peoples in British Settler Colonies, 1830–1910.* Manchester: Manchester University Press, 2003.

Ford, Lisa, and Tim Rowse. *Between Indigenous and Settler Governance.* New York: Routledge, 2013.

Francis, Mark. *Governors and Settlers: Images of Authority in the British Colonies, 1820–60.* Christchurch: Canterbury University Press, 1992.

Freund, Bill. "South Africa: The Union Years, 1910–1948—Political and Economic Foundations." In *The Cambridge History of South Africa.* Vol. 2, *1885–1994*, edited by Robert Ross, Anne Mager, and Bill Nasson, 211–53. Cambridge: Cambridge University Press, 2011.

Girard, Philip. "British Justice, English Law, and Canadian Legal Culture." In *Canada and the British Empire*, edited by Phillip Buckner, 259–77. New York: Oxford University Press, 2008.

Greer, Allan. *The Patriots and the People: The Rebellion of 1837 in Rural Lower Canada.* Toronto: University of Toronto Press, 1993.

Greer, Allan, and Ian Radforth, eds. *Colonial Leviathan: The State in British North America, 1830–1880.* Toronto: University of Toronto Press, 1992.

Harper, Marjory, ed. *Emigrant Homecomings: The Return Movement of Emigrants, 1600–2000*. Manchester: Manchester University Press, 2005.

Harper, Marjory, and Stephen Constantine. *Migration and Empire*. Oxford: Oxford University Press, 2010.

Hickford, Mark. "'Vague Native Rights to Land': British Imperial Policy on Native Title and Custom in New Zealand, 1837–53." *Journal of Imperial and Commonwealth History* 38, 2 (2010): 175–206.

Hiller, James K. "Status without Stature: Newfoundland, 1869–1949." In *Canada and the British Empire*, edited by Phillip Buckner, 127–39. New York: Oxford University Press, 2008.

Jasanoff, Maya. *Liberty's Exiles: American Loyalists in the Revolutionary World*. New York: Alfred A. Knopf, 2011.

Laidlaw, Zoe. *Colonial Connections, 1815–1845: Patronage, the Information Revolution and Colonial Government*. Manchester: Manchester University Press, 2005.

Lake, Marilyn, and Henry Reynolds. *Drawing the Global Colour Line: White Men's Countries and the Question of Racial Equality*. Carlton, Australia: Melbourne University Press, 2008.

Langfield, Michele. "Voluntarism, Salvation, and Rescue: British Juvenile Migration to Australia and Canada, 1890–1939." *Journal of Imperial and Commonwealth History* 32, 2 (2004): 86–114.

MacDonald, Charlotte. *A Woman of Good Character: Single Women as Immigrant Settlers in Nineteenth-Century New Zealand*. Wellington: Bridget Williams Books, 1990.

Marks, Shula. "War and Union, 1899–1910." In *The Cambridge History of South Africa*. Vol. 2, *1885–1994*, edited by Robert Ross, Anne Mager, and Bill Nasson, 157–210. Cambridge: Cambridge University Press, 2011.

Martens, Jeremy. "A Transnational History of Immigration Restriction: Natal and New South Wales, 1896–97." *Journal of Imperial and Commonwealth History* 34, 3 (2006): 323–44.

Perry, Adele. *On the Edge of Empire: Gender, Race, and the Making of British Columbia, 1849–1871*. Toronto: University of Toronto Press, 2001.

Pickering, Paul. "Loyalty and Rebellion in Colonial Politics: The Campaign Against Convict Transportation." In *Rediscovering the British World*, edited by Phillip Buckner and R. Douglas Francis, 102–05. Calgary: University of Calgary Press, 2005.

Trapido, Stanley. "Imperialism, Settler Identities, and Colonial Capitalism: The Hundred-Year Origins of the 1899 South African War." In *The Cambridge History of South Africa*. Vol. 2, *1885–1994*, edited by Robert Ross, Anne Mager, and Bill Nasson, 66–110. Cambridge: Cambridge University Press, 2011.

Ward, Damen. "Constructing British Authority in Australasia: Charles Cooper and the Legal Status of Aborigines in the South Australian Supreme Court, c. 1840–60." *Journal of Imperial and Commonwealth History* 34, 4 (2006): 483–504.

Weaver, John C. *The Great Land Rush and the Making of the Modern World, 1650–1900*. Montreal: McGill-Queen's University Press, 2003.

Woollacott, Angela. *Settler Society in the Australian Colonies: Self-Government and Imperial Culture*. Oxford: Oxford University Press, 2015.

Wright, Nancy E. "'The Lady Vanishes': Women and Property Rights in Nineteenth-Century New South Wales." In John McLaren, A.R. Buck, and Nancy E. Wright, *Despotic Dominion: Property Rights in British Settler Societies*, 190–206. Vancouver: University of British Columbia Press, 2005.

## Chapter 3

Anderson, Clare. "Convicts and Coolies: Rethinking Indentured Labour in the Nineteenth Century." *Slavery and Abolition* 30, 1 (2008): 93–109.

Attard, Bernard. "From Free-Trade Imperialism to Structural Power: New Zealand and the Capital Market, 1856–68." *Journal of Imperial and Commonwealth History* 35, 4 (2007): 505–27.

Béliard, Yann. "Imperial Internationalism? Hull Labour's Support for South African Trade-Unionism on the Eve of the Great War." *Labour History Review* 74, 3 (2009): 319–29.

Bowden, Bradley. "An Economy Ill-Suited to Younger Workers: Child and Youth Workforce Participation in Colonial Queensland, 1886–1901." *Australian Economic History Review* 46 (2006): 111–29.

Burr, Christina. "Some Adventures of Boys: Enniskillen Township's 'Frontier Drillers,' Imperialism, and Colonial Discourse, 1873–1923." *Labour / Le Travail* 51 (Spring 2003): 47–80.

Cadigan, Sean T. *Hope and Deception in Conception Bay: Merchant-Settler Relations in Newfoundland, 1785–1855*. Toronto: University of Toronto Press, 1995.

Cooper, Annabel. "Poor Men in the Land of Promises: Settler Masculinity and the Male Breadwinner Economy in Late Nineteenth-Century New Zealand." *Australian Historical Studies* 39 (2008): 245–61.

Dilley, Andrew. *Finance, Politics, and Imperialism: Australia, Canada and the City of London, c. 1896–1914*. Basingstoke, UK: Palgrave Macmillan, 2012.

Fieldhouse, D.K. "The Metropolitan Economics of Empire." In *The Oxford History of the British Empire*. Vol. 4, *The Twentieth Century*, edited by Judith M. Brown and Wm. Roger Louis, 88–113. Oxford: Oxford University Press, 1999.

Girard, Philip. "'Land Law, Liberalism, and the Agrarian Ideal: British North America,' 1750–1920." In John McLaren, A.R. Buck, and Nancy E. Wright, *Despotic Dominion: Property Rights in British Settler Societies*, 120–43. Vancouver: University of British Columbia Press, 2005.

Green, E.H.H. "The Political Economy of Empire, 1880–1914." In *The Oxford History of the British Empire*. Vol. 3, *The Nineteenth Century*, edited by Andrew Porter and Wm. Roger Louis, 345–68. Oxford: Oxford University Press, 1999.

Hetherington, Penelope. *Settlers, Servants, and Slaves: Aboriginal and European Children in Nineteenth-Century Western Australia*. Perth: University of Western Australia Press, 2002.

Hughes, Heather. "'The Coolies Will Elbow Us Out of the Country': African Reactions to Indian Immigration in the Colony of Natal, South Africa." *Labour History Review* 72 (2007): 155–68.

Hyslop, Jonathan. "The British and Australian Leaders of the South African Labour Movement, 1902–1914: A Group Biography." In *Britishness Abroad: Transnational Movements and Imperial Cultures*, edited by Kate Darian-Smith,

Patricia Grimshaw, and Stuart Macintyre, 90–108. Carlton, Australia: Melbourne University Press, 2007.

Hyslop, Jonathan. "The Imperial Working Class Makes Itself 'White': White Labourism in Britain, Australia, and South Africa before the First World War." *Journal of Historical Sociology* 12, 4 (1999): 398–421.

Kenefick, William. "Confronting White Labourism: Socialism, Syndicalism, and the Role of the Scottish Radical Left in South Africa before 1914." *International Review of Social History* 55, 1 (2010): 29–62.

Lake, Marilyn, and Henry Reynolds. *Drawing the Global Colour Line: White Men's Countries and the Question of Racial Equality*. Melbourne: Melbourne University Press, 2008.

Legassick, Martin, and Robert Ross. "From Slave Economy to Settler Capitalism: The Cape Colony and Its Extensions, 1800–1854." In *The Cambridge History of South Africa*. Vol. 1, *From Early Times to 1885*, edited by Carolyn Hamilton, Bernard K. Mbenga, and Robert Ross, 253–318. Cambridge: Cambridge University Press, 2010–11.

Magee, Gary B., and Andrew S. Thompson. *Empire and Globalisation: Networks of People, Goods, and Capital in the British World, c. 1850–1914*. Cambridge: Cambridge University Press, 2010.

Marks, Shula. "Class, Culture, and Consciousness in South Africa, 1880–1899." In *The Cambridge History of South Africa*. Vol. 2, *1885–1994*, edited by Robert Ross, Anne Mager, and Bill Nasson, 102–56. Cambridge: Cambridge University Press, 2011.

Martens, Jeremy. "A Transnational History of Immigration Restriction: Natal and New South Wales, 1896–97." *Journal of Imperial and Commonwealth History* 34, 3 (2006): 323–44.

Mbenga, Bernard, and Fred Morton. "The Missionary as Land Broker: Henri Gunin, Saulspoort 269 and the Bakgatla of Rustenberg District, 1862–1922." *South African Historical Journal* 36 (May 1997): 145–67.

McCalla, Douglas. "Economy and Empire: Britain and Canadian Developments." In *Canada and the British Empire*, edited by Phillip Buckner, 240–58. New York: Oxford University Press, 2008.

Metcalf, Thomas R. "'Hard Hands and Sound Healthy Bodies': Recruiting 'Coolies' for Natal, 1860–1911." *Journal of Imperial and Commonwealth History* 30, 3 (2002): 1–26.

Northrup, David. "Migration from Asia, Africa, and the South Pacific." In *The Oxford History of the British Empire*. Vol. 3, *The Nineteenth Century*, edited by Andrew Porter and Wm. Roger Louis, 88–100. Oxford: Oxford University Press, 1999.

Reid, Kirsty. *Gender, Crime and Empire: Convicts, Settlers and the State in Early Colonial Australia*. Manchester: Manchester University Press, 2007.

Robbins, Bill. "Governor Macquarie's Job Descriptions and the Bureaucratic Control of the Convict Labour Process." *Labour History* 96 (May 2009): 1–18.

Robbins, William Murray. "Management and Resistance in the Convict Work Gangs, 1788–1830." *Journal of Industrial Relations* 45, 3 (2003): 360–77.

Roberts, David Andrew. "The 'Knotted Hands That Set Us High': Labour History and the Study of Convict Australia." *Labour History* 100 (May 2011): 33–50.

Robinson, Shirleene. *Something Like Slavery? Queensland's Aboriginal Child Workers, 1842–1945*. North Melbourne: Australian Scholarly Publishing, 2008.

Semmel, Bernard. *The Rise of Free Trade Imperialism: Classical Political Economy, the Empire of Free Trade and Imperialism, 1750–1850*. Cambridge: Cambridge University Press, 2004.

Sullivan, Emmett. "Revealing a Preference: Imperial Preference and the Australian Tariff, 1901–1914." *Journal of Imperial and Commonwealth History* 29, 1 (2001): 35–64.

Wilson, Catherine Anne. *Tenants in Time: Family Strategies, Land, and Liberalism in Upper Canada, 1799–1871*. Montreal: McGill-Queen's University Press, 2009.

Woollacott, Angela. "Political Manhood, Non-white Labour and White-Settler Colonialism on the 1830s–1840s Australian Frontier." In *Rethinking the Racial Moment: Essays on the Colonial Encounter*, edited by Alison Holland and Barbara Brookes, 75–96. Newcastle, UK: Cambridge Scholars Publishing, 2011.

## Chapter 4

Adhikari, Mohamed. "Coloured Identity and the Politics of Coloured Education: The Origin of the Teachers' League of South Africa." *International Journal of African Historical Studies* 27, 1 (1994): 101–26.

Bonner, Phillip. "South African Society and Culture, 1910–1948." In *The Cambridge History of South Africa*. Vol. 2, *1885–1994*, edited by Robert Ross, Anne Mager, and Bill Nasson, 254–318. Cambridge: Cambridge University Press, 2011.

Bradbury, Bettina. "Colonial Comparisons: Rethinking Marriage, Civilization and Nation in Nineteenth-Century White Settler Societies." In *Rediscovering the British World*, edited by Phillip Buckner and R. Douglas Francis, 135–57. Calgary: University of Calgary Press, 2005.

Bradlow, Edna. "'The Oldest Charitable Society in South Africa': One Hundred Years and More of the Ladies' Benevolent Society at the Cape of Good Hope." *South African Historical Journal* 25 (1991): 77–104.

Brock, Peggy. "Missionaries as Newcomers: A Comparative Study of the Northwest Pacific Coast and Central Australia." *Journal of the Canadian Historical Association / Revue de la société historique du Canada* 10, 2 (2008): 106–25.

Burley, Stephanie. "Engagement with Empire: Irish Catholic Female Religious Teachers in Colonial South Australia 1868–1901." *Irish Educational Studies* 31, 2 (2012): 175–90.

Byrne, Catherine. "'Free Compulsory, and (Not) Secular': The Failed Idea in Australian Education." *Journal of Religious History* 37, 1 (2013): 20–38.

Carey, Hilary M., ed. *Empires of Religion*. Basingstoke, UK: Palgrave Macmillan, 2008.

Carey, Hilary M. *God's Empire: Religion and Colonialism in the British World, c. 1801–1908*. Cambridge: Cambridge University Press, 2011.

Carter, Sarah. *The Importance of Being Monogamous: Marriage and Nation Building in Western Canada to 1915*. Edmonton: University of Alberta Press, 2008.

Christison, Grant. "Readers and Writers in Colonial Natal (1843–1910)." *English in Africa* 39, 2 (2012): 111–33.

Curtis, Bruce. *Building the Educational State: Canada West, 1836–1871*. London, ON: Falmer Press, 1988.

Durrill, Wayne K. "Shaping a Settler Elite: Students, Competition and Leadership at South African Colleges, 1829–95." *Journal of African History* 41 (2000): 221–39.

Edmonds, Penelope. *Urbanizing Frontiers: Indigenous People and Settlers in 19th-Century Pacific Rim Cities*. Vancouver: University of British Columbia Press, 2010.

Ellinghaus, Katherine. *Taking Assimilation to Heart: Marriages of White Women and Indigenous Men in the United States and Australia, 1887–1937*. Lincoln: University of Nebraska Press, 2006.

Etherington, Norman. "Education and Medicine." In *Missions and Empire*, edited by Norman Etherington, 261–306. Oxford: Oxford University Press, 2005.

Finlay, Henry. "Lawmaking in the Shadow of the Empire: Divorce in Colonial Australia." *Journal of Family History* 21, 1 (1999): 74–109.

Grant, John Webster. *Moon of Wintertime: Missionaries and the Indians of Canada in Encounter Since 1534*. Toronto: University of Toronto Press, 1984.

Grieves, Vicki. "The McClymonts of Nabia: Interracial Marriage, Inheritance and Dispossession in Nineteenth Century New South Wales Colonial Society." In *Rethinking the Racial Moment: Essays on the Colonial Encounter*, edited by Alison Holland and Barbara Brookes, 125–57. Newcastle, UK: Cambridge Scholars Publishing, 2011.

Grimshaw, Patricia. "Faith, Missionary Life, and the Family." In *Gender and Empire*, edited by Phillipa Levine, 260–79. Oxford: Oxford University Press, 2004.

Grimshaw, Patricia. "'That we may obtain our religious liberty ...': Aboriginal Women, Faith and Rights in Early Twentieth-Century Victoria, Australia." *Journal of the Canadian Historical Association / Revue de la société historique du Canada* 10, 2 (2008): 24–42.

Haines, David. "In Search of the 'Whaheen': Ngai Tahu Women, Shore Whalers, and the Meaning of Sex in Early New Zealand." In *Moving Subjects: Gender, Mobility and Intimacy in an Age of Global Expansion*, edited by Tony Ballantyne and Antoinette Burton, 49–68. Urbana: University of Illinois Press, 2009.

Hardwick, Joseph. "Anglican Church Expansion and the Recruitment of Colonial Clergy for New South Wales and the Cape Colony, 1790–1850." *Journal of Imperial and Commonwealth History* 37, 3 (2009): 361–91.

Horne, Julia, and Geoffrey Sherington. "Extending the Educational Franchise: The Social Contract of Australia's Public Universities, 1850–1890." *Paedagogica Historica* 46, 1–2 (2010): 207–27.

Hyams, B.K. "Anti-Intellectualism in the History of the Education of Teachers: England and Australia." *Journal of Educational Administration and History* 11, 1 (2006): 43–49.

Jacobs, Margaret. *White Mother to a Dark Race: Settler Colonialism, Maternalism, and the Removal of Indigenous Children in the American West and Australia, 1880–1940*. Lincoln: University of Nebraska Press, 2009.

Kinber, Julie. "Poor Laws: A Historiography of Vagrancy in Australia." *History Compass* 11, 8 (2013): 537–50.

Laidlaw, Zoë. "'Aunt Anna's Report': The Buxton Women and the Aborigines Select Committee, 1835–37." *Journal of Imperial and Commonwealth History* 32, 2 (2004): 1–28.

Lester, Alan. "Humanitarians and White Settlers in the Nineteenth Century." In *Missions and Empire*, edited by Norman Etherington, 64–85. Oxford: Oxford University Press, 2005.

MacDonald, Charlotte. "Between Religion and Empire: Sarah Selwyn's Aotearoa/ New Zealand, Eton and Lichfield, England, c. 1840s–1900." *Journal of the Canadian Historical Association / Revue de la société historique du Canada* 10, 2 (2008): 43–75.

MacDonald, Charlotte. "Intimacy of the Envelope: Fiction, Commerce, and Empire in the Correspondence of Friends Mary Taylor and Charlotte Brontë, c. 1845–55." In *Moving Subjects: Gender, Mobility and Intimacy in an Age of Global Expansion*, edited by Tony Ballantyne and Antoinette Burton, 89–109. Urbana: University of Illinois Press, 2009.

MacDonald, Robert H. *Sons of the Empire: The Frontier and the Boy Scout Movement 1890–1918.* Toronto: University of Toronto Press, 1993.

Malherbe, Vertrees. "Christian-Muslim Marriage and Cohabitation: An Aspect of Identity and Family Formation in Nineteenth-Century Cape Town." *Journal of Imperial and Commonwealth History* 36, 1 (2008): 5–24.

Marshall, P.J. "Transatlantic Protestantism and American Independence." *Journal of Imperial and Commonwealth History* 36, 3 (2008): 345–62.

Martens, Jeremy C. "'Almost a Public Calamity': Prostitutes, 'Nurseboys,' and Attempts to Control Venereal Diseases in Colonial Natal, 1886–1890." *South African Historical Journal* 45 (Nov. 2001): 27–52.

Martens, Jeremy C. "Polygamy, Sexual Danger, and the Creation of Vagrancy Legislation in Colonial Natal." *Journal of Imperial and Commonwealth History* 31, 3 (2003): 24–45.

Mawani, Renisa. *Colonial Proximities: Crossracial Encounters and Juridical Truths in British Columbia, 1871–1921.* Vancouver: University of British Columbia Press, 2009.

McKenzie, Kirsten. *Scandal in the Colonies: Sydney and Cape Town 1820–1850.* Carlton, Australia: Melbourne University Press, 2004.

Middleton, Sue. "Schooling the Labouring Classes: Children, Families, and Learning in Wellington, 1840–1845." *International Studies in Sociology of Education* 18, 2 (2008): 133–46.

Miller, J.R. *Shingwauk's Vision: A History of Native Residential Schools.* Toronto: University of Toronto Press, 1996.

Mirmohamadi, Kylie. "Melbourne's Sites of Reading: Putting the Colonial Woman Reader in Her Place." *History Australia* 6, 2 (2008): 38.1–38.18.

Morrison, Hugh. "'Little Vessels' or 'Little Soldiers': New Zealand Protestant Children, Foreign Missions, Religious Pedagogy and Empire, c. 1880s–1930s." *Paedagogica Historica* 47, 3 (2001): 303–21.

Neylan, Susan. *The Heavens Are Changing: Nineteenth-Century Protestant Missions and Tsimshian Christianity.* Montreal: McGill-Queen's University Press, 2003.

Parr, Joy. *Labouring Children: British Immigrant Apprentices to Canada, 1869–1924.* Toronto: University of Toronto Press, 1994.

Perry, Adele. *On the Edge of Empire: Gender, Race, and the Making of British Columbia, 1849–1871*. Toronto: University of Toronto Press, 2001.

Pickles, Katie, and Myra Rutherdale, eds. *Contact Zones: Aboriginal and Settler Women in Canada's Colonial Past*. Vancouver: University of British Columbia Press, 2005.

Porter, Andrew. *Religion versus Empire? British Protestant Missionaries and Overseas Expansion, 1700–1914*. Manchester: Manchester University Press, 2004.

Ross, Robert. *Status and Respectability in the Cape Colony, 1750–1870: A Tragedy of Manners*. Cambridge: Cambridge University Press, 1999.

Russell, Penny. *Savage or Civilized? Manners in Colonial Australia*. Sydney: University of New South Wales Press, 2010.

Rutherdale, Myra. *Women and the White Man's God: Gender and Race in the Canadian Mission Field*. Vancouver: University of British Columbia Press, 2002.

Scully, Pamela. *Liberating the Family? Gender and British Slave Emancipation in the Rural Western Cape, South Africa, 1823–1853*. Portsmouth, NH: Heinemann, 1997.

Semple, Rhonda A. "Missionary Manhood: Professionalism, Belief and Masculinity in the Nineteenth-Century British Imperial Field." *Journal of Imperial and Commonwealth History* 36, 3 (2008): 397–415.

Sherington, Geoffrey, and Julia Horne. "Empire, State and Public Purposes in the Founding of Universities and Colleges in the Antipodes." *History of Education Review* 38, 2 (2010): 36–51.

Smart, Judith. "Sex, the State and the 'Scarlet Scourge': Gender, Citizenship and Venereal Diseases Regulation in Australia during the Great War." *Women's History Review* 7, 1 (1998): 5–36.

Stevenson, Maxine. "Learning about Empire and the Imperial Education Conferences in the Early Twentieth Century: Creating Cohesion or Demonstrating Difference?" *History of Education Review* 38, 2 (2010): 24–35.

Swain, Shurlee. "Negotiating Poverty: Women and Charity in Nineteenth-Century Melbourne." *Women's History Review* 16, 1 (2007): 99–112.

Thorne, Susan. *Congregational Missions and the Making of an Imperial Culture in Nineteenth-Century England*. Stanford, CA: Stanford University Press, 1999.

Traue, J.E. "The Public Library Explosion in New Zealand." *Libraries and the Cultural Record* 42, 2 (2007): 151–64.

Twells, Alison. *The Civilising Mission and the English Middle Class, 1792–1850: The "Heathen" at Home and Overseas*. Basingstoke, UK: Palgrave Macmillan, 2009.

Twomey, Christina. "Courting Men: Mothers, Magistrates and Welfare in the Australian Colonies." *Women's History Review* 8, 2 (1999): 231–45.

van Heyningen, Elizabeth. "Poverty, Self-Help and Community: The Survival of the Poor in Cape Town, 1880–1910." *South African Historical Journal* 24 (1991): 128–43.

Van Kirk, Sylvia. *"Many Tender Ties": Women in Fur-Trade Society in Western Canada, 1670–1870*. Winnipeg: Watson and Dwyer, 1980.

Vibert, Elizabeth. "Writing Home: Sibling Intimacy and Mobility in a Scottish Colonial Memoir." In *Moving Subjects: Gender, Mobility and Intimacy in an Age of Global Expansion*, edited by Tony Ballantyne and Antoinette Burton, 67–88. Urbana: University of Illinois Press, 2009.

Wanhalla, Angela. *In/visible Sight: The Mixed Descent Families of Southern New Zealand*. Wellington: Bridget Williams Books, 2009.

Webb, Denver A. "'Tis Here the Young Men and Maidens, the Old Men and Children, Meet to Enjoy Themselves in Their Own Way': Culture, Identity and the King William's Town Public Library at the End of the Nineteenth Century." *Quarterly Bulletin of the National Library of South Africa* 64, 4 (2010): 200–08.

Weir, Christine. "'Deeply Interested in These Children Whom You Have Not Seen': The Protestant Sunday School View of the Pacific, 1900–1940." *Journal of Pacific History* 48, 1 (2013): 43–62.

Wilson, Alan. "The Clergy Reserves: 'Economical Mischiefs' or Sectarian Issue?" *Canadian Historical Review* 42, 4 (1961): 281–99.

## Chapter 5

Bell, Duncan. "The Idea of a Patriot Queen? The Monarchy, the Constitution, and the Iconographic Order of Greater Britain, 1860–1900." *Journal of Imperial and Commonwealth History* 34, 1 (2006): 3–21.

Berger, Carl. *The Sense of Power: Studies in the Idea of Canadian Imperialism, 1867–1914*. Toronto: University of Toronto Press, 1970.

Bickford-Smith, Vivian. "Revisiting Anglicization in the Nineteenth-Century Cape Colony." In *The British World: Diaspora, Culture and Identity*, edited by Carl Bridge and Kent Fedorowich, 82–95. London: Frank Cass, 2003.

Buckner, Phillip. "Casting Daylight upon Magic: Deconstructing the Royal Tour of 1901 in Canada." In *The British World: Diaspora, Culture and Identity*, edited by Carl Bridge and Kent Fedorowich, 158–89. London: Frank Cass, 2003.

Buckner, Phillip. "The Royal Tour of 1901 and the Construction of an Imperial Identity in South Africa." *South African Historical Journal* 41 (Nov. 1999): 324–48.

Coates, Colin M. "French Canadians' Ambivalence to the British Empire." In *Canada and the British Empire*, edited by Phillip Buckner, 181–99. New York: Oxford University Press, 2008.

Codell, Julie F. *Imperial Co-histories: National Identities and the British and Colonial Press*. Madison, NJ: Fairleigh Dickinson University Press, 2003.

Coombes, Annie, ed. *Rethinking Settler Colonialism: History and Memory in Australia, Canada, Aotearoa New Zealand and South Africa*. Manchester: Manchester University Press, 2006.

Crais, Clifton, and Pamela Scully. *Sara Baartman and the Hottentot Venus: A Ghost Story and a Biography*. Princeton, NJ: Princeton University Press, 2009.

Damousi, Joy. *The Labour of Loss: Mourning, Memory, and Wartime Bereavement in Australia*. Cambridge: Cambridge University Press, 1999.

Darian-Smith, Kate. "Images of Empire: Gender and Nationhood in Australia at the Time of Federation." In *Britishness Abroad: Transnational Movements and Imperial Cultures*, edited by Kate Darian-Smith, Patricia Grimshaw, and Stuart Macintyre, 153–68. Carlton, Australia: Melbourne University Press, 2007.

Deacon, Desley. "Location! Location! Location! Mind Map and Theatrical Circuits in Australian Transnational History." *History Australia* 5, 3 (2008): 81.1–81.16.

Dubow, Saul. "Colonial Nationalism, The Milner Kindergarten and the Rise of 'South Africanism,' 1902–10." *History Workshop Journal* 43 (1997): 53–85.

Dubow, Saul. "How British Was the British World? The Case of South Africa." *Journal of Imperial and Commonwealth History* 37, 1 (2009): 1–27.

Dubow, Saul. "South Africa and South Africans: Nationality, Belonging, Citizenship." In *The Cambridge History of South Africa*. Vol. 2, *1885–1994*, edited by Robert Ross, Anne Mager, and Bill Nasson, 17–65. Cambridge: Cambridge University Press, 2011.

Fletcher, Ian Christopher, Laura E. Nym Mayhall, and Philippa Levine, eds. *Women's Suffrage in the British Empire: Citizenship, Nation and Race*. London: Routledge, 2000.

Graham, Morris. "Newcastle Rallies to the Flag, February 1902: Arthur Hill Griffith and Opposition to the Boer War." *Journal of the Royal Australian Historical Society* 89, 1 (2003): 53.

Hall, Catherine. "What Did a British World Mean to the British? Reflections on the Nineteenth Century." In *Rediscovering the British World*, edited by Phillip Buckner and R. Douglas Francis, 21–37. Calgary: University of Calgary Press, 2005.

Harper, Marjorie. "'Personal Contact Is Worth a Ton of Textbooks': Educational Tours of the Empire, 1926–1939." *Journal of Imperial and Commonwealth History* 32, 3 (2004): 48–76.

Heaman, Elsbeth. *The Inglorious Arts of Peace: Exhibitions in Canadian Society during the Nineteenth Century*. Toronto: University of Toronto Press, 1999.

Inglis, K.S., and Jock Phillips. "War Memorials in Australia and New Zealand: A Comparative Survey." *Australian Historical Studies* 24, 96 (2008): 179–91.

Jones, Aled, and Bill Jones. "The Welsh World and the British Empire, c. 1851–1939: An Exploration." In *The British World: Diaspora, Culture and Identity*, edited by Carl Bridge and Kent Fedorowich, 57–81. London: Frank Cass, 2003.

Jordan, Caroline. "Progress versus the Picturesque: White Women and the Aesthetics of Environmentalism in Colonial Australia 1820–1860." *Art History* 25, 3 (2002): 341–57.

Kelly, Veronica. "Shakespeare in Settler-Built Spaces: Oscar Asche's 'Recitals' of *Julius Caesar* in the Melbourne and Sydney Town Halls." *Contemporary Theatre Review* 19, 3 (2009): 353–66.

Kirk, Neville. "The Conditions of Royal Rule: Australian and British Socialist and Labour Attitudes to the Monarchy, 1901–11." *Social History* 30, 1 (2005): 64–88.

Lambert, John. "Britishness, South Africanness, and the First World War." In *Rediscovering the British World*, edited by Phillip Buckner and R. Douglas Francis, 285–304. Calgary: University of Calgary Press, 2005.

Landau, Paul S. "Transformations in Consciousness." In *The Cambridge History of South Africa*. Vol. 1, *From Early Times to 1885*, edited by Carolyn Hamilton, Bernard K. Mbenga, and Robert Ross, 392–448. Cambridge: Cambridge University Press, 2010–11.

Lester, Allan. *Imperial Networks: Creating Identities in Nineteenth-Century South Africa and Britain*. London: Routledge, 2001.

Lorimer, Douglas. "From Victorian Values to White Virtues: Assimilation and Exclusion in British Racial Discourse, c. 1870–1914." In *Rediscovering the British World*, edited by Phillip Buckner and R. Douglas Francis, 109–34. Calgary: University of Calgary Press, 2005.

Lowry, Donal. "The Crown, Empire Loyalism and the Assimilation of Non-British White Subjects in the British World: An Argument against 'Ethnic Determinism.'" In *The British World: Diaspora, Culture and Identity*, edited by Carl Bridge and Kent Fedorowich, 96–120. London: Frank Cass, 2003.

MacDonald, Robert H. *Sons of the Empire: The Frontier and the Boy Scout Movement 1890–1918*. Toronto: University of Toronto Press, 1993.

MacKenzie, John M. *Museums and Empire: Natural History, Human Cultures and Colonial Identities*. Manchester: Manchester University Press, 2009.

MacKenzie, John M. *Propaganda and Empire: The Manipulation of British Public Opinion, 1880–1960*. Manchester: Manchester University Press, 1984.

MacKenzie, John M. with Nigel Dalziel. *The Scots in South Africa: Ethnicity, Identity, Gender and Race, 1772–1914*. Manchester: Manchester University Press, 2007.

Marks, Shula. "Class, Culture, and Consciousness in South Africa, 1880–1899." In *The Cambridge History of South Africa*. Vol. 2, *1885–1994*, edited by Robert Ross, Anne Mager, and Bill Nasson, 102–56. Cambridge: Cambridge University Press, 2011.

McCreery, Cindy. "Rude Interruption: Colonial Manners, Gender and Prince Alfred's Visit to New South Wales, 1868." *Forum for Modern Language Studies* 49, 4 (2013): 437–57.

Meany, Neville. "Britishness and Australia: Some Reflections." In *The British World: Diaspora, Culture and Identity*, edited by Carl Bridge and Kent Fedorowich, 121–35. London: Frank Cass, 2003.

Miller, Carman. *Painting the Map Red: Canada and the South African War, 1899–1902*. Montreal: McGill-Queen's University Press, 1993.

Montana, Andrew. "From the Royal Academy to a Hotel in Kapunda: The Tour of William Powell Firth's *Derby Day* in Colonial Australia." *Art History* 31, 5 (2008): 754–85.

Moore, Tom. "Liberal Imperialism in Australian Political Thought, 1902–14." *Journal of Imperial and Commonwealth History* 43, 1 (2015): 58–79.

Nasson, Bill. "World War I in South Africa's Memory." *Matériaux pour l'histoire de notre temps* 1, 113–14 (2014): 156–60.

Pickles, Katie. *Female Imperialism and National Identity: Imperial Order Daughters of the Empire*. Manchester: Manchester University Press, 2002.

Pickles, Katie. "A Link in 'The Great Chain of Empire Friendship': The Victoria League of New Zealand." *Journal of Imperial and Commonwealth History* 33, 1 (2005): 29–50.

Potter, Simon J. "Communication and Integration: The British and Dominions Press and the British World, c. 1876–1914." In *The British World: Diaspora, Culture and Identity*, edited by Carl Bridge and Kent Fedorowich, 190–206. London: Frank Cass, 2003.

Radforth, Ian. *Royal Spectacle: The 1860 Visit of the Prince of Wales to Canada and the United States*. Toronto: University of Toronto Press, 2004.

Raibmon, Paige. "Theatres of Contact: The Kwakwaka'wakw Meet Colonialism in British Columbia and at the Chicago's World Fair." *Canadian Historical Review* 81, 2 (2000): 157–90.

Riedl, Eliza. "Teaching Empire: British and Dominion Women Teachers in the South African War Concentration Camps." *English Historical Review* 120, 489 (2005): 1316–47.

Russell, Penny. "Girl in a Red Dress: Inventions of Mathinna." *Australian Historical Studies* 43 (2012): 341–62.

Sargent, Lyman Tower. "Utopianism and the Creation of New Zealand National Identity." *Utopian Studies* 12, 1 (2001): 1–18.

Scott, Joanne, and Ross Laurie. "Colonialism on Display: Indigenous People and Artefacts at an Australian Agricultural Show." *Aboriginal History* 31 (2007): 46–62.

Sheftall, Mark. "Mythologising the Dominion Fighting Man: Australian and Canadian Narratives of the First World War Soldier, 1914–1939." *Australian Historical Studies* 46 (2013): 81–99.

Storey, Kenton Scott. "'What Will They Say in England?': Violence, Anxiety, and the Press in Nineteenth Century New Zealand and Vancouver Island." *Journal of the Canadian Historical Association* 20, 2 (2009): 28–59.

Tietze, Anna, and Nicholas Botha. "Civilising the Cape: Public Art Exhibitions and Cape Visual Culture, 1851–1910." *Journal of South African Historical Studies* 40, 6 (2014): 1177–91.

Trapido, Stanley. "Imperialism, Settler Identities, and Colonial Capitalism: The Hundred-Year Origins of the 1899 South African War." In *The Cambridge History of South Africa*. Vol. 2, *1885–1994*, edited by Robert Ross, Anne Mager, and Bill Nasson, 66–101. Cambridge: Cambridge University Press, 2011.

Vance, Jonathan. *Death So Noble: Memory, Meaning, and the First World War*. Vancouver: University of British Columbia Press, 1997.

van der Wang, Ian. "Hugh Wyndham, Transvaal Politics and the Attempt to Create an English Country Seat in South Africa, 1901–14." In *The British World: Diaspora, Culture and Identity*, edited by Carl Bridge and Kent Fedorowich, 136–57. London: Frank Cass, 2003.

van Heyningen, Elizabeth. "The Concentration Camps of the South African (Anglo-Boer) War, 1900–1902." *History Compass* 7, 1 (2009): 22–43.

van Heyningen, Elizabeth. "'The Healing Touch': The Guild of Loyal Women of South Africa 1900–1912." *South African Historical Journal* 47 (Nov. 2003): 24–50.

Walden, Keith. *Becoming Modern in Toronto: The Industrial Exhibition and the Shaping of a Late-Victorian Culture*. Toronto: University of Toronto Press, 1997.

Woollacott, Angela. *To Try Her Fortune in London: Australian Women, Colonialism, and Modernity*. Oxford: Oxford University Press, 2001.

## Conclusion

Buckner, Phillip, ed. *Canada and the End of Empire*. Vancouver: University of British Columbia Press, 2005.

Levine, Philippa. "Decolonization." In *The British Empire: Sunrise to Sunset*, Chapter 11. Harlow, UK: Pearson, 2007.

# Index